Postdevelopmental Approaches to Pedagogical Observation in Childhood

Postdevelopmental Approaches to Childhood
Series Editors: Jayne Osgood and Mona Sakr

Troubling traditional developmentalist logic, this series brings together post-developmental approaches that offer fresh ways to reconsider firmly established ideas about childhood from observations, to policy, curriculum, environment and materials. Postdevelopmental Approaches to Childhood gathers a range of international scholars in a series of edited collections that unsettle traditional approaches to practice, pedagogy and research in childhood. Providing a home for innovative, experimental and creative approaches and a diverse range of theoretical and methodological orientations, the series opens up new ways of becoming-with children in both practice and research.

Also Available in the Series:

Postdevelopmental Approaches to Childhood Research Observation,
edited by Jayne Osgood
Postdevelopmental Approaches to Pedagogical Observation in Childhood,
edited by Mona Sakr, Jennifer Rowsell and Kortney Sherbine

Forthcoming in the series:

Postdevelopmental Approaches to Digital Arts in Childhood,
edited by Marissa McClure and Mona Sakr

Postdevelopmental Approaches to Pedagogical Observation in Childhood

Edited by
Mona Sakr, Jennifer Rowsell and
Kortney Sherbine

BLOOMSBURY ACADEMIC
LONDON • NEW YORK • OXFORD • NEW DELHI • SYDNEY

BLOOMSBURY ACADEMIC
Bloomsbury Publishing Plc, 50 Bedford Square, London, WC1B 3DP, UK
Bloomsbury Publishing Inc, 1385 Broadway, New York, NY 10018, USA
Bloomsbury Publishing Ireland, 29 Earlsfort Terrace, Dublin 2, D02 AY28, Ireland

BLOOMSBURY, BLOOMSBURY ACADEMIC and the Diana logo are trademarks of
Bloomsbury Publishing Plc

First published in Great Britain 2023
Paperback edition published in 2025

Copyright © Mona Sakr, Jennifer Rowsell and Kortney Sherbine and contributors, 2023

Mona Sakr, Jennifer Rowsell and Kortney Sherbine and contributors have asserted
their right under the Copyright, Designs and Patents Act, 1988, to be
identified as Author of this work.

Series design by Grace Ridge
Cover image © Sally Anscombe / Getty Images

All rights reserved. No part of this publication may be: i) reproduced or transmitted
in any form, electronic or mechanical, including photocopying, recording or by means
of any information storage or retrieval system without prior permission in writing from
the publishers; or ii) used or reproduced in any way for the training, development or
operation of artificial intelligence (AI) technologies, including generative AI technologies.
The rights holders expressly reserve this publication from the text and data mining
exception as per Article 4(3) of the Digital Single Market Directive (EU) 2019/790.

Bloomsbury Publishing Plc does not have any control over, or responsibility for, any
third-party websites referred to or in this book. All internet addresses given in this
book were correct at the time of going to press. The author and publisher regret
any inconvenience caused if addresses have changed or sites have ceased
to exist, but can accept no responsibility for any such changes.

A catalogue record for this book is available from the British Library.

A catalog record for this book is available from the Library of Congress.

ISBN: HB: 978-1-3503-6964-1
PB: 978-1-3503-6968-9
ePDF: 978-1-3503-6965-8
eBook: 978-1-3503-6966-5

Series: Postdevelopmental Approaches to Childhood

Typeset by Deanta Global Publishing Services, Chennai, India

For product safety related questions contact productsafety@bloomsbury.com.

To find out more about our authors and books visit www.bloomsbury.com and
sign up for our newsletters.

Contents

List of Illustrations	vi
List of Contributors	viii
Series Editors' Foreword	xii
Introduction *Mona Sakr, Jennifer Rowsell and Kortney Sherbine*	1
1 The Rhythm: Posthuman Perspectives on Childhoods and Classroom Observation *Kortney Sherbine*	9
2 Togetherness in Early Childhood Art: Observation *with* Young Children *Shana Cinquemani*	27
3 Movements, Synchronicities, Choreographies: Attuning to Young Children's Drawing *Sylvia Kind*	37
4 Hacking Observational Literacy Tools in Early Childhood Education *Karen Nociti and Mindy Blaise*	57
5 Reconceptualizing Observations with Infants and Toddlers: Perspectives from Aotearoa, New Zealand *Kiri Gould, Marek Tesar and Jen Boyd*	81
6 'What's Happening *Here*?': Speculative Routes to Observation in Early Art Teacher Education *Christopher M. Schulte*	99
7 Alone-Together: Exploring Children's Material/Digital/Analogue Engagements through Intergenerational Research *Mark Shillitoe, Harriet Hand, Scarlett Shepherd, William Squire and Jennifer Rowsell*	119
8 Hidden Mothering and Mutated Modest Witnessing with Hop(scotch) Studio *Marissa McClure*	141
9 Posthuman Babies: Reconceptualizing a Baby's First Year *Sara Sintonen and Alexandra Nordström*	157
10 Experimental Analysis of Photography and Video in Postdevelopmental Observations of Early Childhood Art in the Family Home: Thinking with Barthes' *Camera Lucida* *Mona Sakr*	175
Index	191

Illustrations

Figures

2.1 and 2.2	Students exploring the provocation of coloured lights	28
2.3 and 2.4	Children observing and documenting the shadow puppet performances	29
2.5 and 2.6	The children and I engaging in reflective storytelling about last week's art class	33
3.1	The liveliness of drawing	40
3.2	Joining with the hospitalities of drawing	45
3.3	The generosities of drawing	47
3.4	The beginning of a drawing-dance	51
4.1	Gabbiljee (the watery place at the end of Derbarl Yerrigan)	58
4.2	The observational literacy tool	62
4.3	A section of the messed-up observational literacy tool	68
4.4	Wardong and creek	71
7.1	Clockwise from top left: Mapping sound, Identical brunch; Favourite part of the room; Mapping the magical story box; Where we were; Inside/Outside spatial sound map; 50 sounds of me; Soundscape performance score; Sewing circle reflection	127
7.2	Map: Favourite part of the room	129
7.3	Inside/outside spatial map	130
7.4	What can we learn from sewing a circle?	132
7.5	Soundscape performance score	134
8.1	The sticky machine	142
8.2	Hidden Mother	144
8.3	Views of Hopscotch Studio, before, at the beginning and throughout the first year of ARIM	146
8.4	Stella's altered dolls in Hopscotch Studio	151

8.5	One of Luca's selfies in Hopscotch Studio	153
8.6	Hopscotch Studio at present	154
10.1	Series of stills showing E's action	183

Table

| 7.1 | Selected Mapping Encounters | 126 |

Contributors

Mindy Blaise is Vice Chancellor's professorial research fellow and the co-director of the strategic research centre, Centre for People, Place and Planet at Edith Cowan University, Perth, Western Australia. Mindy is co-founder of the Common Worlds Research Collective and #FEAS, Feminist Educators against Sexism. She conducts feminist postdevelopmental and postfoundational research and is committed to generating and telling different kinds of stories about gender and children's worldly relations.

Jen Boyd is an early childhood teacher and graduate student, who holds a special interest in exploring posthumanist, new materialist and post-qualitative approaches to research.

Shana Cinquemani is assistant professor in the Department of Teaching + Learning in Art + Design at the Rhode Island School of Design, USA, and a past-president of the Early Childhood Art Educators interest group through the National Art Education Association. Her research interests are grounded in theories of early childhood art education, the conceptualization of children's art as a meaningful sociocultural practice, connections between art and play, curriculum inquiry and theory, ethical research practices with children and relationships between children and adults in the art classroom space.

Kiri Gould is lecturer in Early Childhood Education at the University of Auckland, New Zealand. She has a growing interest in how postdevelopmental approaches in early childhood education can support teachers to respond to the challenges of the anthropocene in their work with children and families.

Harriet Hand is a designer, educator and PhD candidate in the School of Education at the University of Bristol, UK. Her research takes an experimental and participatory approach to explore the ways mapmaking gives access to complexity and generates new possibilities for transforming young people's sense of self and the world around them.

Sylvia Kind is faculty instructor in Early Childhood Education at Capilano University, Canada, and an *atelierista* at the Capilano University Children's Centre. Her work is guided by a/r/tography and research-creation practices and is motivated by an interest in young children's studio practices, their lively material improvisations and collective experimentations, and in developing an understanding of studio research in early childhood contexts. She has co-authored the book *Encounters with Materials in Early Childhood Education*, co-edited *Drawing as Language* and has written several journal articles and book chapters on studio practices in early childhood.

Karen Nociti is lecturer and PhD candidate in the School of Education (Early Childhood Studies) at Edith Cowan University, Perth, Western Australia. Her research is influenced by feminist new materialisms, walking methodologies and posthuman theories of literacy. She is particularly interested in troubling normative place-based practices that separate children from Place with the intention of generating new pedagogies that (re)situate Place and children within shared common worlds.

Alexandra Nordström is a postdoctoral researcher at the Faculty of Educational Sciences, University of Helsinki, Finland. Her research interests include affect, literacy, and play in early childhood education, post-approaches in educational research and figurations of children and childhood. In her doctoral thesis, Alexandra examined young children's joy and literacy practices from sociocultural and posthumanist theoretical perspectives.

Jennifer Rowsell is professor of digital literacy in the School of Education at the University of Sheffield. Her research seeks to expand what literacy is and can be in contemporary, multimodal times. She is particularly interested in conducting ethnographic research with children and young people from a lived, post-digital approach to meaning making.

Mona Sakr is senior lecturer in education and early childhood at Middlesex University, UK. Her research focuses on digital technologies in childhood, with a particular focus on how the digital re-shapes creative, playful and art-making experiences for young children. Currently, she is researching Early Years (EY) practitioners' use of video to engage in reflective interpretations of children's art-making and how they perceive their role in facilitating creativity and playfulness among children. Previous research projects include a phenomenological analysis of children's experiences of digital augmentation during history learning, observation studies of collective digital art-making in the EY classroom and a case study of parent-child art-making with different technologies in the home.

Christopher Schulte holds the position of Endowed Associate Professor of Art Education in the School of Art at the University of Arkansas, USA, where he also serves as director of the Center for the Study of Childhood Art. Grounded in childhood studies and informed by a range of postdevelopmental approaches, Dr Schulte's scholarship, teaching and community engagement focus on the artistic, play-based and aesthetic practices of young children, with special attention given to the study of drawing in childhood.

Scarlett Shepherd completed her undergraduate degree in educational studies at the University of Bristol.

Kortney Sherbine is an independent researcher based in Pittsburgh, Pennsylvania, USA. Her research examines children's encounters with popular culture in early childhood and elementary classrooms. Her work has appeared in the *Journal of Early Childhood Literacy*, the *Journal of Curriculum and Pedagogy* and the *Journal of Language and Literacy Education*, among other journals and edited volumes.

Mark Shillitoe is an art educator. A creative technologist and innovator, he is passionate about creating opportunities for curious learners to explore and uncover their creative potential through developing web, media and invention literacies in an exciting evolving digital landscape.

Sara Sintonen works as a professor of early childhood education at the Faculty of Education, University of Turku, Finland (2023–24). She is also a senior lecturer at the University of Helsinki's Faculty of Educational Sciences. She holds titles of adjunct professor on media education (University of Helsinki) and on children's digital cultures (University of Turku). Her research interests include arts, literacy, and materiality in early childhood education, as well as post-approach theoretical and methodological aspects.

Marissa McClure is an artist, educator and researcher, interested in contemporary theories of children's art, community-based art education, feminist theory and curriculum inquiry and design. She is currently assistant chair of the Department of Art and Design, associate professor of Art Education, coordinator of the Art Education Program and women's and gender studies affiliate faculty at Indiana University of Pennsylvania, USA. Before coming to higher education, she was an early childhood art educator in rural and urban settings and in art museums.

Will Squire is an undergraduate student who completed his undergraduate degree at the University of Bristol.

Marek Tesar is associate professor and associate dean international at the University of Auckland, New Zealand. His research is focused on philosophical methods, childhood studies and early childhood education. His latest research focuses on the construction of childhoods and methodological and philosophical thinking around ontologies and the ethics of researching these notions.

Series Editors' Foreword

This book series, Postdevelopmental Approaches to Childhood, brings a lively collection of edited volumes together that directly trouble developmentalist logic underpinning dominant ideas about what children can or should (be able to) do at certain stages of development. Although seemingly common sense and benign, developmentalism is taken up in ways that can lead to the marginalization of children who do not fit normative expectations, and as a consequence are perceived as deviant, abnormal or substandard (Burman, 2016; Cannella & Viruru, 2004). Through multiple theoretical and practice lenses post developmentalism offers alternative ways to be with and learn from children through childhood. It opens up new possibilities for celebrating differences among children and paying closer attention to the unfolding of children's everyday experiences. The series therefore aims to support pedagogues and researchers to experience children and childhood differently, to refuse labels and codification against normative expectations and instead embrace richer perspectives grounded in overt commitments to social justice.

To extend the series, two books focusing on postdevelopmental approaches to observation in childhood are launched simultaneously. The curation of these twin volumes underlines how profoundly significant observation is within early childhood. Observation is fundamental to both childhood pedagogies and childhood research and the way observations take shape in contemporary practice builds on long and rich histories, which generates a complex, critical dialogue between developmental and postdevelopmental ways of encountering the world, and the child within the world. This particular volume, edited by Jennifer Rowsell, Kortney Sherbine and Mona Sakr, focuses on pedagogical observations in childhood and what might emerge when such observations are mobilized in ways intended to disrupt developmentalism.

Throughout its ten chapters, contributed by a renowned panel of international researchers, writers and pedagogues, the book offers a robust challenge to dominant developmental approaches to and protocols for observation in childhood pedagogies. It questions the preoccupation in pedagogical observations of 'capturing' development as it unfolds for children and instead positions observation as a means for learning in a deep sense, where both educators and children learn together and from one another. It provokes questions around the most basic assumptions we tend to make about pedagogical observations in childhood, for example, that observations will be conducted by adults with a focus on children. Engaging with posthumanism, feminist new materialism, social semiotics, sociocultural approaches and much more, the book wonders about what might be done, seen and lived differently in relation to pedagogical observations. It is radical in both the challenge it makes and the alternative possibilities it brings into the arena.

For too long, pedagogical observations have typically been used as a way by educators to seemingly know and 'fix' the developing child against normative trajectories. Educators are trained to use observations as the basis for pinning down what a child can and cannot do. For example, prescriptive observational techniques are taught as standard in early childhood education courses throughout the world and in practice, popular marketplace observation tools prioritize the interpretation of children's behaviours according to an increasingly narrow set of expectations. Educators are often encouraged to make short video observations of young children that are then accompanied by the completion of an age-bound checklist, pinning down not just the child but also that particular moment of experience in a deeply restrictive manner. This book looks again at the pedagogical foundations of this kind of practice, but it also presents a range of exciting forays into what might happen if we were to instead prioritize the richness of childhood experiences as the basis for observational practice.

Excitingly, the book contains contributions that span experiences from babyhood and parents' (often unwitting) pedagogical observations of their own very young children to explorations of teachers' more codified observational practice in educational contexts and the influence this can have on particular children. Chapters in this volume emerge from a diverse set of theoretical orientations and take up a range of key concepts, that illustrate the potential for posthumanism and (feminist) new materialism to exist in dialogue with postcolonial place literacies and socio-material and ecological perspectives to foster new ways of thinking about and doing pedagogical observations. The chapters' diverse approaches respond to a fundamental aim of the Postdevelopmental Approaches to Childhood series, which seeks to encourage and enable dialogue across theoretical boundaries, where there is a common desire to unsettle the dominance of developmentalism and reconceptualize childhood and children in more expansive and equitable terms.

Introduction

Mona Sakr, *Middlesex University*; Jennifer Rowsell, *University of Sheffield*; and Kortney Sherbine, *Independent Researcher*

Welcome

In this introduction, we set up what to expect from this volume of the series Postdevelopmental Approaches to Childhood. We begin by explaining what postdevelopmentalism means to us and why we particularly need to apply a postdevelopmental approach to pedagogical observations of children's experiences and interactions. Borrowing phrases from the chapter in the volume by Mark Shillitoe and colleagues, we present the 'sparks', 'flows' and 'pulses' that resonate across the contributions when taken as a whole. Working with the playful logic of sparks, flows and pulses enables us to see how chapters exist in dialogue with one another, without reducing the specific contribution made by each one. The final section of the introduction offers an overview of the individual chapters in the volume.

Postdevelopmental Approaches to Childhood Observation

This book challenges dominant developmental models of observation in early childhood pedagogy. It deconstructs traditional approaches to observation, which tend to focus on 'capturing' development in action. It explores alternative ways of thinking about and doing observations in early childhood, particularly pedagogical observations carried out typically by adults as part of learning and teaching practices. The contributors are inspired by a diverse range of theoretical perspectives that challenge traditional developmentalist approaches, including posthumanism, feminist new materialism, social semiotics and sociocultural approaches.

Observations are a fundamental aspect of early childhood pedagogies. Observation is a dominant mode of enquiry used in pedagogical practice to pursue ways of knowing (and fixing) the developing child against normative expectations. Educators are taught how to go in search of particular knowledge about children and childhood that can be revealed through careful, directed and prescribed observational techniques. Typically, how we think about and conduct observations is deeply connected with dominant developmental paradigms in early childhood, where the observation tracks the processes through which the child is becoming-adult. Troubling developmentalism and its capacity to both marginalize children that do not fit 'normal' patterns of development (Burman, 1994, 2008) and miss the richness of childhood experiences (Sakr & Osgood, 2019) therefore means also troubling our approach to observations in early childhood. The prevailing approaches to observation in childhood pedagogy are limiting and present social justice dilemmas that we propose need to be unsettled, dismantled and reimagined. Approaching observations in new, experimental and innovative ways can enable us to both expand the theoretical field of postdevelopmentalism and develop new, more open-ended and deeply respectful ways of engaging in pedagogical observations of children's experiences and interactions.

Sparks

Across chapters in the collection there are sparks that jump off the page to disrupt normative, straitjacket framings of children's development. Sparks allow authors to voice their frustrations and anger at the ways that children and their immense capacities are often underestimated and undervalued by top-down, autonomous developmental perspectives on what a child should do, accomplish and be. Sparks throw into relief sharp contrasts between the research that you will read in this book and the developmental perspectives frequently foregrounded in international childhood learning policies and curricula. Observing sparks entails locating, situating and naming tensions or constraints to a child's agency within and across early years contexts.

Developmental observations tend to sit within a 'doing school well' autonomous model that all of the authors call into question. There are powerful sparks in Sherbine's chapter featuring ten children in a US classroom completing group work and assignments in original ways, yet constrained by quite deficit framings of their work. DJ, in particular, is a child who became absorbed in a double-bubble map that he made with friends and during its composition he exhibited vitality (Boldt, 2020) that seemed quite invisible to the teacher. Moving beyond developmental perspectives to post-perspectives, specifically posthuman perspectives, allows Sherbine to recognize and celebrate children's relational becoming and dynamism in early years contexts. Schulte offers a powerful spark in the form of the question 'What's happening here?' which he discusses using with student-teachers as they explore observations of childhood art. Asking this question repeatedly can enable observers to unpick their own assumptions and expectations about what should be happening and instead attend to and attune to the threads of what is actually unfolding.

Sparks do not necessarily have to involve disruption, sparks can jump off the page as agentive forces for children. Take Gould, Tesar and Boyd's chapter about observations in early childhood education and care settings in Aotearoa New Zealand. Observing closely children's ecological sense-making and their relational moments with materials and nature. Like Sherbine, the authors foreground sparks within learning stories that illustrate relational moments with matter and embodied understandings of nature. Sparks can emerge through disruptive methods, such as the hacking used by Nociti and Blaise in their chapter as a method to 'find, intervene and transform weaknesses in systems'.

Flows

Across chapters in the collection there are flows which invite attentive, tacit, sensory, engaged thinking and being that takes place in the moment and middle of meaning-making. Flows move bodies, hearts, minds, spaces and places into an as-if realm that allows a child to engage in speculative, creative practices filled to the brim with their own agency. Flows attune people to their thoughts and desires and move them into an immersive experience with learning. Observing flows happen when researchers listen carefully, step back and co-experience moments across contexts that unfold in the book.

Flows are evident in every chapter. In the flurry of McClure's hopscotch studio; in Kind's attentive listening to children's drawings; in Nociti and Blaise's intra-actional account of children's ways of knowing in nature and in Sakr's account of punctum in a child's photographs. Flows capture desire, immersion and uncontrollability. Flows unsettle routines and invite what Sakr calls 'wormholes' of discovery and vitality.

Pulses

Across chapters there are pulses that rupture regulatory time-space constraints and boundaries to move children into a line of flight. Pulses can happen together or alone, but their essence rests on a discovery or denouement of thought, feelings or experience. Think of pulses as a bit like *punctum* in photographs (as applied in Sakr's chapter based on Barthes theorizing of images). Pulses unsettle a moment, but they also drive it and compel us to recognize the qualitative difference between being in flow, attuned, at ease and co-present vs. being weighed down and undermined by assumptions, structures and expectations.

In Cinquemani's chapters, pulses manifest as provocations with light, shared with children in the context of a Saturday morning art class for young children. Through the shared response of these provocations there emerged a radical commitment to collaboration, which in turn enabled the children involved to access new kinds of joy and delight in art-making.

Pulses in Sintonen and Nordström's chapter come in the form of materializations of baby memories and milestones in their memory books and the ways that parents signal key aspects and affections for their children in books that celebrate a baby's first year. Baby books explored in the chapter are framed as cultural artefacts intimately tied to social relations and figurations of the child. These books respond to and construct popular conceptualizations of the child, childhood and childhood observation, and the pulses celebrate and sediment how babies are becoming.

Chapter Summaries

Sherbine explores the entanglements of children in an American elementary school as they intra-acted (Barad, 2007) with one another, their teachers, a university researcher and the objects and things in their grade two classroom. Particular attention is given to research involving one child's entanglements with two clipboards during a small group book discussion about *The Gospel of Cinderella* and the ways in which the child-clipboard-discussion expectations-teacher-researcher assemblage produced a specific mo(ve)ment of literacy and classroom identity. In highlighting this assemblage, care is taken in examining how particular images of childhood were reified in the moment when the child-with-clipboards was reprimanded for not behaving as expected. Drawing on posthumanist concepts to examine the relationships between bodies and things, this chapter argues that being a child, a learner, a reader and a participant are emergent and always in relation.

In Chapter 2, Cinquemani examines the possibilities for togetherness in pedagogical observations in the context of early childhood art education. The chapter thoughtfully considers how our perceptions as educators can be altered when we observe *with* children as opposed to simply observing them. In doing so, Cinquemani explores how thinking can be extended when we fully open ourselves up to the interconnectedness of the child and the adult, rather than positioning the child and the adult as an actor and acted upon. Cinquemani's method of observation involves art-making, teaching and researching with young children that pursue the idea of collective relationships – rejecting an idea that the teacher is omniscient and that children and adults alike learn together and co-construct knowledge together. In this way, sparks, flows and pulses emerge from art, relations and inviting agentive spaces of belonging.

Kind's chapter considers observation and documentation of young children's artistic engagements, and drawing in particular, as processes of attuning to and finding a rhythm and synchronicity with what is going on, and as acts of finding one's way towards corresponding *with* rather than collecting information *about* a child's artistry. The chapter draws on new materialism, Ingold and the experimental work of Manning and Massumi, as it considers thinking through making (Ingold, 2013) and thinking through doing (Manning & Massumi, 2014). This shifts the intention in observations from learning about children's processes and artistry and observing from a distance, to questions of how mark-making, drawing, ideas, materials and bodies move together and how we might respond and work with children's approaches and co-compositional processes. It aims to know things differently through motional-relational knowing and a bodied feeling-knowing (Manning & Massumi, 2014).

In Chapter 4, Nociti and Blaise trouble settler perspectives of Place and literacies by experimenting with unmapping Place literacies. Unmapping Place literacies aim to disrupt the normative ways in which literacies are observed and mapped in early childhood education. The chapter is based on a study about Place literacies emerging from Gabbiljee, a wetlands area in Perth, Western Australia. The study took place over a series of walking events where the researcher (Karen) walked with a class of school-age children and their educators during their weekly visits to the wetlands. In contrast to traditional observations that aim to progress children along a continuum, paying attention to literacies emerging from Place–children encounters invites responses that ask, 'What is our shared responsibility for what happens next?'

In their chapter, Gould, Tesar and Boyd locate observation within a socio-material and ecological perspective aligned with *Te Whāriki*, which is curricular framework out of New Zealand. Filled with vivid and moving engagements between children and nature, readers can get lost in the chapter. Observations sit within learning stories that draw significantly on post-qualitative and Indigenous lenses on the ways that children learn across formal and informal contexts. The chapter thereby explores a broad range of approaches that researchers and teachers can apply from gaze, film and camera, written documentation and other methods to capture and describe children's experiences across early childhood spaces. There is a secondary emphasis in the chapter on children's tacit ecological sense-making and relational meaning-making with materials. Filled with sparks, pulses and flows, the chapter anchors children's meaning-making within human and more-than-human engagements.

In Chapter 6, Schulte focuses on the question 'What *is* happening here?' and what might happen to observations when we ask this question as postdevelopmental researchers. While subtle, this particular question stands to both broaden and complicate how we orientate ourselves to children's engagements with the visual arts. It stretches the frames of reference we have become accustomed to using and troubles the interpretive values we lean on most to rationalize this use. To ask this question is to take seriously the iterative act of wondering how, why and in what ways, right *here*, children's making is actually inviting us, at times nudging us, into a 'wormhole' (Sakr, 2021) of difference and reconfiguration. The chapter contemplates the conceptual and pedagogical relationship of this question to early art teacher education, specifically the ways in which it refigures observation as a speculative act, one that materializes new and unsettling routes to think and be with childhood art.

Mark Shillitoe, Harriet Hand, Jennifer Rowsell, Scarlett Shepherd and William Squire turn their attention to the ways in which the 2020 pandemic forced teachers around the world to dramatically change how they organized pedagogical spaces for children. With a sudden movement online, children not only grappled with the precarity and uncertainty of Covid-19 but also adapted in short order to digital spaces and virtual learning. Observing, documenting, thinking and writing together across two contexts, the authors explored how children entangle themselves with objects and modes with little adult input other than occasional chats, reinforcements and inquiries. In one year four classroom, Shillitoe transformed his primary teaching context into a space where 'serendipitous concurrences' (Burnett et al., 2020) happen, spark and take flight (Shillitoe, 2020). The chapter presents this exploratory research study with a focus on children's spatial and more-than-human engagements and their implications for ways that researchers approach childhood observation.

In Chapter 8, applying a feminist theoretical framework, McClure, as an artist, scholar and educator, gives readers a bird's eye view of two toddlers working in 'Hop{Scoth} Studio Lab'. By filming the two young children's art-making experiences. Sparks are in abundance in this chapter with a deep dive into art-making and DIY work with children and adults together making, thinking and being. In the chapter, McClure maps children's movements through activities from a visual essay to collaborative narrative portraits. Making illustrations and installations together, adults and children navigate their own emotions and embodied sensations with artistic improvisations. The chapter is a living record of the flows, pulses and sparks that ensure when creative processes and practices (and their attend vulnerabilities are elicited). Observations in the chapter make visible complex ways of knowing and being by the toddlers and the ways that they can get lost within developmental observations of young children.

In their chapter, Nordström and Sintonen explore the use of baby journals as a way for parents to track their baby's development and moments of joy and growth in the first year. Deconstructing examples of popular journals in Finland, they explore how a posthumanist approach can de-centre a child's biological growth as the main aspect of this momentous experience for new families. They explore what alternative conceptualizations of the child and childhood might become possible when the documentation of a baby's first year of life is approached differently.

In Chapter 10, Sakr explores how to approach the analysis of photography and video as part of postdevelopmental childhood observations. The chapter considers how when we play with how we analyse photographs and videos that are part of childhood observation, we are opening up, questioning and deconstructing a much deeper set of assumptions about children and childhood. Theory can support us in this experimentation and, in this chapter, Sakr explores the invitations to think differently about photographs offered by Barthes in his work *Camera Lucida*. Taking Barthes' reconceptualizations of photography as a starting point, she experiments with an analysis of a four-second video fragment of her nephew E engaged in art-making in the family home. She shows how, when thinking with Barthes, the focus re-orientates to new details in the action and interaction which in turn opens up new lines of questioning. Rather than putting the child in the evaluative gaze of the adult, these new lines of questioning create a foundation for authentic curiosity and co-presence – two potential pillars of a postdevelopmental approach.

References

Barad, K. (2007). *Meeting the universe halfway: Quantum physics and the entanglement of matter and meaning.* Duke University Press.

Boldt, G. (2020). Theorizing vitality in the literacy classroom. *Reading Research Quarterly, 56*(2), 207–221.

Burman, E. (1994). *Deconstructing developmental psychology* (1st ed.). Routledge.

Burman, E. (2008). *Deconstructing developmental psychology* (2nd ed.). Routledge.

Burnett, C., Merchant, G., & Neumann, M. (2020). The appearance of literacy in communicative practices: Interrogating the politics of noticing. *Cambridge Journal of Education, 50*(2), 167–183.

Ingold, T. (2013). *Making: Anthropology, archaeology, art and architecture*. Routledge.

Manning, E., & Massumi, B. (2014). *Thought in the act: Passages in the ecology of experience*. University of Minnesota Press.

Osgood, J., & Sakr, M. (2019). *Postdevelopmental approaches to childhood art*. Bloomsbury.

Sakr, M. (2021). 'She's nice company and a good friend': Thinking with Haraway to reconceptualise children's playful interactions with Alexa in the family home. In J. Mikats, S. Kink-Hampersberger, & L. Oates-Indruchova (Eds.), *Creative families: Gender and technologies of everyday life* (pp. 167–88). Palgrave Macmillan.

Shillitoe, M. (2020). Arts-based practice: A tactical pedagogy. In C. McLean & J. Rowsell (Eds.), *Maker literacies and maker identities in the digital age* (pp. 94–117). Routledge.

1

The Rhythm

Posthuman Perspectives on Childhoods and Classroom Observation

Kortney Sherbine
Independent Researcher

Introduction

Like others who engage in classroom research alongside young children (cf, Davies, 2014; Jones et al., 2010; Leafgren, 2009; Leander & Boldt, 2013; Lenz Taguchi, 2010; Olsson, 2009; Sellers, 2013; Thiel, 2015), I am interested in how posthumanist philosophies can help us (re)think what is involved in coming into relationship with children and research. Posthumanism involves an onto-epistemology that demands a shift from representational thinking about the individual to speculative thinking about the collective; it involves considerations of entanglements among bodies and objects that are driven by becomings and affect and that are always productive with the potential for transformation and reinvention.

In this chapter, I experiment with posthumanist concepts in consideration of what matters in childhood and observations of children in classrooms. To do so, I return to data from an ethnographic study at a public elementary school in the southeastern United States. I begin with a vignette that I developed from expanded field notes, jotted over the course of about thirty minutes one morning in Mrs L's second-grade classroom. The vignette highlights the complexity and vitality of the classroom as bodies and objects move and engage in a myriad of activities across contexts. I then interrogate the developmental perspectives that positioned and classified the children in particular ways that morning before offering a posthumanist analysis that seeks to understand the entanglements of childhood and research in affective and emergent ways.

An [A]Typical Morning

It was the beginning of the literacy workshop in Mrs L's second-grade classroom. I leaned against the wall, near the video camera, watching the children as they moved around the classroom. It took a few moments for everyone to settle in to their activities for the morning. Ten children read books – either at their desks or on cushions on the floor around the classroom. Two children played sound-letter correspondence games on the computer. Ray-Ray[1] and Mello worked together on drawing a basketball comic at their table. Gabby pinched Million Dollar Man on the arm, drawing the ire of Track Star, who immediately rushed to tell the student teacher, Ms M, about the assault on his best friend. Ms M suggested that Track Star return to his seat, which he did after he stomped away and yelled, 'I was trying to help him!'

Ms. M glided around the room and tapped a few children on the shoulder. As she moved from one to the next, each gathered supplies and walked to the small group learning space on the carpet. Suddenly, Track Star was at my side. 'Ms. Sherb', he said, 'Gabby hurt my best friend's feelings. She pinched him.'

'I'm really sorry that happened,' I tried to assure him. 'It is kind of you to look out for your friend.'

As Track Star moved towards his desk once again, I focused in on the small group of children congregating with both teachers on the carpet. Mrs L was distributing papers with an image of a double-bubble map, a graphic organizer with approximately ten circles connected by lines, that was often used to support students as they compare and contrast ideas from texts. Ms M sat slightly behind her, preparing to watch her mentor teach the lesson. The children either sat cross-legged with clipboards on their laps or stretched out on their stomachs, propped up on their elbows. Pencils were nearby. As I slid into a chair nearby with my field notebook, the lesson began.

'Today we're going to practice comparing and contrasting with our double-bubble maps', said Mrs L. 'Remember that when we compare, we think about how things are the same and when we contrast, we think about how they are . . .?'

'DIFFERENT!' the children called out in chorus.

'Right', Mrs L continued. 'This is *The Gospel Cinderella* (Thomas & Diaz, 2004). We've already read it, so you know what happens. But we're going to take a picture walk through the book to get some good ideas that will help us remember a book that has already been read. Think about the characters in the book and one of the historical figures we're learning about in social studies.' Mrs

L turned the pages of the book. Some children leaned in as they scrutinized the illustrations. Others glanced from the book to their clipboard and around the room at their classmates. DJ laid down with two clipboards, holding his pencil between his thumb and index finger and flipping it back and forth so that the eraser and lead tapped each clipboard over and over again, a rhythmic beat emerging in the taps. *Tap tap taptap taptap. Tap tap taptap taptap.* DJ then stuck his pencil in the hole along the top edge of one of the clipboards.

As Mrs L closed the book, Bella raised her hand and spoke. 'She [Cinderella] was just like Martin Luther King because she was standing up for herself.' Mrs L smiled.

'I liked it because . . . because . . . ', DJ chimed in. He attempted to articulate his ideas a few times before he was hushed by the other children.

'How many clipboards, DJ?' asked, Mrs L.

'Only one,' he replied.

'Could you put the other one away?'

DJ stood to return one of the clipboards to the basket on the shelf as Mrs L asked the children to consider the historical figure they were learning about in social studies and compare and contrast that person with the characters from *The Gospel Cinderella*. She instructed them to write down one idea before returning to their desks to work independently.

'Is your name on your paper?' she asked DJ as he looked at his classmates. 'We've got too much to do today for you to be messing around.'

DJ wrote his name on his paper and then asked, 'Can I work with you today, Mrs. L?'

'Not today,' she replied. 'Finish up writing down your idea, everyone, and then show me flat pencils.' DJ put his head down for a moment and then began filling out the first bubble on his paper. 'Okay, I'd like to see flat pencils,' Mrs L repeated. 'Are you ready, DJ?'

'Yes, I'm ready,' he replied.

'So where should your pencil be?' Mrs L asked.

DJ placed his pencil not flat on his clipboard, as Mrs L expected, but back in the hole of the clipboard. He glanced down and moved the pencil to the surface of the clipboard. The other children shared the ideas they wrote on their papers before all were excused to finish completing the double-bubble map at their desks. A clatter of bodies, clipboards, pencils and papers came like a wave as the children stood and began to move around the room.

DJ stopped when he saw me watching him. 'Can you help me with this?' he asked.

'Look, DJ, you've got this. You've already written down some great ideas. I think Mrs L wants you to do this on your own today,' I told him, though in the moment, I wanted nothing more than to walk with DJ to his desk, hear his ideas and offer support as he wrote those ideas on paper.

'I can't do it, it's too hard,' DJ mumbled as he walks to his seat.

I was completely enthralled in the children and the double-bubble maps, mostly because the lesson and activity seemed so out of character for Mrs L and her students. In this classroom, children generally had much more choice in what they read and how they responded. During the literacy workshop, students milled about the room independently, applying concepts from reading and writing mini lessons taught by Mrs L and the student teacher while drawing on texts and experiences that mattered personally to them and that were inspired by to their interests and preferences (see Sherbine, 2019, 2020). While Mrs L had grown frustrated with what she perceived as DJ's misbehaviour during the six months that I had been doing research in this classroom, he seemed particularly targeted on this day as a focus of her redirection. It made me feel uneasy as I reflected on the research indicating that Black students, like DJ, Bella and the majority of their classmates, are statistically more likely to be recommended for special education services (Blanchett, 2006) or suspended from school entirely (Milner, 2013).

I moved around the classroom and stopped periodically to sit with students as they wrote ideas on their double-bubble maps. 'Why are we doing this?' Bella asked as I shifted my body in the empty chair next to her. Admittedly, I shared Bella's concern about the authenticity of the assignment, which seemed so disconnected from the norm of the classroom.

Mrs L must have heard Bella, too, because it was she who responded, 'We need something to show your parents on Parent Night.'

'I'm going to share this picture!' Pickle exclaimed, holding up an illustration of a sports broadcaster he had been working on instead of his double-bubble map.

DJ and Million Dollar Man glanced up from their double-bubble maps to look at Pickle's drawing and then immediately looked back down and continued writing. DJ seemed to hear music as he bobbed his shoulders up and down in synch with a rhythm only he could hear. He must have sensed me watching. He looked my way, smiled, and said, 'I'm almost finished!'

What are we to make of these encounters between children, teachers, stories, clipboards, pencils, double-bubble maps, researcher, and . . . and . . . and? More specific to this chapter, and inseparable from the first question, how might we consider what it means to observe and be part of the children's entanglements with humans and objects in a classroom space where, at times, they seemed ostracized for not meeting the expectations of teachers and classmates?

As I take up these inquiries and reflect on my time as a university researcher learning alongside DJ, Ray-Ray, Mello, Gabby, Bella, Pickle, Million Dollar Man, Track Star, their classmates and teacher, I think-with posthumanist philosophies in order to recognize and amplify the children's ways of being in the classroom which, through a lens of developmental psychology, would be (and often are) considered abnormal or unacceptable. Further, I consider the movements of my observational research alongside DJ and his classmates as I sought to learn more about how literacy unfolded and the myriad ways children demonstrate their competencies in the classroom.

After a brief introduction to the children, teachers and the research site, I describe a number of concepts that I then plug into the vignette that opens this chapter in order to engage with the relationships between and among bodies and objects in Mrs L's classroom. I conclude with a consideration of how an ethics of immanence (Lenz Taguchi, 2010) might provide teachers and researchers with productive and loving ways to consider how children are always becoming in-the-moment in the classroom.

Situating the Rhythm

The morning that DJ and his classmates met with Mrs L to discuss *The Gospel Cinderella* and began completing their double-bubble maps occurred about six months into an eight-month-long ethnographic study of a second-grade classroom in the southeastern United States. As I have detailed elsewhere (Sherbine, 2019, 2020, Under Review), I was initially drawn to Mrs L and the children in the classroom because of the amount of choice that was embedded into the children's literacy encounters. Typically, Mrs L organized literacy instruction around a workshop model, wherein she taught a brief reading or writing mini lesson that focused on a particular skill or strategy and then offered ample time for students to practice that skill or strategy with texts of their choosing. Much of the children's encounters with texts were collaborative and play-filled as they created narratives that blended and remixed storylines and characterizations from popular television shows, music and sports events. In other words, Mrs L and her students engaged in what Dyson (2003a, 2003b) termed a 'permeable curriculum', one that built connections between school-based literacies and home-based interests. The basketball comic created collaboratively by Ray-Ray and Mello was just one example of students working and playing together as they co-constructed meaning with texts and artefacts that were meaningful to them (see Sherbine, 2020 for an in-depth analysis of the children's encounters with WWE wrestling figurines).

As I noticed the children engaging with ideas from popular culture in their literacy encounters, I jotted field notes in a small brown notebook that I carried with me as I joined the children in their reading and writing. The children soon recognized the notebook as a space where I was writing down my observations and, frequently, the details of their conversations. On more than one occasion, a child asked me to read what I had written down or looked carefully at the words scribbled on the page that I would elaborate upon later with my own questions, theoretical connections and notes about my emotional responses. I video-recorded each session and viewed the recordings as I expanded field notes, looking for details and intra-actions that were occurring simultaneously to whatever moment I may have been focused on. The video camera was, at first, quite an oddity to the students as I took care to set it up each morning in a corner of the classroom that would, ideally, record a wide shot of the space as bodies and objects moved around during instruction and independent practice. For the first week or so, the students took turns moving the tripod, turning the camera on and off, and working with the zoom feature. By my third week in the classroom, Million Dollar Man had taken it upon himself to set up the camera for me each morning upon my arrival.

I also had audio recorders that I placed with different groups as children worked together on various projects. The children were just as fascinated with this technology as they had been with the camera, though they grew accustomed to the presence of the small metal boxes and got in the habit of turning the microphone towards whoever was speaking in the group at a given time. In the days following the small group work with *The Gospel Cinderella*, Ray-Ray shared the basketball comic with me and became distracted and amused by his capacity to alter the movement of the lines on the voice recorder app of my iPhone by changing the volume and inflection of his voice (I had forgotten the bag with the audio recorders that day and had to make do with what I had with me). The children were becoming co-researchers with me as they made decisions about whose spoken discourse was amplified and how it was amplified in particular moments.

My focus on the children's encounters with data collection technologies is critical here because the classroom ethnography that unfolded in Mrs L's classroom focused on the relationships and interconnections between bodies and objects. That is, the objects and people whose purpose was to observe and generate data about the happenings of the classroom quickly became part of those happenings, entangled with the children's movements around the classroom. There was a constant blending of child-object-technology-researcher throughout the study; permeable boundaries in an exploration of a permeable curriculum.

DJ, Classmates, Clipboards, And . . . And . . . And . . .

Throughout this chapter, I draw heavily on philosophical concepts described by Deleuze and Guattari (1977, 1987) as I consider the opening vignette. I appreciate Deleuze and Guattari's focus on potential and possibility in their conceptual philosophy. For them, playing with concepts allows for new ways of thinking about what it *might* mean to be in the world. That is, rather than focusing on representations of being that always refer to familiar representations of reading, writing, playing, observing and researching, thinking with concepts in creative ways allows us to disrupt what we think we know to speculate on what else *might* be possible.

Deleuze and Guattari (1977, 1987) put forth the concept of *assemblage* as one that carries the potential to think differently about relationships in the classroom. Assemblage can be described as a coming-together of heterogeneous parts in a way that new experiences and emotions are felt, and new affects are registered on the body. As Leander and Boldt (2013) write, the assemblage is 'the collection of things that happen to be present in any given context. These things have no necessary relation to one another, and they lack organization, yet their happenstance coming together in the assemblage produces any number of possible effects on the elements in the assemblage' (p. 25). While I name part of the introductory assemblage as DJ-classmates-clipboards-teachers-double-bubble map-researcher, I do not mean to suggest that the assemblage is a static thing that serves as a representation of a moment. Assemblages, rather, are doings or makings, always in-process, changing and producing newness from one moment to the next.

The DJ-classmates-clipboards-teachers-double-bubble map-researcher assemblage comprises what MacClure (2010) describes as a 'glow' in the data. It simultaneously slows down and speeds up my considerations of childhood in the classroom as it beckons me to look deeper at the interconnectedness of bodies and objects while also cultivating more connections with other bits from my field notes and interview transcripts. There was an affective response involved in encountering the glow that morning as I become attuned to Mrs L's impatience with DJ and DJ's emotional response. The attunement continues now as I reread my field notes and review video data. Their displays of emotion register on my own body and in my psyche as I desire to speak up on DJ's behalf, fretting that his ideas and contributions did not matter as much as how he behaved during instruction.

This particular assemblage glows, reaches out and beckons further scrutiny, in part, because the small group mini lesson was such an anomaly given the more typical ways that literacy unfolded in the classroom. The rigid structure of the worksheet and number of clipboards permitted, the demands that pencils be positioned a certain way, the time constraints put on children to think and write, and the public identification of DJ's failure to meet expectations functioned to convey a limited view of *what counted* as literacy learning and participation that day.

Developmental Perspectives on Childhood [Observations]

These reductive notions of *what counts* as appropriate in the classroom emerge from 'the hegemony of developmental psychology', (Tarr, 2003, p. 7), wherein the focus is not on the potentialities of the collective assemblage, but on the individual and the individual's efforts based on a universal trajectory towards a predetermined outcome (Genishi & Dyson, 2009; James et al., 1998; Sellers, 2013; Sherbine, 2016). As Sellers (2013) writes, developmental paradigms at once normalize and pathologize and 'overlook the fact that valorizing normalcy limits possibilities for children, and positions those who define what is "normal" – adult experts, most likely white, middle class – at the top of a hierarchy of power' (p. 36).

Further, developmental perspectives involve fixed notions of thinking about childhood which lead to taken-for-granted ideas about who children should be, how they should behave, how they should learn, what their limitations are, etc. (Lenz Taguchi, 2010; Sellers, 2013; Yelland, 2010). As Sakr and Osgood (2019) suggest, '[d]evelopmental paradigms contribute to the marginalization of children who do not fit the norms that are inevitable within a developmental model' (p. 2).

To consider the DJ-classmates-teachers-clipboards-double-bubble maps assemblage from a developmental perspective would involve scrutinizing the children's behaviours in comparison to an ideal. For example, Bella engaged with Mrs L's assignment in a way that Mrs L deemed appropriate as she answered the prompt for the lesson directly. Her behaviours were normalized through Mrs L's verbal and nonverbal responses to her during small group instruction and through the absence of hushing from her classmates when she shared her ideas aloud.

Developmental paradigms might suggest that DJ was a distracted student playing with clipboards who was not attentive enough to formulate an idea to share with his classmates and who relied too much on adult assistance to complete an assignment. These perspectives were reified in the verbal redirections from Mrs L and the impatience demonstrated by his classmates as he attempted to respond to the teacher's prompt; there was a particular way to *do school* during small group instruction and it was clear that DJ did not meet those expectations. In my view, this developmental perspective on childhood is one that sees only deficit in children like DJ and conflicts with perspectives that are oriented towards ethics and care.

Likewise, developmental perspectives on observations of and research about children involve formulations and protocols that assume there is an outcome that can be *known* or *understood* and that there is a question that can be *answered*. The focus on the individual rather than the collective positions the observer/researcher on the outside looking in thereby removed from the child's encounters and taking note of what is occurring without recognizing one's own function in the assemblage. In a developmental paradigm, observations are made based on the predetermined assumptions about what children can or cannot and should or should not do; there is little room for considering the unexpected, experimentative, playfulness that is such a part of children's lived experiences (Olsson, 2009).

Posthumanist Perspectives on Childhood Observation

I am drawn to posthumanist philosophical perspectives, informed by the work of Deleuze and Guattari (1977, 1987), Barad (2007), and Bennett (2010) because, in their attentiveness to relationships, connections and entanglements, they centre an emergence of ethics and care. Posthumanisms recognize multiple ways of being and becoming in the world as always in-the-moment and always in relation with another. Further, the relationships are not limited to only the human; posthumanisms consider the comings-together of human and non-human objects in consideration of what matters, the conditions under which they matter and what is generated in the mattering (Barad, 2007). The entanglements between humans and non-humans are productive as assemblages create opportunities for transformation and change. Thus, there is quite a chasm between developmental perspectives, which seek to categorize children in relation to a known outcome and posthumanist perspectives, which are interested in that which is contextualized, relational, nonrepresentational, and emergent (Leander & Boldt, 2013).

As I move beyond developmental perspectives in considerations of research with children in Mrs L's classroom, I invoke the concepts of *becoming* (Deleuze & Guattari, 1987) and *thing power* (Bennett, 2010) to think about the dynamic and interconnected nature of childhood and the observation of children.

In a Pinch: Becoming-Child-Researcher

Deleuze and Guattari (1987) elaborated on the concept of *becoming* in order to disrupt what they felt was the West's preoccupation with identity. They were interested in movements, flows and processes, rather than static or fixed notions of being. They wrote, 'to become is not to progress or regress along a series ' (p. 238). Thus, whereas identity in relation to developmental paradigms is always situated along a continuum, becoming is a verb involving relationships, connections and the emergence of difference. This difference is a change or a transformation, even at micro levels (Davies, 2014).

Becoming is always a becoming-with and so for those of us who are interested in thinking about childhood and observations of children from posthumanist perspectives, it is not enough to think of individualization and universals. Rather, becoming entails a transmission of affect, or potential, when bodies and objects come into relationship with one another in assemblages. These potentials lead to ongoing transformations – new possibilities for how we might be in the world, always in relationship, always entangled with others. Lenz Taguchi (2010) described the relationship between becoming and pedagogy:

> A pedagogy that deals with becomings basically means that we move – simultaneously – between what is (the actual), and what might become (the virtual). What Deleuze calls the virtual is the reality of the potentialities of all organisms in the interconnectedness with everything around us. Drawing upon Deleuze, we strive for the *virtual* potentialities of a child, an organism or an event, which allows for the child (and yourself as teacher) to reinvent herself or himself with each event, and to be affirmative of learning as a state of transformation. (p. 176)

To think-with becoming and the vignette that opens this chapter is to consider the ways in which the humans and objects in the assemblage were involved in affective transformations or reinventions from one moment to the next. Ray-Ray and Mello, in their relationships with comic-making materials and basketball discourse and through their collaborative drawing and storytelling, were becoming-comic, becoming-sports broadcasters and becoming-artists. Their pencils became microphones as they announced the game, stopping to add speech bubbles. They talked over one another as they drew the elements of their comic and appropriated language from broadcasts they had seen on television. A familiar sports genre became entangled with what was happening in-the-moment as the marks on the page took on a narrative of their own. If even for a moment, the process of being part of the children-comics-basketball assemblage created an opportunity for the boys to experience writing – and basketball and comic-making and being in the classroom – differently.

The assemblage that emerged when Gabby pinched Million Dollar Man created an opportunity for Gabby, who might be described as a passive and quiet student, to experience becoming-instigator while Track Star was becoming-protector and becoming-mediator. Through my observation of the pinch and a verbal beckon from Track Star, I was pulled into the fluid assemblage as well, becoming-empathy and possibly becoming-attentive as, somewhat deliberately, I wanted to validate Track Star's effort to demonstrate empathy for his friend.

In the Gabby-pinch-Million Dollar Man-Track Star-stomping assemblage, the children and I were in processes of engaging in affective encounters with one another, transformed by the collision and movements of bodies, the words in raised voices, and the beat of stomps across a linoleum floor. I did not observe this assemblage passively. Rather, I was attuned to my increased heart rate as Track Star spoke with me *after* he'd talked to his teacher as the children – or at least Track Star in that moment – recognized me as having some level of authority in the classroom space. How might I offer him something different than what Ms M did when he shared his frustrations with her? How might what I offer him be from a place of empathy and care while not subverting the student teacher's redirection? These questions might not emerge when the focus of the observation is on checking boxes on an observation sheet or quickly writing anecdotes that 'capture' a moment. As Lenz Taguchi (2010) writes,

> If we believe that the child in learning is a process of transformation and becomes anew in intra-actions and interconnectedness with the rest of the world, then it becomes impossible to exclusively adhere to the pre-formulated stages of

maturity or learning specific contents, as in the case of constructivist theories of learning and developmentally appropriate practices. (p. 177)

Posthumanist observation – and pedagogy, for that matter – involve *becoming in the moment*, which for observers and teachers involves being actively attuned to the connections as well as the dissonance that emerges in relationships with the children.

Rhythm and Marginalization: Becoming-DJ-Clipboards

During my observations in Mrs L's classroom, DJ and his relationships with objects in the classroom reminded me of how interconnectedness matters. I have written elsewhere about DJ's entanglements with stuffed toy cows (Sherbine, Under Review), wrestling figurines, and how the encounters between DJ and objects tended to amplify his many competencies in the classroom (Sherbine, 2019). Bennett (2010) defines this capacity of objects to do things, to 'make a difference, produce effects, alter the course of events' (p. viii) as *thing power*. Drawing on Latour, Bennett described thing power as 'the curious ability of inanimate objects to animate, to act, to produce effects dramatic and subtle' (p. 6). Inanimate objects do not act on their own, however, but are always in relationship with other human and non-human bodies. Extending Deleuze and Guattari's (1987) assemblage, Bennett (2010) envisages an 'agentic assemblage' (p. 111) that is a coming-together of the animate and inanimate (Jackson & Mazzei, 2016).

To think-with thing power and the DJ-teacher-pencil-clipboard-double-bubble map-researcher as an agentic assemblage is to speculate on what might have been produced by the entanglements between the human and non-human that morning. It seems that the pencil, clipboards and double-bubble map in concert with Mrs L, the discourse of Parent Night, and DJ's prior experiences participating in literacy instruction (Sherbine, 2019) produced pressures to perform and conform. The pencil-clipboard-double-bubble map functioned to confine DJ's – and his classmates' – thinking in a way that demanded a particular type of articulation that could be organized into small circles spread across an eight-and-a-half by eleven-inch piece of paper. The pencil-clipboard-double-bubble map also disrupted the children's notion of what literacy learning in Mrs L's classroom entailed. The structure provided by the objects in the small group stripped away the choice that the children were accustomed to, creating a palpable sense of uncertainty and apprehension at that moment.

It could also be that the pencil and clipboard opened something up for and with DJ: a space to create a rhythm. Perhaps the rhythm created an opportunity for him to *make* something in a moment when his contributions to the group were overlooked. The rhythm created a slight spectacle that drew Mrs L's attention to him when his contributions were quieted by his classmates. Perhaps the rhythm that started with the clipboards and pencil carried DJ's thinking later as he sat at this desk and wrote down his ideas: *DJ seemed to hear music as he bobbed his shoulders up and down in synch with a rhythm only he could hear. He must have sensed me watching and he looked my way, smiles, and said, 'I'm almost finished!'*

Bennett (2010) writes that 'a theory of vibrant matter presents individuals as simply incapable of bearing *full* responsibility for their effects' (p. 37); it is always the body 'and . . . and . . . and . . . ' (Deleuze & Guattari, 1987, p. 25) in the assemblage that creates new ways of becoming. This carries implications for classroom observation, as the focus of one's attention is never truly limited to just the children or just the children and teacher. Thinking with thing power in observation demands an account of the fluid and ephemeral relationships among human *and* non-human bodies. This means a careful consideration of not only the intra-actions between teachers and children but among texts, writing utensils, curricular materials, the classroom space itself, research equipment, etc. While setting up a camera in the corner of the classroom in order to get a wide shot might be one part of classroom observation, watching intently as children intra-act with objects, listening carefully as children and objects become entangled across contexts and being willing to speculate about the becomings that might emerge in those entanglements are part of posthumanist observation.

A willingness to speculate means letting go of the notion that we can ever truly see or understand what it is that we observe in classroom. Like bodies and objects, meaning is always on the move as assemblages shift and change, becoming new from one moment to the next (Gannon, 2016; St. Pierre, 2013). Thinking and acting with the concept of thing power enables us to attend to non-human objects, to recognize the potential that they carry in relationships with teachers and children and to engage more carefully with those relationships.

An Ethics of Immanence and Attunement to Potentialities

These reflections on entanglements and becomings among the human and non-human in the classroom led me to wonder about how posthumanist perspectives on observation might create new opportunities for teachers observing, working with and learning alongside children. In attending to the potentials, of what *might* be emerging in the relationships in the classroom, it seems that there is space to attend to what Lenz Taguchi (2010) described as an 'ethics of immanence', which honours who children are and their becomings in-the-moment. She writes, 'an ethics of immanence in education is concerned with the inter-connections and intra-actions in-between human and non-human organisms, matter and things, the contents and subjectivities of students that emerge through learning events' (pp. 175–6).

In an ethics of immanence, teachers recognize that children are *always* changing. To reduce them to some predetermined classification only ignores the potential that is emergent in their entanglements and becomings with other humans and objects. In this way, an ethics of immanence is focused on potentialities: on what *might* be, rather than on what should be. Stewart (2007) suggests that in attending to affect and becomings, we are able to 'slow the quick jump from representational thinking and evaluative critique long enough to find ways of approaching the complex and uncertain objects that fascinate because they literally hit us or exert a pull on us' (p. 4). Just as the glow in data provokes further scrutiny, speculating on becomings that emerge in the vital entanglements and agentic assemblages of a classroom opens up space to consider broader, and perhaps more inclusive, possibilities for what it means to be, become and belong.

On a pragmatic level, this means remaining attuned to affect, open to potential and cognizant of one's own entanglements with children and objects in moments of observation. An ethics of immanence suggests that we slow down and linger with the entanglements we notice among the human and non-human and that we refrain from drawing broad conclusions about what those entanglements might mean or how they might define children. Further, an ethics of immanence recognizes that there is *always* potential in classroom assemblages. Revisiting pedagogical documentation, anecdotal records, photographs of children's learning and play, and the like from different theoretical perspectives while plugging new philosophical concepts into assemblages creates opportunities to read things in new ways. In doing so, we attend to the ongoing potentialities of what it means to be alive and in relationship.

An ethics of immanence in observation suggests that new and emergent becomings are inevitable in the contexts surrounding teaching. In always looking at what *might* be, rather than what is, we remain in-the-moment, attentive to our own becomings as we come into relationship with the potentialities of childhood over and over again. Finally, Lenz Taguchi (2010) offers helpful insights on the power of potentialities when she alludes to work by Colebrook: 'Colebrook writes that ethics for Deleuze is about a "love for what is", and not an ethics of knowledge and a search for some truth, justification or foundation beyond, outside of or transcendent to what is' (p. 176). A love for what is. A love for DJ, the clipboards, pencil and rhythm that they created together. A love for Bella and her enthusiasm to share her ideas. A love for Track Star, Million Dollar Man, Gabby and a pinch that provided an opportunity to navigate friendships and limits. A love for Pickle's drawing and Pickle's love for his drawing. A love for comics. A love for basketball journalism. A love for the relationships and entanglements that speak to the vitality and lived-ness of the classroom.

Note

1 All of the children's names are pseudonyms selected by the children. Many of the names reflect the children's interests in popular culture at the time. Gabby's favourite gymnast was Gabby Douglas. Mello was an NBA fan whose favourite player was Carmello Anthony. Million Dollar Man watched WWE wrestling on television every Thursday evening.

References

Barad, K. (2007). *Meeting the universe halfway: Quantum physics and the entanglement of matter and meaning.* Duke University Press.
Bennett, J. (2010). *Vibrant matter: A political ecology of things.* Duke University Press.
Blanchett, W. (2006). Disproportionate representation of African American students in special education: Acknowledging the role of white privilege and racism. *Educational Researcher, 35*(6), 24–28.
Davies, B. (2014). *Listening to children: Being and becoming.* Routledge.
Deleuze, G., & Guattari, F. (1977). *Anti-Oedipus: Capitalism and schizophrenia.* Penguin Books.
Deleuze, G., & Guattari, F. (1987). *A thousand plateaus: Capitalism and schizophrenia.* University of Minnesota Press.
Dyson, A. (2003a). *Brothers and sisters learn to write: Popular literacies in childhood and school cultures.* Teachers College Press.
Dyson, A. (2003b). Popular literacies and the "all" children: Rethinking literacy development for contemporary childhoods. *Language Arts, 81*(1), 61–70.

Gannon, S. (2016). 'Local girl befriends vicious bear': Unleashing educational aspiration through a pedagogy of material-semiotic entanglement. In C. Taylor & C. Hughes (Eds.), *Posthuman research practices in education* (pp. 128–148). Palgrave MacMillan.

Genishi, C., & Dyson, A. (2009). *Children, language, & literacy: Diverse learners in diverse times*. Teachers College Press.

Jackson, A., & Mazzei, L. (2016). Thinking with an agentic assemblage in posthuman inquiry. In C. Taylor & C. Hughes (Eds.), *Posthuman research practices in education* (pp. 93–107). Palgrave MacMillan.

James, A., Jenks, C., & Prout, A. (1998). *Theorizing childhood*. Teachers College Press.

Jones, L., Holmes, R., MacRae, C., & MacClure, M. (2010). 'Improper' children. In N. Yelland (Ed.), *Contemporary perspectives on early childhood education* (pp. 177–191). Open University Press.

Leafren, S. (2009). *Reuben's fall: A rhizomatic analysis of disobedience in kindergarten*. Left Coast Press.

Leander, K., & Boldt, G. (2013). Rereading 'a pedagogy of multiliteracies': Bodies, text, and emergence. *Journal of Literacy Research, 45*(1), 22–46. https://doi.org/10.1177/1086296X12468587

Lenz Taguchi, H. (2010). *Going beyond the theory/practice divide in early childhood education: Introducing an intra-active pedagogy*. Routledge.

MacClure, M. (2010). The offence of theory. *Journal of Education Policy, 25*(2), 277–286.

Milner, R. (2013). Why are students of color (still) punished more severely and frequently than white students? *Urban Education, 48*(4), 483–489.

Olsson, L. (2009). *Movement and experimentation in young children's learning: Deleuze and Guattari in early childhood education*. Routledge.

Sakr, M., & Osgood, J. (2019). *Postdevelopmental approaches to childhood art*. Bloomsbury.

Sellers, M. (2013). *Young children becoming curriculum: Deleuze, Te Whāriki and curricular understandings*. Routledge.

Sherbine, K. (2016). Emerging childhoods & immanent becomings: Considering difference in one child's encounters with popular culture. *Discourse: Studies in the Cultural Politics of Education, 37*(5), 785-797.

Sherbine, K. (2019). Wrestling with competency and everyday literacies in school. *Journal of Language & Literacy Education, 15*(2), 1–22.

Sherbine, K. (2020). Track Star + thing power: Be[com]ing in the literacy workshop. *Journal of Early Childhood Literacy, 20*(4), 613–630.

Sherbine, K. (Under Review). Choke holds and Chick-Fil-A cows: Intimate literacies in the elementary classroom.

St. Pierre, E. (2013). The appearance of data. *Cultural Studies ⇔ Critical Methodologies, 13*(4), 223–227.

Stewart, K. (2007). *Ordinary affects*. Duke University Press.

Tarr, P. (2003). Reflections on the image of the child: Reproducer or creator of culture? *Art Education*, *56*(4), 6–11.

Thiel, J. (2015). "Bumblebee's in trouble!": Embodied literacies during imaginative superhero play. *Language Arts*, *93*(1), 38–49.

Thomas, J., & Diaz, D. (2004). *The gospel Cinderella*. Amistad.

Yelland, N. (2010). *Contemporary perspectives on early childhood education*. Open University Press.

2

Togetherness in Early Childhood Art

Observation *with* Young Children

Shana Cinquemani
Rhode Island School of Design

In the fall of 2014, I designed and taught a ten-week Saturday morning art class for young children (aged —three to five years old) on the campus of a large university in the South West United States. Within these classes, the children engaged primarily in voluntary art-making experiences, where they were given access to a wide variety of materials, yet no specific guidelines for how these materials should be used. On the seventh Saturday of this class, the children walked into our class (a college seminar room transformed into an early childhood art classroom) and saw, among the typical art studios set up, a provocation of light. There were three tripods each holding a metal clamp lamp with a different-coloured lightbulb inside. These lights stood in front of a white sheet which was suspended from a clothing rack. There was space in front of and behind the white sheet.

After drawing in their sketchbooks and settling into the morning, some of the children came up and began to interact with the light. There were no rules or guidelines presented, so they freely explored. They turned the lights on and off. They moved the lights so they pointed to the sheet directly in front of them, to the floor and to the ceiling (see Figure 2.1). They moved the tripods into different spots to see how that changed the experience and even shifted the lights so they pointed at each other in a triangular format. The tripods and lights were then shifted to behind the sheet, rather than in front of it. As the children played with these materials, I engaged alongside them. I commented on their actions and what I noticed – colours, shadows, shapes, etc. There were fourteen children in this class, and most of them wove in and out of this provocation. At moments they directly engaged or collaborated with peers to move or interact with the

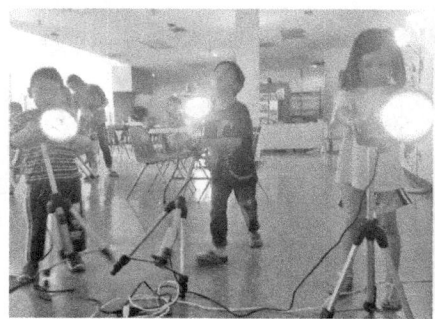 

Figures 2.1 and 2.2 Students exploring the provocation of coloured lights.

lights (see Figure 2.2). Some stood back and simply watched and others chose not to participate at all.

I offered the children a second way to engage after this initial experience – through the creation of shadow puppets. I gave the children black paper, scissors, tape and wooden skewers and showed them how they could use these materials to create 'puppets' that could perform behind the white sheet, creating shadows. Many of the children became busily engaged in creating characters that could act behind the screen, but ultimately seemed much more interested in the art of performing itself. Thus, an audience was needed (see Figure 2.3). I sat along with other children (who were either patiently waiting for their turn to perform or simply observing) to watch the stories unfold behind the screen. Working with their peers, the children's puppets came alive and acted out fantastical tales full of drama, movement and sound, but these stories were ultimately hard to interpret. Despite that hurdle, the children observing were enthralled and took bits and pieces from these performances into their own work.

There was a great deal of joy that stemmed from this experience which primarily surrounded the act of performing, observing and documenting. The creation of the puppets (what some might see as the core of the 'artmaking' experience here) was simply a means to an end. This element did not really excite the children. They used the crude shapes they drew and then cut out to tell stories of imaginary spaces and creatures that played and fought with each other. They wanted to put on a show and they wanted people to watch this show. At the same time, those of us in the audience were not simply viewing, but carefully observing and documenting as well (see Figure 2.4). The children used the digital cameras available within the classroom to record the performances of their peers, and then share and watch the recordings alongside the performers. Most often I sat in the audience alongside the children viewing

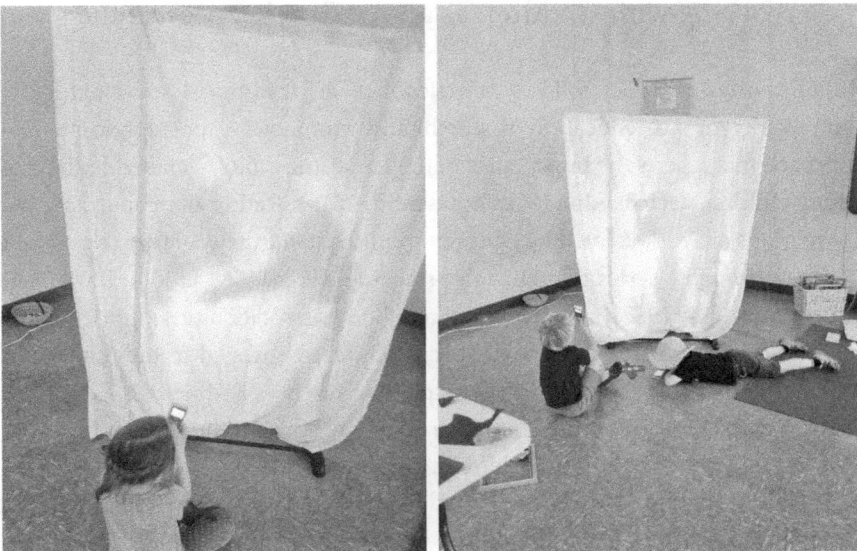

Figures 2.3 and 2.4 Children observing and documenting the shadow puppet performances.

or waiting for their turn to perform, documenting as well, but not always. At times I simply observed, talking with the children seated next to me about what was happening in the story. Within these moments, the children and I formed a collective, producing things that would not be possible alone (Mazzei & Jackson, 2012).

Yet I wonder what we each observed in these moments, and how these observations came to impact us. As I reflected later that day about watching the children perform, I recalled instances where I could have intervened, moments that challenged my own ideas about the power of the adults in charge. Should I have acted rather than just observed? Told the children performing to stand closer, speak louder, move their puppets more slowly or shift their bodies to the side so their own shadow did not overwhelm the silhouette of their puppet? While observing the children in action these thoughts ran through my head. But I did not act. I simply sat and observed alongside the other children. I wonder what the children observed while watching. Were they also paying attention to the lack of clarity? Or were they observing the joy of playing out your ideas in front of an audience? The way your puppet can move behind the screen, illuminated by the colourful light? The way the audience will be able to hear your voice but not necessarily hear your words? The fact that everyone else is watching you?

Working with Children as an Art Teacher-Researcher

Broadly, my practice follows a rejection of traditional developmental frameworks of art education research and embraces a postdevelopmental approach that asserts the importance of the social and cultural embeddedness of young children's art-making (Sakr & Osgood, 2019). Rather than analysing the anonymous artwork created by children to understand the way that they might develop through a series of predictable stages (Kellogg, 1967 [2007]; Lowenfeld & Brittian, 1964 [1987]), my own research follows a sociocultural model that is built around 'close observations of specific children engaged in the practice of making images and objects, in the company of teachers and peers' (Thompson et al., 2015, p. 399). This kind of practice takes into account the art-making event itself and all that contributes to children's ideas and making.

However, my practice is also grounded in my own positionality as teacher-researcher, and not simply researcher alone. This is an important distinction to note because I am interested in new ways that art educators can re-think the relationships they have with the children they teach and also how these relationships can come to inform both curriculum and pedagogy. Therefore, this work is more than simply observing children as they create and engaging with them in meaningful ways during this creation – but also thinking about how we can do this work as art classroom teachers and not guests within a classroom. Through this lens, the experiences shared within this chapter are grounded in ideas about observing *with* children more specifically, and having the opportunity to use observation to '[wonder] with children about what they see, think, and feel, and how they make sense of experiences' (Gandini et al., 2005, p. 2).

Most of my work in art-making, teaching and research with young children explores the idea of collective relationship, which rejects the teacher as an all-knowing figure who passes on their knowledge to students. Rather, I am interested in exploring what relationships between adults and children can look like if they were based on dialogue, fostering a co-construction of knowledge. I believe this is accomplished by working with children as collaborators and partners in exploration. It pushes back against notions of educators not interfering in children's art-making and simply allowing the false inherent creativity of the children to come forward (McClure, 2011). Rather, I am more interested in moments where young children and adults work together (Cinquemani, 2014, 2019; Cinquemani & Kraehe, 2020) to create something new. The examples I share within this chapter are drawn from a specific research project that was grounded in the notion of challenging issues of power, authority and knowledge in early childhood art education. In order to work through these ideas, the studio was built around art-making experiences created, led or inspired by the children themselves. I was eager to discover what could occur when adults took a step back from the typical early childhood art curriculum of either process or product, and let the children simply make or play with materials. In this view, play and making with materials extend beyond process but provide a way for children to learn the language of materials (a Reggio Emilia-inspired practice), allowing them to understand how they can use and manipulate art media to communicate their ideas. Additionally, this approach reaches beyond the artefacts of art-making to consider the interconnectedness between young children and materials.

Rejecting Power + Control: Observations *with* Children

Within the context of the art classroom described earlier, observation and documentation played a central role. It was a way to begin to understand the interests of the children, which was essential to the classroom itself (as it was designed to inherently reject teacher/adult control and lean into children's ideas more fully). Additionally, throughout this project, I was deeply interested in the ways in which the relationships between children and adults would form and change when children had control over their own art-making and explorations of materials. Via Vecchi (2010) writes that observation and documentation allow us to 'illustrate the extraordinary, beautiful and intelligent things children [know] how to do . . . [leading] to a much greater sense of respect for them and a desire to know them better' (p. 132–3). However, I was not interested in illustrating these things alone, but more so with the children. Therefore, I viewed all the elements of my role in the classroom as a collaborator, grounded in the idea of *with*.

This notion rejects commonly held ideas about art in early childhood or early elementary classrooms. Within these kinds of spaces, children create based on lessons that are carefully designed by adults, which often result in children having created a piece of art following step-by-step directions that look very similar to the art of their peers. Observations of this kind of art-making tend to be grounded in ideas about following directions, the creation of a 'successful' final project, or determining if children's use of tools or materials (or even their artwork itself) aligns to traditional developmental milestones. The idea of observation with young children also rejects ideas about power and control in traditional classroom spaces. As Canella and Viruru (2004) note, 'the gaze has been accepted as appropriate for all childhood spaces as a physical structure of power' (p. 109). This kind of gaze is grounded in the idea that children must always be watched over, positioning them in positions of inferiority. In contrast, observation with rather than on or about pushes back against these ideas about adult surveillance, power, control and a successful/correct final product. Rather, when we observe with or alongside children, we can create spaces of collective experience and communication.

Observation *with* the children in this art classroom developed organically. Because the adults in the space (myself and two undergraduate art education students) were actively involved with what the children were doing, making and thinking, it became almost impossible for us to observe alone. The children understood us as 'a different sort of adult' (Christensen, 2004, p. 174) – a kind of adult that would collaborate with them, pay attention to their ideas and help them bring their artistic visions to life. Sometimes this kind of adult also simply observed as they engaged in material exploration and making not typically sanctioned within the art classroom. However, as we modelled a deep engagement with what the children were doing and making (asking questions, writing down their ideas, taking photographs and videos and recording audio) the children did this as well. They often watched other children use materials or engage with provocations before they themselves tried them out. They would ask questions of their peers to learn a new technique or strategy. And often they would simply observe their peers alongside us as adults. Because this classroom was grounded in voluntary art-making experiences, the children were compelled to observe as a starting point for ideas.

Narrating in the Threshold – Telling Stories *with* Children

Vea Vecchi (2010) explains that observation and documentation can tell stories of children with complexity and tenderness. Yet I did not just want to tell stories 'of' children – I wanted to tell stories 'with' children. In order to do this, I embraced a kind of reflective storytelling where the children and I could re-live shared documentation as a way to *observe with each other*. This practice involved a kind of reflective storytelling. Drawn from observation and documentation collected from the previous art class, each Saturday I would invite the children to listen to 'stories from last week'. Using notes, audio recordings, photographs

Figures 2.5 and 2.6 The children and I engaging in reflective storytelling about last week's art class.

and videos (created by the children and the adult art teachers present) I created stories that told my memories of what had occurred during the previous week. I shared moments that were especially exciting for me (like collaborating with a student on a project), interactions that I saw between children and materials, as well as moments that I witnessed in passing that I wanted to know more about or examples of the children's art that needed additional context. I carefully wrote down these stories so I could read them back to the children alongside the images/videos (see Figures 2.5 and 2.6). Then, I asked for their ideas about my story – did I leave anything out? Was there something more they could tell me about their art or experience? Was anything I said incorrect? I used various ways to collect the children's ideas – from writing down their words on physical documentation next to their images to simply jotting down notes on my own.

What remains interesting for me about this experience was the way in which the children and I engaged in observation together about past moments, thus creating more layers of interpretation and understanding. I believe that our understanding and experiences can shift or change when we are able to see through someone else's perspective. The children saw images of themselves and their artwork narrated through my own point of view, yet were given the chance to alter the story. Thus, together we created new knowledge and ideas that were not possible alone. To borrow from Mazzei and Jackson (2012), we were thinking in the 'threshold' – a space 'between the two' that is 'both/and' (p. 450). Within the threshold, 'bits and pieces of each other' (p. 451) can be found in our work. Mazzei and Jackson go on to describe that this between or threshold space is, 'not a process of working individually to contribute to the whole but is a process of producing something not possible outside the space of the threshold where the "two" produce thinking not possible otherwise' (p. 451). The experience of storytelling with the children was messy and incomplete. Yet it created opportunities for collective remembering and experiencing where the observations were not mine alone but something all of the children could engage with.

Togetherness in Artmaking

Throughout this classroom, the acts of observing, documenting, creating and making *with* one other were ever present. Because the curriculum followed an emergent model and was inspired by the children's interests, there was a great deal of freedom for them to create the kinds of art that they wanted to, or just explore materials. Additionally, because there was time and space for children to sit back and observe (without the pressure of always being asked to make), the children were also able to internalize others' experiences and transform them into something new. There were many moments of the children being inspired by one another in new and exciting ways. The ideas for artworks and material explorations wove throughout the room and spanned time, some ideas coming back after weeks later.

The nature of this classroom and the focus on collaboration fostered a space where the children found joy and value in observing each other, with adults and by themselves. And they drew inspiration from those moments. The value of this kind of observation and making *with* was that it encouraged the children to lean into the idea of the collective rather than the singular. What they all created was not possible without observing the experiences of each other. Thus, the art created and the art-making experiences that occurred were more meaningful and dynamic since all of us had a hand in their creation. It was not simply the teacher telling the students what to create, or even the children 'copying' each other. Rather a collective inspiration occurred from the threshold spaces we embodied. We moved back and forth, and in and out, of private and collaborative making. Ultimately creating things that would have been impossible without each other.

References

Canella, G. S., & Viruru, R. (2004). *Childhood and postcolonization: Power, education, and contemporary practice*. Routledge Falmer.

Cinquemani, S. (2014). Entering the secret hideout: Fostering newness and space for art and play. *The Bank Street College of Education Occasional Papers, 31*. http://bankstreet.edu/occasional-paper-series/31/part-i/entering-the-secret- hideout/

Cinquemani, S. (2019). Working with children in the spaces between. In C. Schulte (Ed.), *Ethics and research with young children: Personal pedagogies* (pp. 77–88). Bloomsbury Press.

Cinquemani, S., & Kraehe, A. (2020). Thinking alongside children: Explorations of Artistic Practice and Research in Early Childhood. *Art Education, 73*(6), 4–11. (Editorial).

Christensen, P. H. (2004). Children's participation in ethnographic research: Issues of power and representation. *Children and Society, 18*, 165–176.

Gandini, L., Hill, L., Cadwell, L., & Schwall, C. (Eds.). (2005). *In the spirit of the studio: Learning from the atelier of Reggio Emilia*. Teachers College Press.

Kellogg, R. (1967 [2007]). *Rhoda Kellogg child art collection*. https://www.early-pictures.ch/kellogg/archive/en/

Lowenfeld, V., & Brittain, W. L. (1964 [1987]). *Creative and mental growth*. Prentice Hall.

Mazzei, L. A., & Jackson, A. Y. (2012). In the threshold: Writing between-the-two. *International Review of Qualitative Research, 5*(4), 449–458.

McClure, M. (2011). Child as totem: Redressing the myth of inherent creativity in early childhood. *Studies in Art Education, 52*(2), 127–141.

Sakr, M., & Osgood, J. (Eds.). (2019). *Postdevelopmental approaches to childhood art*. Bloomsbury Press.

Thompson, C. M., McClure, M., Schulte, C., & Sunday, K. (2015). New directions in researching young children's art making. In O. Saracho (Ed.), *Handbook of research methods in early childhood education: Review of research methodologies volume II* (pp. 393–432). Information Age.

Vecchi, V. (2010). *Art and creativity in Reggio Emilia: Exploring the role and potential of ateliers in early childhood education*. Routledge.

3

Movements, Synchronicities, Choreographies

Attuning to Young Children's Drawing

Sylvia Kind
Capilano University, Canada

This chapter considers observation and documentation of young children's artistic engagements as processes of attuning to and finding a rhythm and synchronicity with what is going on, and as acts of finding one's way towards corresponding *with* rather than collecting information *about* a child's artistry. It draws on the experimental work of Manning and Massumi, Ingold, Kontturi and artists' practices as it considers thinking through making (Ingold, 2013) and thinking through doing (Manning & Massumi, 2014). This shifts the intention away from learning *about* children's processes and artistry and observing from a distance to an immersive and responsive listening and attention. It orients us to questions of how mark-making, drawing, materials and bodies move together and how we might respond and work with children's rhythms, approaches and co-compositional processes. It aims to know things differently through 'motional-relational' (Manning and Massumi, 2014, p. 42) knowing, and bodied feeling-knowing (Manning, 2012).

If we think of making, artistic creation, or drawing as a project (Ingold, 2013) then we focus on the processes and productions, as if it is a trajectory from idea to form. As if the child has an idea in mind and through materials brings this idea into form. Or in the case of very young children, we may focus on the pleasure of the explorations and processes as if there is no intended result or on their progressions from rudimentary marks to more differentiated images. But what if we think of making differently as a process of correspondence (Ingold, 2013) taking shape within a field of forces, and the child as a participant in a world of active materials (Pacini-Ketchabaw et al., 2017), then it demands other attunements, perceptual engagements and ways of attending. Rather than a descriptive process, inquiring into children's artistry becomes a delicate process of thinking about what is going on while learning to move with the compositions, where nothing can be 'captured' just responded to.

In this chapter I trace the beginning of an ongoing inquiry into drawing with infants and toddlers, ages one to three years, that I am engaged in as atelierista alongside early childhood educators in a university campus Children's Centre. In doing this I open up our processes of paying attention, documenting, engaging with and responding to the emerging insights. Rather than situating these processes as 'observation' I am particularly interested in what it might mean to attend, pay attention and develop responsive attunements to what is taking place. From the Latin *attendere,* the word 'attend' suggests stretching towards. Ingold (2018) elaborates on this by describing acts of attention as caring, listening, waiting, being present, going along, joining with and longing as in 'the stretching of a life' (p.21). In similar ways, I understand attunement as a sensitive reciprocity, a symbiotic orchestration or movement *with*, rather than knowledge about someone or something. To attune to something is to pay close attention, orient towards it and find a rhythm and synchronicity with it (Kind, 2020). Attunement can be understood as tuning-to, as in tuning a musical instrument to another, entering into the rhythms and tempos in harmony with or in counterpoint to what is going on, and having a sense of what matters and what is taking shape in *this* situation. It reflects acts of reaching towards, leaning closer into, stretching ourselves beyond what we might typically hear, see or notice, in attentive and bodied *responsive*, not just receptive, listening. To attend, and to listen, is to become open to being affected (Davies, 2014).

In the Children's Centre, particularly in the infant and toddler rooms drawing is typically encountered as a time of collective gathering where educators often join with children in drawing alongside each other. Through this project, along with the educators, I hope to open more vibrant spaces of drawing together, responding and cultivating conditions for sensitive response-ability in correspondence with the events. In drawing together, to do more than simply echo what children are doing, and to respond to more than the mark. The intent of our inquiry then isn't to 'learn more about' young children's drawing, although we do hope for more nuanced and intimate understandings, but to invigorate life-living pedagogies in new ways and to engage in documentation and these acts of attention as processes of way-finding and curriculum-making (Vintimilla & Kind, 2021). As Cristina Delgado Vintimilla (n.d) discusses, pedagogy is not just interested in describing existing conditions but in 'activating possible orientations that will provoke educational processes to invent a living curriculum that experiments with alternative propositions and intentions' (para. 7). This project takes shape at the intersections of art and pedagogy, where collective drawing and the hope for a more vibrant engagement with the textures, tonalities, rhythms and co-compositions of drawing meets this desire. The pedagogical impulse of the project is concerned with creating a life together, activating new ways of knowing, being and creating together.

Situating Drawing

In considering young children's drawings, attention is typically drawn to the moment of mark-making when pastel, crayon or pencil meets paper and an image begins to form. There is the hope that by observing and listening to the child, attending to the characteristics of the marks made, and to the emerging processes, verbalizations and stories, one can discover what their drawings are about. This situates drawing as a form of self-expression, language or communication that offers insight into children's inner worlds, invented narratives and symbolic and representational efforts. It considers the child as the central protagonist and instigator of graphic and verbal narratives. Within this frame it makes sense to observe the child, document individual processes, take note of how drawings take shape from the first mark to the finished image, consider the progression of images and the ways that meanings and stories are formed and articulated. Situating drawing of infants and toddlers in this way also tends to frame their efforts within developmental processes of learning to draw with attention given to how mark-making and use of materials becomes more fluid and differentiated over time. So that their ways of drawing are perceived as phases they go through in developing more sophisticated approaches and representations.

Certainly, what children's drawings say, mean, represent and communicate matters and there is rich beauty and variance in the marks, lines, images, words, stories and the perspectives and interpretive insights that are generated (see Vecchi & Ruozzi, 2015). The singularity of each child, their processes, visual narratives and their artistic growth and learning matter a great deal. Yet if we think outside of representation, art as a project or object and a reflection of a child's knowledge or skill, other possibilities open up. Rather than centring, observing or looking at the child as if the child holds the meaningfulness of the drawing if we see the child as a participant within an ecology of materials and relations, the focus shifts to *looking-with* drawing as it unfolds and becomes active within a field of intersecting forces. This frames drawing as an event, always a collective, a multiplicity of relations in movement together. Spaces, places, materials, surfaces, child, educator, bodies,

Figure 3.1 The liveliness of drawing.

ideas, verbalizations, sonorities, gestures, actions of drawing, emerging marks and images are in movement together so that drawing moves beyond the bounds of the paper and is more than ideas made visible. Drawing in this way takes shape in concert with the exchanges, mutualities and intra-actions so that drawing becomes 'an animated, lively, and transmutable thing' (Penn, 2021, p. 151) (Figure 3.1).

In resonance with Kontturi (2018), this considers drawing as always in-process, and in 'perpetual movement' (p. 9). Thus, the meaning isn't located in individual works, marks and images, or in or with a child, but is produced in the living, doing, making of it, and in the entanglements, relationalities and assemblage of influences. The primary concern then, becomes how a work *works*, its doings and activations and what it makes possible or sets in motion. This means being attentive to drawing in-the-making, and its unfoldings and relations. 'To follow, then, is to embrace the "work" of art, its material, affective, and relational doings that push it beyond the representational function, offering something new instead of what is already known' (Kontturi, 2018, p. 10).

Drawing as Dance

We begin to attend to infants and toddlers drawing by reading John Matthews (2003) together as a way of enlarging our understanding of what might be part of the actions of mark-making. Matthews, working from an artistic development perspective, richly describes the kinaesthetic, haptic, bodied, gestural, action drawings of very young children. He offers nuanced insight into the bodied acts of drawing which helps us notice more of the details and particularities of children's drawing actions, but it's the proposition to consider drawing as 'a patterned dance in space and time' (p. 34) that lingers and becomes our propelling curiosity. What happens when we see drawing in this way, when drawing, as choreography, 'becomes a field for movement expression when the body becomes an intensive participant with the evolving milieu rather than simply the instigator of the action' (Manning, 2013, p. 101)?

O'Sullivan (2006) describes how 'art becomes predetermined by the questions you have asked' (p. 14). Thus, if we start with the proposition that young children's drawing could take shape as a dance-like choreographic event, then the aim is not so much to understand or gain more knowledge about children's images and intentions, or to prove Matthews's assertions, but to engage with the proposition, enter in and feel the rhythms, movements, and collective improvizations and discover what is brought into view and becomes undone in the process. Engaging with Manning's (2013) choreographic thinking, we consider drawing as a way of moving, creating and composing within a field of relations, improvising with others and with the rhythms, tempos, gestural expressions and co-emergences. So that it's not just an individual child's way or aspect of a child's artistic development that they move through and leave behind, but the shape of the event. Attending to drawing in this way is shaped by thinking-doing or motional-relational knowing where 'the what-if is moving thinking itself out' (Manning & Massumi, 2014, p. 43). As Kontturi (2018) describes, 'it is about entering a wave of life unfurling: about being taken up in its motion, moving with it' (p.8). This generates questions of how drawing moves in choreographic ways. What movements, marks, rhythms, reciprocities, invitations and temporalities are shaping drawing, and what might this mean for how we could attend to its 'performative aspect, what it does and makes us do' (O'Sullivan, 2006, p. 20)? What kinds of experiences and co-motions would this produce? This shifts the focus from looking at or observing children as if what is seen can be directly known, to *looking-with* and opens us to processes of *moving-with*, sensing-with and attuning to symbiotic co-becomings (Vintimilla & Kind, 2021).

In these drawing choreographies we also attend to the responsiveness of the materials, spaces and situations as 'a dance of attention is not attentiveness of the human to the environment but attentiveness of the environment to its own flowering' (Manning & Massumi, p. 6). It is an attention that emphasizes the 'immediacy of mutual action' (p. 6) of human and non-human others. To cultivate these relationalities and collectivities, drawing spaces are situated in central and open areas, as visible invitations to gather. The educators, sensitive to drawing materials that work with the tone and orientation of the inquiry and the movements of young children, have available pastels, soft pencils, charcoal and graphite. Chalk pastels and soft fat water-based wood-encased pastel-pencils in particular, are the primary media as they blend, spread, co-mingle, move easily between surfaces and bodies, and gently mark us along with the traces left on paper, surfaces and children's hands. The harmonious range of colours allows for layers of marks and continuous blendings and transformabilities, and gives aesthetic visibility to the movements and exchanges over time and enhances a sense of fluidity, mutuality, responsiveness and co-implication. The pastels and pencils are washable so the space itself can be hospitable to the movements and traces of materials and marks. Long papers are laid out on the floor, cover walls and low wooden platforms to invite and facilitate gatherings and wanderings, with small papers available to open to various movements and travelling. Time is fluid and there is a flow of children in their comings and goings.

The space itself is responsive, hospitable and in movement. This has been carefully cultivated by educators over the years making it possible to improvise with the gravitational pull of certain transparencies and relational elements in the room, such as children's draw to drawing on windows that look into the adjoining room and the trees outside, and on photos of children that are posted on the wall. In response, a drawing-gathering space is reconfigured by inserting a large plexiglass easel-like panel in between two low wooden benches to echo the draw of the windows and to amplify the relationality of drawing and ways of drawing with others. A few photos of children are printed on transparencies and posted on the plexiglass to add layers to the relationality. In small responsive gestures we attend to and compose with the aesthetic and fluid qualities of the room, materials and children's movements. We attend to the choreographies of the everyday, to spaces, situations, bodies and drawings in movement together.

In considering everyday choreographies and attuning to choreographic ways of drawing we consider the work of dance artist Justine A. Chambers. In her practice she considers

> how choreography can be an empathic practice rooted in collaborative creation, close observation, and the body as a site of a cumulative embodied archive. Privileging what is felt over what is seen, she works with dances 'that are already

there' – the social choreographies present in the everyday. (National Arts Centre, n.d., para. 1)

I was fortunate to attend a few presentations where she discussed aspects of her work and was intrigued by how she composes dances by gathering and rearticulating everyday gestures. In her performance *Family Dinner* (Chambers, n.d) for instance, she explores the choreography of dining by gathering and composing with the gestures of the people she dines with. She investigates the intimate vocabularies of gesture and conceptualizes body as an archive where the gestures of others are remembered and held in her body and become the language of her movement practice. Bringing her work into conversation offers us a path to begin and a way to become attuned to and compose with the relational choreographies of drawing.

Documentation Processes

We enter the speculative propositions through video recording drawing events, focusing on relationalities, co-compositions and instances of drawing where children are in interaction with others. To move away from individualistic and developmental orientations we deliberately focus on moments of exchange and mutuality. The videos, moving images, bodies, materials, gestures, enactments, sonorities, voices and various and shifting perspectives allow for thinking in movement (Manning & Massumi, 2014) and give glimpses into ways materials, children and educators are in correspondence together. Video also has the potential as an expressive, interpretive and artistic medium and enables reconfigurations and juxtapositions that draw attention to particular ideas-in-formation through the editing processes (Cooley, 2007; Kind & Argent, 2017). We have been careful to consider video not just as a straightforward, linear or objective record or repetition of what happens, but to work with its interpretive and poetic possibilities and how the processes of filming, editing, viewing and considering the work together can help us develop deeper attunement and invite more sensitive and diverse ways of knowing, seeing, sensing and responding.

The video recordings of events are divided into short segments, intervals or 'phrases', in order to highlight instances of co-composition and draw attention to particular emergent ideas, small moments, gestures and reciprocities. Each video-phrase is an effort to bring attention to particular ideas in their formation. Taken out of the linear sequence of events, reconfigured and grouped together around common concerns they draw attention to emergent insights and resist the straightforward narrative of *what* happened. We create an archive of video phrases, collections of 'gestures' that resonate together.

We have informal conversations when I am present with the children and educators during drawing events, and we meet together to view and discuss the video segments in biweekly virtual meetings. In our discussions we aim to open up the details, nuances and particularities of how things flow and move together and give shape to this through forming propositional concepts, which in turn helps inform, direct and refine what we attend to and in subsequent drawing events. As Manning (2012) discusses, 'To create concepts is to move with language's prearticulations. In this mode of thinking/feeling, language does not yet know what it means. It has not yet defined where it can go' (p.5). Through these processes and over time we begin to consider emergent relationalities, co-compositions, materialities, reciprocities, gestures, flows, rhythms, sonorities, synchronicities, hospitalities, generosities, transparencies, convergences and alliances. The concepts give propositional shape to how these events flow and what propels them. These are not categories and nothing is fully defined or distinct, but overlapping, intertwined and in play with each other.

To help to give shape to the concepts-in-formation I select particularly resonant instances to describe in writing. This is a process of trying out language and descriptive terms to help us become more attentive and sensitive to the moving compositions and to give speculative shape to what is germinating. It is not a process of applying already known concepts, simply adding interpretive or theoretical perspectives, or trying to objectively explain the events, but a process of articulating and giving shape to immanent and emergent concepts and ideas and to stay in-the-making. I look for 'larval ideas' (Vintimilla in Nuxmalo, Vintimilla & Nelson, 2018, p. 437), and things not yet fully formed, yet vibrant in their suggestions.

There is a particular impossibility in translating video segments directly into written words as if the descriptions could accurately convey the experience. But this isn't the purpose. The experience will always be more that the representation of it, and so I aim to convey the heart, the tempo, the being and doing of the moments as we give shape the experiences in written form. Writing at first feels fragmented and inadequate, but in the re-viewings and re-writings it begins to find its way to the heart of the matter. When it touches the pulse and lived relationalities, and reveals something previously not considered, it speaks back to us and begins to feel as if it has a life. I aim for language that 'feels the world' (Manning, 2012, p. 215) that senses, moves with and is immersed in its textures

Figure 3.2 Joining with the hospitalities of drawing.

and tonalities that creates as much as it describes. These processes help us more fully articulate and bring into view what we are noticing and what is present in its nascent form so we can become more attuned to the rhythms, flows and movements of drawing, feel things coming into being, create responsive situations and offer small improvisational openings and activations. I aim to compose at the edge of the not yet and activate the potential or the germ of the event so that 'knowledge is crafted in the processes of art in the making' (Kontturi, 2018, p. 11). In this way our processes of attention, documentation, video recording, discussions and writing become recursive way-finding processes (Figure 3.2).

Ingold (2013) writes 'to correspond with the world . . . is not to describe it, or to represent it, but to *answer to it*' (p. 108). Thus, the intent is not to simply describe, learn about or even 'know what to do next', but to join with and activate the potential so that this dance of attention is not just to what appears to us in these moments, but also to what is still to come, like minor or small gestures that propel us towards something more. Drawing on Deleuze and Guattari, Manning (2016) describes the minor gesture as 'the gestural force that opens experience to its potential variation. It does this from within experience itself, activating a shift in tone, a difference in quality' (p. 1). And so with subtle shifts, small gestures still in improvisational form and with growing attunement, we respond to and join with the movements and propositions of the events.

Generosities, Hospitalities and Invitations

MJ, an educator, is sitting with Sage on her lap. There are drawn marks on the plexiglass, on the paper lining the benches and on the paper covering the adjacent wall as layers made over time. Sage is watching what is going on, not yet enveloped in drawing. When Justine joins, the actions of drawing are paused.

> *Justine moves close to the two, momentarily sits beside them, then walking around begins to collect the fragments of chalk pastels from under the bench. She collects them in two small clear containers, offers a pastel to me, walks to MJ, considers her open hand, and in wanderings between, begins to offer pieces one at a time to me, MJ, and to Sage. MJ's open hand welcomes each offering but each time Justine offers a piece to Sage there is a pause as Sage considers it then shakes her head in refusal. These rhythms of generosity continue as Justine walks between us and offers chalk pastels, and each time extends one to Sage in spite of her quiet refusals. Justine extends a chalk pastel, looks at Sage and immediately shakes her own head as if in acknowledgement that Sage is not receptive to this material. But she still continues with a vibrant smile as if with a sense of joy and generosity in the opening of invitations. There is no demand, just a sense of open hospitality.*
>
> *Earlier I had noticed Sage drawing with a fine line black pen, creating tiny delicate wavy lines. I extend a similar pen to Justine who tries it out on the plexiglass easel then offers it to Sage who immediately receives it. Justine waits, watches, turns again to me to offer more pastels, expands her gathering to other materials, and continues her offerings. In the meantime, the pen has drawn Sage into drawing on the paper covered bench. It draws in Justine as well as she takes up another pen and joins in with Sage.*

There are hospitalities in the open hand, the containers, multiple pastels and pen, and in the acceptance of refusals and the way that they open other possibilities, along with the waiting and joyful hope for others to join and the weaving wandering walking lines joining bodies together. We see how drawing for children as well as for ourselves is a process of attuning to others. Justine's momentary embrace of Sage's head-shake opens wonderings of how children collect the gestures of others in drawing and how we might as well, not just through the practicalities of video recording, but in a bodied feeling-knowing where, as Justine A. Chambers articulates, body becomes an archive. We also wonder what other gestures, invitations and hospitalities are extended and reciprocated? What draws us to drawing?

It's early in the morning and as children are arriving educators Rachel and Lily, along with Cedar, Harper, and Sunny are gathered around a low wooden platform covered with a large sheet of paper. Pastel-pencils are exchanged between hands, one hand holds a pencil then both hands, bodies move around the platform, and there is a constant tap-tap-tap of the pastel-pencils making dot-like marks on the paper covered wooden surface as if in an invitation to gather. The chorus of tapping is interspersed with smooth fluid drawn lines and the fluid moving lines of the children's wanderings. Children come and go, climb on the drawing surface, enter in the drawings, move away to greet the incoming children, and move back to drawing. The tap-tap continues as a sonorous call to drawing.

Justine is drawing on paper beside MJ, an educator, in view of Heloisa, Sage, and Ava. She draws repeating lines on the paper, on the plexiglass panel, then a few tap-tap-tap marks and a pause with her hand drawn back as if in an invitation. MJ responds to her tapping with her own tap-tap-line marks which becomes a tapping-line-drawing conversation, at times as a rhythmic exchange, and at times a synchronous harmony of lines, sounds, and marks in moving bodied resonance and improvisation with each other. Justine's tapping marks are momentarily directed at Sage who is directly in her view on the other side of the plexiglass, who hasn't joined in the drawing yet but is keeping a close watch on the pen in Ava's hand. It appears as if Justine is moving in rhythm with MJ while at the same time offering sonorous invitations for Sage to join in as well.

Figure 3.3 The generosities of drawing.

We begin to see these drawing events as the gathering of gestures, sound-marks, rhythms and invitations (Figure 3.3).

Reciprocities and Relationalities

Gabi, an educator, and Madi are sitting across from each other and are drawing together on a long paper laid out on the floor. On the paper there are layers of drawings made over several weeks, traces of other children and other intersections, silently suggesting that each instance of drawing is not an isolated event but comes into being in the company of others.

> *Gabi selects a charcoal pencil and draws continuous circular lines on the paper with charcoal, looks at Madi and draws her hand back. Madi selects a stick of graphite, draws a circular shape beside Gabi's rotations. The sliding smooth quality of the graphite lends itself to fast moving lines and continuous movement. With fluid, sliding, movements she extends her circle over Gabi's drawing with a slight increase in intensity as if in an acknowledgement of Gabi's marks and an invitation to continue. She lifts the graphite off the paper and there is a slight pause. Gabi responds to this increase in intensity and with a slightly faster tempo and energy draws around both circles. There is a pause, Madi looks at the marks, glances up at Gabi, back at the marks, and with a slight smile, vigorously responds by drawing her own circles over Gabi's circular lines. The energy of the lines seems to move through her, from her bare feet, through her body to her arms, hands, graphite, and paper.*
>
> *As if in an unspoken agreement, a back and forth rhythmic exchange takes shape. Draw-look-pause-exchange-draw-pause-repeat, with Gabi and Madi responding to each other in similarity of shape, intensity, tempo, and rhythm until Gabi shifts the flow and tempo. She lines the drawn circular rotations with short, tap-tap-tap sound-marks. Madi's eyes follow the path. There is a longer pause as Madi looks at her, her hand moves to her forehead and into her hair, and after another momentary hesitation offers an even more intense and prolonged circular response as if to indicate to Gabi that she had been playing the game wrong. Gabi, leaning in, matches the intensity in her drawn circular response, and the back and forth dialogue of circular drawings continues, but this time with a slight increase in intensity and shorter pauses between the exchanges.*
>
> *Gabi shifts the tempo again with slower, calmer, and more deliberate lines, drawing attention to the smooth, rich, soft, blackness, and variability of the charcoal. Madi's hand moves back to her head, in what we see as momentary*

puzzlement, and responds again with vigorous rotations, extending the duration of her drawing-time as if to emphasize attention to a particular intensity. Gabi responds in rhythm and intensity, but this time sustains her invitation and the charcoal's potential to expand the back and forth conversation. In each exchange she offers slight variances in the tap-tap marks that line the evolving circular drawings while still keeping with the established tempo of the exchanges. The rhythms of the exchanges continue. Then in a brief moment Madi welcomes Gabi's tapping sonorous lines by incorporating them into her circular response. A circular line, 5 short quick tap-tap marks, then more continuous circular rotations.

As the rhythmic quality of this 'game' comes into view we attend to how the tempo, intensity, intervals and reciprocities of drawing and pausing create the event. We notice the invitational potency of the pause, and how Madi and the graphite instigate and propel the tempo and rhythm which Gabi finds her way into, while Gabi and the charcoal expand the conversation through slight variances in the marks which Madi joins with. The charcoal, graphite, Madi, Gabi, marks and circular rotations in composition together. In this instance, drawing takes shape as co-implication and co-composition, with each reaching towards the other in a symbiotic interplay. As Manning (2016) elaborates, 'reaching-toward foregrounds the relationality inherent in experience, a kind of feeling-with the world' (p. 2). The repetitive gestures, rhythm, force and intensity, draw us back to Justine A. Chambers (2020, January 6) and her collaborative work *One hundred more*, a dance performance composed of iterative gestures and small rhythmic movements, portraying gestures of resistance. The force and intensity of the gestures are moving and powerful, and are bodily felt in the viewing. This sensing, feeling-knowing exceeds words and is carried with us as we continue to wonder about the intensities, rhythms and gestures present in these everyday acts of drawing.

Gestures, Rhythms and Sonorities

To attend more closely to the rhythmic nature of drawing we are drawn to subtle invitations, fleeting gestures and tiny moments. Each instance on its own is somewhat inconsequential, yet gathered they resonate together. In continuous speculative and tenuous gestures of listening and responding, of trying out the rhythms for ourselves, feeling the tempos, intensities and intonations, more of the choreographic nuances of the events come into presence. Each act of attention and response echoes into the next, offering ways for us to enter *with* children in their gestures, rhythms and sonorities.

> *Madi makes several long slow curving lines followed by short quick straight intersecting lines. She repeats this in flexible ways, each rendition a repetition with variance moving between slow-quick, and circular-vertical. It isn't a predictable or set pattern, but there seems to be an intrinsic rhythmic structure to her marks.*

> *Will draws a line, a drawn out long line on paper, then an increase in speed as his hand and the pastel continue the line in the air as if taking flight. This continues with variance – slow slightly curving long line that makes a swishing sssshhh sound as the pastel moves along the paper, then lift-off as his hand continues the line in the air accompanied by his voiced sssshhhh sound. His hand suspended in the air releases the pastel and the line continues as it falls to the ground. Lines are marked on paper, in the air, and in sound.*

> *Ava, Goldie, and MJ, an educator, are drawing outside on drawing boards leaning against the fence. Antonio is to the side making repeating melodic sounds that have an arc-like sliding quality, high-low-and up again sounds. MJ borrows this sound and repeats it as she draws high-low-sliding rhythmic lines. Ava responds by drawing on and beside the sound-marks, and Antonio, closely attending to MJ and the repeating singing-sounds and lines, joins in with other sonorous tapping and sliding marks creating a brief melodic conversation.*

We continue with our attention to the particular and select small video segments, most under half a minute long instances where hands, fingers, pastels, bodies, lines and marks are moving in synchronous harmony and create new compositions or video poems of gestural synchronicities. This draws attention to the intimacies and nuances of bodied 'social choreographies' where children and educators, hands, lines and marks, are momentarily in rhythmic correspondence together. As we watch the videos with gestures in repetition and feel the pulsations and reverberations, the intensities move through us and we find ourselves embracing them in a bodied feeling-knowing. To bring visibility to these synchronicities, and to keep us immersed in intensities that are felt and not just seen and to enliven a rhythm and feel for drawing, MJ brings in her flute to play the rhythms as children draw and educators gather with the children around some of the video segments playing on a laptop. These moments are as much about our own attunement as it is in drawing children's attention as we join together in feeling-with, moving-with and responding-to. As the videos play children and educators return the sounds and rhythms in inventive ways, a

Movements, Synchronicities, Choreographies 51

Figure 3.4 The beginning of a drawing-dance.

child echoes the sounds which reverberates among others, bodies move around the space and no one is silent or still.

This is thought in movement or thought in the act (Manning & Massumi, 2014), where every work is an experiment, a process of invention and thinking otherwise while trying to activate a collective and reciprocal rhythm (Kind, 2020) and at the same time proposing new configurations that produce small variances. This is not a typical search for children's meanings so we can identify, extend or elaborate on children's interests or even understand their drawing processes, but a search for joining in the co-motion and co-compositions, where we are learning to move together in a responsive and ongoing exchange. Manning (2013) describes this as a symbiotic 'expression-with' (p. 11) and a 'preconscious tuning-with that sparks a new set of relations that in turn affect how singular events express themselves in the time of the event' (p. 11). These processes move us in response, drawing us closer to *moving-with* the rhythms of the events (Figure 3.4).

> *MJ, Sage, Alexis, Justine, are gathered with Linden in front of a long length of paper taped to the wall. Linden, standing on a low woven ottoman, begins. As she lifts her arm to draw the anticipation seems to vibrate through her body, then, making long vertical repeating lines her bodied drawing-dance moves to the paper. Alexis, an educator, joins in to one side with one long line. Linden pauses, hand drawn back,*

studies Alexis' moving line, then joins in again along with MJ, an educator, on the other side creating a rhythmic, sonorous, chorus of lines on paper. The repeating vertical lines simultaneously reverberate from her fingers and arms to her toes and down the length of the paper. MJ and Alexis enter the invitation that Linden's delight extends and the pulse of the lines seem to move through their bodies in motional-relational responding and rhythmic correspondence with Linden and with her lines. The chorus continues until, moving into the lines and living the drawn lines, Linden becomes the line as she grasps the ledge high above the paper and hangs suspended.

Justine A. Chambers (Early Childhood Pedagogy Network, 2021) describes her process of getting to know others through their movements, while 'trying to embody other bodies so we don't forget them' (30:15). In this way body becomes archive and we carry others with us through their motions, indications and beckonings. Through this we are finding our way to following lines in movement and rhythms in formation, while thinking through their sensations with things not yet fully formed or articulable. Manning (2012) describes an event in-the-making as 'a thought at the cusp of articulation – a prearticulated thought in motion' (p. 5). So that 'choreographic thinking is the activation, in the moving, of a movement of thought. It expresses itself not in language per se but as the pulses across embodiments and rhythms' (Manning, 2013, p. 103) generating temporalities, relationalities and moving compositions.

Choreographies

Giving value to small moments helps us attune to the nuances and reciprocities, appreciate more of the flow, cadence, pace and tempo of the events and brings into view the nature of the relationalities and co-compositions that characterize young children's drawing. We see the vibrancy of infants and toddlers' processes and how the event of drawing is expanded, giving more space and visibility to the rhythmic generosities and exchanges with others. And it proposes other 'what-ifs' as I wonder what if we saw these events, not as phases children go through, but some of the very structures and impulses of drawing itself. How could this be kept alive throughout the centre and with older children as well?

> *I enter the toddler room during a refrain of generosities. Goldie is trying out the new 'mini pens' we bought in response to Sage's affinity for the pen. As*

children arrive she offers them one and soon rhythms of giving and receiving take shape as small pieces of paper, pens, pastels move between hands and travel with bodies. Pens make a mark, are offered to others, hands exchange drawing media, and more marks are made. Paper is torn into small strips, offered to others, momentarily take flight, and are marked, twisted, and extended to and exchanged with others. These moving, rhythmic exchanges, generosities and hospitalities draw others into the space and small gatherings begin to form around the large wooden block that is covered with paper and the paper taped the wall. It is impossible to see drawing as an individual self-expressive act or concerned primarily with the representation or mark. The first dance here is one of generosity and hospitality and undoes perceptions of the self-focused, self-expressive, individualistic drawing-child.

Heloisa, an educator, and Goldie move to drawing side by side on the long lengths of paper on the wall, their small circular repetitions have a varied yet visual harmony. The lines on paper act as an invitation and one by one Linden, Ava, Avery and Judianne, an educator, join. There are repeating moments of rhythmic correspondence as one hand follows another, with educator and child in moving response to each other where at times the educator leads and at times the child. Linden joins beside Judianne in drawing slow mid-size circular lines, their arms, hands, graphite and lines moving in tempo with each other. Ava and Avery briefly are in synchronous rhythm as they stand shoulder to shoulder, bodies touching, with their repeating pastel vertical lines keeping time.

It is a play not just of lines and marks, but of movements and intensities while sensing and feeling the power of the lines: the more gentle downward line, the dynamic energy of upward strokes, the fluidity of the arc, the sharp tap-mark that draws attention to itself, and the horizontal line that refuses to be followed. Like Justine A. Chambers (in Zakharova & Chambers, 2021, April 19) we consider 'the force of a gesture' (1:23:46) not just the gesture itself.

Pastels and pens are exchanged and move between hands in constant hospitalities to each other. The paper itself, in layers reflecting weeks of drawing, invites attention to the underneath and immersive compositions. There is the physicality of drawing, with lines moving through bodies, from arms to toes. There are momentary interludes and in each pause the lines of a drawer beginning again brings others back into the dance. This brings attention to what the lines do rather than what they mean or represent affirming Manning's (2016) proposition that 'when something does, new relational fields are forming, and with them, new modes of existence' (p. 30).

We catch glimpses of children in synchronous rhythm with each other, and the ways that gestures, rhythms, marks and materials move between children as they borrow, elaborate on and enter into each other's movements and intensities. We see gesture as a mutual beckoning, as something still in formation and open to the hospitality, response and improvisation of the other: the open hand, the shake of a head, the flight of a line, the invitational pause at the end of a drawn line, the tap-tap of the pastel-pencil, the ssshhhh lines of the chalk pastel. As we feel the marks and intensities the gestural vocabulary of drawing expands and with it our attention to the moving co-compositions.

That educators join in these encounters with children is a highly sensitive endeavour and requires increasing and ongoing pedagogical and artistic attunement and continuous resistance to simply gathering information and applying insights. The hope is to hold open our emerging understandings, enter in yet not take over, join *with* without being certain, and find our way to composing alongside children while in responsive, rhythmic resonance and immersive attunement to the fluxes, flows, variances, tempos, intensities and choreographies of the event. In doing this we gather and offer small movements, modest propositional invitations and minor gestures with the hope of activating potentialities and alternative ways of being together. As Manning (2016) writes, 'the minor gesture invents new modes of life-living' (p. 8) and 'new forms of existence, and with them, in them, we come to be' (p. 2). Through bodied *responsive* attentiveness and in resonance with Justine A. Chambers' processes, we do this by creating conditions, 'putting a set of propositions in motion' (Chambers in Zakharova & Chambers, 2021, April 19, 31:21), and staying responsive without directing or determining what will happen.

This symbiotic process of moving-with and becoming-with offers vibrant openings for thinking otherwise, for resisting instrumentalities, conventions of the self-expressive or developing child, educator as initiator or facilitator-observer, young children's drawing as primarily the mark or developmental progressions, and knowledge gained through detached, objective, observation. We anticipate spending an extended time in these processes and in our attention to drawing. These are not insights easily attained, applied or generalizable, rather situational where cultivating a relational context and a generous space for these speculations is as vital as the growing attunement to what is taking place. And so, we walk slowly through this, taking our time inventing and reconfiguring as we go. This becomes our daily work and we continue to cultivate life-living pedagogies and find drawing gatherings enriched, enlivened and vibrant with hospitalities, relationalities, synchronicities, symbiotic co-becomings and ourselves altered in the process.

Acknowledgement

I am particularly grateful to the educators who have been engaging in this project and their sensitivity to the processes: Alexis Conlinn, Deb Fayle, Ivy Lam, Heloisa Porto Alves Alcantara Martim, Gabi Neves, M. J. Paculan, Nicole St Laurent, Judianne Tompson, Lily Wan and Rachel Weal.

References

Chambers, J. A. (2020, January 6). *One hundred more.* Justine A. Chambers.
Chambers, J. A. (n.d.). *Family dinner.* Justine A. Chambers. https://justineachambers .com/family-dinner-the-lexicon/
Cooley, M. (2007). Video poems: Seeking insight. *Canadian Review of Art Education Research & Issues, 34*(1), 88–98.
Davies, B. (2014). *Listening to children: Being and becoming.* Routledge.
Early Childhood Pedagogy Network. (2021). *In dialogue with contemporary art* [video]. https://www.ecpn.ca/events/exposures/past/dialogue-contemporary-art
Ingold, T. (2013). *Making: Anthropology, archeology, art, and architecture.* Routledge.
Ingold, T. (2018). *Anthropology and/as education.* New York: Routledge.
Kind, S. (2020). Wool works, cat's cradle, and the art of paying attention. In C. Schulte (Ed.), *Ethics and research with young children: New perspectives* (pp. 49–61). Bloomsbury Publishing.
Kind, S., & Argent, A. (2017). Using video in pedagogical documentation: Interpretive and poetic possibilities. In A. Fleet, C. Patterson, & J. Robertson (Eds.), *Pedagogical documentation in early years practice* (pp. 35–42). Sage.
Kontturi, K. (2018). *Ways of following: Art, materiality, collaboration.* Open Humanities Press.
Manning, E. (2012). *Relationscapes: Movement, art, philosophy.* The MIT Press.
Manning, E. (2013). *Always more than one: Individuation's dance.* Duke University Press.
Manning, E. (2016). *The minor gesture.* Duke University Press.
Manning, E., & Massumi, B. (2014). *Thought in the act: Passages in the ecology of experience.* University of Minnesota Press.
Matthews, J. (2003). *Drawing and painting: Children and visual representation* (2nd ed.). Paul Chapman Publishing.
National Arts Centre. (n.d.). *Dance artist.* Justine. A. Chambers. https://nac-cna.ca/en/ bio/justine-a.-chambers
Nuxmalo, F., Vintimilla, C. D., & Nelson, N. (2018). Pedagogical gatherings in early childhood education: Mapping interferences in emergent curriculum. *Curriculum Inquiry, 48*(4), 433–453. https://doi.org/10.1080/03626784.2018.1522930

O'Sullivan, S. (2006). *Art encounters Deleuze and Guattari: thought beyond representation*. Palgrave Macmillan.

Pacini-Ketchabaw, V., Kind, S., & Kocher, L. (2017). *Encounters with materials in early childhood education*. Routledge.

Penn, L. R. (2021). Wow we're stepping on the weeds: Animation and aliveness in children's classroom drawing(s). In H. Park & C. Schulte (Eds.), *Visual arts with young children: Practice, pedagogy, learning* (pp. 139–58). Routledge.

Vecchi, V., & Ruozzi, M. (Eds.). (2015). *Mosaic of marks, words, material*. Reggio Children.

Vintimilla, C. D., & Kind, S. (2021). Choreographies of practice: Mutualities and sympoetic becomings in early childhood teacher education. In H. Park & C. Schulte (Eds.), *Visual arts with young children: Practice, pedagogy, learning* (pp. 33–46). Routledge.

Vintimilla, C. D. (n.d.). *What is pedagogy?* Early Childhood Pedagogies Collaboratory. https://www.earlychildhoodcollaboratory.net/what-is-pedagogy

Zakharova, T., & Chambers, J. A. (2021, April 19). *The materiality of play: Early childhood education research in diffractive dialogue with dance as an artistic practice* [video]. Disrupting early childhood: Inheritance, pedagogy, curriculum. https://www.earlychildhoodcollaboratory.net/disrupting-early-childhood

4

Hacking Observational Literacy Tools in Early Childhood Education

Karen Nociti and Mindy Blaise,
Centre for People, Place, and Planet, Edith Cowan University, Boorloo (Perth), Western Australia

Djilba (Noongar season of transition and growth) sun is strengthening. Characterised by a mix of cold and warmer days that eventually transition into hot Kambarang (Noongar season of transformation), this particular Djilba day is a warm one. Sunlight, trees and soft wind mingle, creating shadows, flickering on drying earth. Walking along the grey sandy path, shoe prints leave their mark. We wonder, what other creatures might be leaving their tracks in this path? We notice how the sandy path transitions into damp, spongy earth. This subtle change underfoot, along with the musty smell of decomposing leaf litter tells us that the creek is nearby.

Arriving at the creek, we glance down at our clipboards that hold a literacy observational tool that we have been provided. This tool is used by the teachers to make observations about childrens' literacy skills and knowledge.

A group of children, teachers, and a water ecologist are crowded at the edge of the creek, testing the floatability of paper boats. Crouching, two boys launch their boats into the flowing creek, and then run to the top of the bridge to watch it move with the currents. One of the boats has slowed down to a standstill. We wonder what might have caused this pause? The exposed roots of the trees lining the banks of the creek reach well below the surface of the water. Perhaps the boat is caught on a tree's root.

Looking down at our clipboards, we are troubled by the limitations of what is written on the paper compared to what we are noticing in this moment. There is nothing on the tool that describes the ways in which children might notice and describe the relations between the creek and the trees lining its banks, or how they might make connections between the flow of the creek and the season. We realise that this tool is far from adequate in describing the types of literacies that are emerging from and with Place in this moment. (taken from field notes and dialogue between Karen and Mindy, 16th August 2021)

This encounter with creek, trees, wind, sun and much more took place during a walking event on Noongar Country, in Boorloo (Perth), Western Australia. Over several months, the authors (Karen and Mindy) walked-with a group of twenty, six and seven-year-old children and their three teachers during weekly visits to Bush School. Bush School is modelled on European Forest School programmes (Elliot & Chancellor, 2014). Adapted to suit an Australian climate and cultural context, children attending Bush School spend part or all of the school day outside of the classroom and in local bushland environments. At this Bush School we walk-with Gabbiljee, a wetlands ecosystem known by Noongar peoples as the watery place at the end of Derbarl Yerrigan (Swan River) (Figure 4.1).

Figure 4.1 Gabbiljee (the watery place at the end of Derbarl Yerrigan).

This particular group of children have attended Bush School over the past two years and is familiar with the wide variety of bird life, insects and vegetation that is characteristic of the wetlands. The weekly programme varies but is typically planned in response to changes in local weather conditions. Some walks include pre-planned activities, such as cubby building or wood whittling while others emerge in response to childrens' interests on the day. There is a strong focus on the inclusion of Aboriginal cultural knowledges with each walk commencing with an Acknowledgement of Country.[1] The children know that Gabbiljee has particular significance for the Whadjuk Noongar group and that the wetlands were an important seasonal food source (City of Melville, n.d.). This area also holds strong spiritual significance to Noongar Dreaming. Derbal Yerrigan and Dyarlgarro Beeliar (Canning River), both of which feed into the wetlands, were created by the Waugal, a rainbow serpent that made Noongar peoples the custodians of the land (https://www.noongarculture.org.au/spirituality/). Less familiar to the children are accounts of uneasy relations between Noongar peoples and settlers during a historical period of colonization (City of Melville, n.d.). When we walk-with Gabbiljee, we acknowledge that we are also walking-with these uneasy histories and with the tensions that come with walking alongside other ways of knowing this Place[2] (Sundberg, 2014).

Our presence on the walks was planned as a part of Karen's PhD, a year-long inquiry into Place stories emerging from Place–children encounters during Bush School. One of the key aims of the project was to understand alternative ways of approaching place-based pedagogies by troubling how Western education separates children from Place. With education recognized as playing a crucial role in responding to environmental crises, an examination of the ways in which education currently conceptualizes place is not only timely but also essential to our future survival (Common Worlds Research Collective, 2020). Place-based models of learning, where children visit and learn about local places, have become an increasingly popular response to calls for education to make sustainability a curriculum priority (Barrable & Booth, 2020). Many of these programmes teach environmental literacies, with the intent that children will develop the knowledge and skills for enacting sustainable futures (Barrable & Booth, 2020; Elliot & Chancellor, 2014). One critique of these programmes is that they are typically built on stewardship models that view children as the solution to the world's problems (Taylor, 2013). By positioning children as being able to fix nature in this way, this approach works to separate children from a nature in which they are already embedded (Taylor, 2013).

The concept of Place literacies opens up possibilities for thinking about how education might approach place-based education, along with the literacies required for thinking and learning *with* Place, differently (Somerville, 2007). Place literacies emerge from Place–children relations, with Place equally agentic as children in the generation of literacies. Thinking about Place and literacies in this way is not easy. It requires a radical reimagining of the normative ways in which adults think and work with children in early childhood education. However, the evidence is mounting that current approaches to environmental and sustainability education will not make any significant impact should it carry on in this way. The only option is for education to do something radically different (Common Worlds Research Collective, 2020).

A more expansive understanding of Place and literacies requires teachers to think and do literacies differently while still working within the constraints of mandated curriculum and assessment. This otherwise response calls for a creative reimagining of the norm, a disruption to a 'business as usual' mentality. This paper argues that hacking as a method opens up spaces for rethinking and repurposing habitual observational practices in early childhood (Hamilton et al., 2021). The aim of our hack at Bush School was twofold. First, we wanted to dismantle and reconfigure the constraints of a typical literacy observational tool to make space for more expansive understandings of literacies emerging from and with Place. Second, we see hacking the tool as a way of demonstrating how educators might approach observations of literacies otherwise while still working within the constraints of predetermined curriculum and assessment tools.

History of the Literacy Observational Tool

Observational tools such as the literacy template we were provided are designed based on developmental theories of literacy acquisition (Clay, 1991). Developmental perspectives of literacy learning have been prevalent since the 1920s. These early approaches to teaching reading were grounded in the idea that children would learn to read only when developmentally ready (Kuby et al., 2019b). Using the term emergent literacy, Marie Clay theorized that the road to becoming literate is a gradual process, beginning from birth and influenced by an individuals' environment and experiences (Clay, 1991). Since the 1970s the terms literacy, emergent literacy and its plural form literacies have been used to describe a broad range of skills, conceptual understandings, knowledges and dispositions. Over time these have been organized into various iterations of continua that outline expected achievements for children by age or stage of development (Clay, 1991; Rees et al., 1997). These are understood as proposed trajectories that point towards an eventual outcome of the child becoming a literate adult who is enabled to participate as an active member of society.

While developmental perspectives of literacy acquisition have prevailed over time, a consensus on a shared conceptualization of literacies has never been reached (Snow, 2006). Societal change has meant that definitions of literacies have needed to continually expand and adapt in response to a rapidly changing world (Kuby et al., 2019b). These definitions have become increasingly complex to incorporate the recognition of influences such as culture, identity and individual contexts on literacy development. Concurrently, large-scale quantitative studies that focus on the science behind reading have worked in direct opposition by reducing the complexity of literacies to phonics and skills-based instruction (see Ehri et al., 2001 for a meta-analysis of studies). These varied and often conflicting perspectives have resulted in a wide range of pedagogical practices that educators employ to teach basic reading skills alongside communicative and critical literacy practices. Oral, written, visual, digital and multimodal texts form the basis of early literacy experiences as children learn to read, view, compose and critically analyse through and with multiple modes of communication. These types of experiences typically take place inside the classroom and often act as a support for the learning that is planned for place-based programmes. For example, on their return to the classroom, children might talk, read or create texts about what they observed or learnt about while outdoors. Or, through the shared reading of a non-fiction text, children might learn new vocabulary that can be used to describe what they might observe in the outdoor environment. While it is acknowledged that learning occurs in outdoor environments, literacies are typically planned for, taught and observed within the four walls of the classroom.

The Observational Literacy Tool We Were Given

The observational literacy tool that we were given (see Figure 4.2) is grounded in a developmental logic that privileges the skills and knowledge that a child is expected to demonstrate at a particular stage of reading development (Burman, 2017). These are organized into five broad areas that are universally recognized as being essential to reading development (Snow, 2006). Each area

Sem 2 Grade	Phonemic Awareness: Focus on oral manipulation	Phonics: Spelling/Code Knowledge	Fluency: Word and/or Text Level Reading	Comprehension: Listening/Reading	Vocabulary: Tier 2
			Year One		
A	Can add, delete and substitute initial, any medial, final sounds in CVC, CVCC, CCVC CCVCC CCCVCC words with accuracy and speed. Can blend and segment four/five/six sounds words with accuracy.	Can read and spell CVCC, CCVC words and multisyllabic words using a range of vowel digraphs mostly accurately. Uses suffixes like -ed -ing with accuracy. Chooses alternate spellings with accuracy.	WPM 100+ Blending of extended code is automatic. Use of intonation in response to punctuation and to enhance meaning. Reads accurately with fluency and expression.	Can locate specific information in written texts. Uses background knowledge to make inferences. Makes connections from text to build on own current knowledge. Seeks clarification with well-structured questions.	Can use context knowledge to work out the meaning of unknown words. Uses a wide range of vocabulary to express ideas. Can use well-chosen vocab to add detail and interest.
B	Can add and swap some initial, medial, final sounds in CVC, CVCC, CCVCC, CCCVCC words. May have difficulty deleting adjacent consonants at beginning and end of words in CCVC, CCVC, CCCVCC words. Is able to delete, add, swap initial, medial, final sounds in CVC words. Can blend and segment four/five/six sounds words with accuracy.	Experiments with using a range of vowel digraphs to represent phonemes. Attempts to spell common derivational suffixes such as -ed -ing but may still represent phonetically e.g. jumpt	WPM 80-90 May sound out words that are multisyllabic, unfamiliar or contain less frequently used code. Reasonable speed and reading rate are maintained even if some words are sounded out.	Uses background knowledge to predict and makes inferences with ease. Can predict and infer. Retells stories with details. Can compare and contrast with detail and justification. Asks questions to enable clarification. Responds to texts explaining connections and links texts to personal experiences. Retells stories including many events using connectives/adjectives/detailed vocabulary.	Uses a variety of adjectives (to build detail and precision) to describe, retell, and summarize. Learns tier 2 vocab with ease and uses new vocabulary appropriately. Speaks with grammatically correct sentences. Enquires about word meanings.
C	Able to delete, swap and add sounds into and from CVC words. Can blend and segment CCVC, CVCC sound words with accuracy. Needs assistance to be able to manipulate adjacent consonants in CCVC/CCVC words.	Can read and spell CVCC, CCVC words containing consonant digraphs and taught vowel digraphs. Can read one and two syllable words containing initial code, consonant digraphs and taught vowel digraphs. Can read common derivational suffixes such as -ed and -ing.	40-60WPM Can read CVC words and nonwords with automaticity. Can read CVC nonwords. Can decode or read CVCC, CCVC words and nonwords successfully. Large bank of known HF words 100+ Sounds out a word and retains it to read it again on subsequent pages. Self corrects/rereads Can decode simple multisyllabic words. Reading at sentence level with ease.	Recounts/describes sequenced ideas from simple texts they have read or listened to. Demonstrates understanding by making personal connections. Can make inferences by interpreting familiar texts and texts with predictable structure.	Uses a variety of simple and more interesting adjectives, verbs, adverbs. Learns tier 2 vocab. Uses some content specific vocabulary.

Figure 4.2 The observational literacy tool.

has then been divided into neat categories of skill subsets that are organized to match up with an A–D grading system. This type of tool is often used by a teacher to determine where a child fits within a continuum of reading skills and knowledge. It is often applied as a method to track a child's progress or to communicate to various stakeholders about a child's level of achievement (or lack of) in certain areas. A rubric such as this one might also inform a teacher about what to plan for next so that a child may continue on the desired trajectory towards reading mastery. When used as a tool for observation, its purpose is to direct the educators' attention towards a child's demonstrations of the skills and knowledge that correspond with what is written on the tool. Although this is useful for observations of certain types of literacy skills and knowledge, it is problematic because of the ways in which it narrows observations to focus only on particular types of bodies, while at the same time ignoring others.

Privileging Certain Types of Material Bodies

Due to its grounding in developmental logic, the tool privileges a universal description of what counts as 'normal' reading development. The normal child fits within one of the neat and tidy boxes on the observational literacy tool. Although developmental maps might claim to allow for individuals to follow their own pathway, the trajectory towards eventual mastery is non-negotiable (Rees et al., 1997). The definition of the standardized child is historically grounded in Westernized models of education that privilege only those who are 'white and rational, schooled and sensible' (Truman et al., 2020, p. 4). Cultural upbringing, caregiving practices, linguistic diversity, etc. are just some of the factors that are not countered in the design (Burman, 2017). This privileging of universal human bodies has an implicit impact on the ways in which educators use the tool to make observations of children. For example, materials, time and resources might be organized in ways that allow children opportunities to demonstrate what they know and can do in ways that are described on the tool. Consequently, in their effort to monitor reading development, educators devote more of their time to observing, teaching and planning for the children who are most likely to fit the criteria on the tool, thus contributing to an ongoing cycle of social inequality (Burman, 2017).

Not only does the tool privilege certain types of *human* bodies, it privileges the human as the sole producer and consumer of literacies. For example, the tool does not consider the more-than-human elements of Place as literate bodies capable of generating literacies. Seeking to dismantle the hierarchical structures that permeate Western education systems, literacy researchers are looking towards a more expansive understanding of what counts as a literate body. Much of this work has been in response to wider ontological shifts in the social sciences. Often called the material turn, this perspective brings to light the inherent vitality of matter and recognizes its agency in being able to shape and alter events (Bennet, 2010). Grouped under the broader term of posthuman literacies, early childhood literacy scholars are drawing from feminist new materialism theory as a way of disrupting the focus on the human as the sole producer and consumer of literacy knowledge, relations and realities (Hackett & Somerville, 2017; Kuby & Rowsell, 2017).

Karen Barad's theory of agential realism, along with its integral concept of intra-action, has been particularly fortuitous in providing these researchers with an alternative space for understanding how literacy materials (e.g. books, paper, writing implements) encounter time, space and people to produce literacies (Barad, 2007). Intra-act, different to interact, affords the material as having agency, with literacies understood as emerging from the intra-actions between humans and materials (Hackett & Somerville, 2017). Where Westernized models of education promote individual knowledge over the collective, this perspective draws attention towards literacies as collective meaning-making emerging from 'intense movements and soundings' from both human and more-than-human elements of Place (Hackett & Somerville, 2017, p. 380).

When agency is distributed across the human *and* more-than-human elements of Place, as in a relational ontology, there are opportunities for noticing the ways in which Place actively contributes to shaping worlds in which we live (Hackett et al., 2020). Critical to this work is the understanding that a relational ontological view of the world has always been central to Indigenous cosmologies. Framed by the concept, Place-Thought, Indigenous peoples understand Place as 'alive and thinking' and impossible to separate from knowing (Watts, 2013, p. 21). In early childhood education, Catherine Hamm proposes Place-Thought walks as a decolonizing practice when walking-with Place and children in an Australian context (Hamm, 2015). During walks on Country, Hamm foregrounds situated Indigenous knowledges as a practice that supports the development of different ways of being affected by Place (Hamm, 2015).

Several scholars working in the space of posthuman literacies have found it helpful to think-with Indigenous ways of knowing and being as a way to understand literacies as emerging from childrens' relations with Place (Nxumalo & Cira Rubin, 2019; Somerville, 2007). The practice of foregrounding situated Indigenous Place stories ensures that Place is acknowledged as already storied and in doing so opens up possibilities for decolonizing Place in early childhood education and research (Nxumalo & Cira Rubin, 2019). As two non-Indigenous women[3] walking and thinking-with Noongar Country, this practice presents several challenges. It has required us to acknowledge the colonial influence of our own education and how this education has offered only a partial and subjective way of knowing the world. The practice of thinking-with Aboriginal ways of knowing and being with Place has been central to the process of our own unlearning, while making specific Place stories and histories visible has been a deliberate practice that contributes to what Sundberg describes as enacting 'the world as pluriverse' (Sundberg, 2014, p. 41).

Privileging Particular Bodies of Thought

Observational literacy tools such as the one we were given, are designed in a way that draws a teacher's attention towards particular bodies of thought, specifically bodies of thought about what counts as literacy and as a literacy event (Truman et al., 2020). For instance, it does not immediately lend itself to considering Place as literacy. It points towards a definition of literacy that is future orientated, in that it focuses a teacher's attention in always looking towards the child's eventual mastery of reading. By always looking towards future achievement, it is all too easy to ignore what is actually happening in the moment. Furthermore, by looking for demonstrations of knowledge and skills, the attention is always on the production of literacies (Kuby et al., 2019a). This is hardly surprising since the epistemology of literacies (i.e. how we know and how children learn literacy) has long been the focus of literacy research in early years education. However, by attending to Karen Barad's argument for an ethico-onto-epistemology in that knowing, becoming and doing cannot in fact be separated, then education must begin to consider different types of questions about what counts as literacy knowing (Barad, 2007). This might include questions such as what are literacies, how are they produced and how do literacies produce the worlds in which we live (Kuby et al., 2019a)?

Drawing on the scholarship of Barad, Kuby and colleagues propose that education begins to think-with an ontology of literacies; where the focus shifts from thinking of only humans as agentic in the production of literacies and towards the ways in which materials, space, time and children intra-act to generate new literacies (Kuby et al., 2019a). For example, an attunement towards Place-child(ren) *relations* as opposed to Place and child(ren) as separate subjects, makes space for noticing how literacies are emerging in the moment and contributing to Place-making. It shifts the focus from always looking for literacies as a product of human knowledge and towards literacies as an entanglement of Place-child(ren) knowing, becoming and doing (Kuby et al., 2019a). Rather than continuing to reproduce what we already know and can do, an ontology of literacies invites the possibility for new relations, new literacies and ultimately, new realities for the worlds in which we live (Kuby et al., 2019a).

Hacking as a Feminist Method of Critical Inquiry

While the term hacking is used across a variety of contexts, in recent years it is most commonly used when referring to unauthorized access to computer systems. Not unlike computer hacking, hacking as a method of critical inquiry seeks to find, intervene and transform weaknesses in systems. Hacking as a method of critical inquiry has been used by teachers who seek to transform normative practices by disrupting the dominant social powers that operate within education systems (Andrzejewski et al., 2019). Hacking can also be understood as a distinctly feminist practice in that the intent of hacking is to transform and act upon systemic practices that privilege certain types of bodies over others (Clover & Williamson, 2019). An example of feminist hacking, the Feminist Museum Hack, engaged in creative acts of intervention as a 'pedagogy of possibility' for reimagining how museums privilege certain narratives, genres and aesthetics (Clover & Williamson, 2019, p. 1). Through the implementation of various hacking tactics, the hack opened up possibilities for new ways of engaging with museums.

In the archives of *Hacking the Anthropocene*, Astrida Neimanis describes hacking as a process of experimentation that involves collective thinking and action (Neimanis, 2021). Like Neimanis, we understand experimentation to be an uneasy, vulnerable and imperfect doing (Neimanis, 2021). It is through the *doing* of walking, conversing, grappling, thinking, learning and listening with Place, with one another and with children that we were able to employ hacking tactics. The concept of a tactical type of response offers an approach to hacking that is both intentional and strategic. Tactics are also defined as 'the art or skill of employing available means' (Merriam-Webster, n.d.). This meaning is particularly helpful in that it illustrates the ways in which our hack is not about doing away with what is already happening. Rather, hacking tactics invite possibilities for reimagining the ways in which early childhood education currently engages with place-based education and literacies through the repurposing of an observational literacy tool. The concept of grappling was central to the implementation of each tactic. To grapple with something implies that there is some sort of tension (Merriam-Webster, n.d.). Grappling with the tensions that come into play when thinking-with concepts that don't conform to universal ideas about Place, literacies and children is difficult work. It requires a shift from an orientation towards a presupposed outcome and towards an openness to uncertainty.

For our hack of the observational literacy tool, not only do we intend to trouble normative definitions of literacies and literacy events, but we also seek to expand the definition of literate bodies to include the more-than-human elements of an agentic and interconnected Place. We wonder how Place literacies might be understood if the rubric was reconfigured to also include the more-than-human elements of Place? And what might happen if the literacy tool was reconfigured so that the focus was shifted towards relations and the collective rather than the individual child?

Hacking the Observational Literacy Tool

On a particular afternoon at Bush School, we are each walking-with clipboards that hold the literacy observational tool (see Figure 4.1) that we had been provided. The tool directs us to look for childrens' demonstrations of knowledge and skills that correspond to what is written on the rubric. If we were to use the tool as intended, we might look from our clipboard to the children and back again and ask ourselves questions such as, what vocabulary are the children using? Can children use this vocabulary to express their ideas? Can children make connections between the vocabulary they have learnt in the classroom and what is happening today at Bush School? We might highlight specific indicators on the tool as a way of recording when we observe something that corresponds with the phrases on the rubric.

We notice how the words used on the tool are bound by certain definitions of literacy. An example is how the tool refers to child(ren) as being able to make connections, respond to and recount *texts*. The Western Australian curriculum defines *text* as, 'A means for communication. Their forms and conventions have developed to help us communicate effectively with a variety of audiences for a range of purposes. *Texts* can be written, spoken or multimodal and in print or digital/online forms' (School Curriculum Standards and Authority, [SCSA], 2014). This definition of *text* directs us to look for examples of children using texts that fit within the confines of this definition. Sometimes children bring a type of digital text, an iPad, to Bush School. The iPads are used to take photographs and videos and to create new multimodal texts as children record their voices, tell stories and use drawing apps. On this particular day, the children don't have their iPads, but they have listened to the reading of a non-fiction text prior to leaving for Bush School. If we were to use this tool in

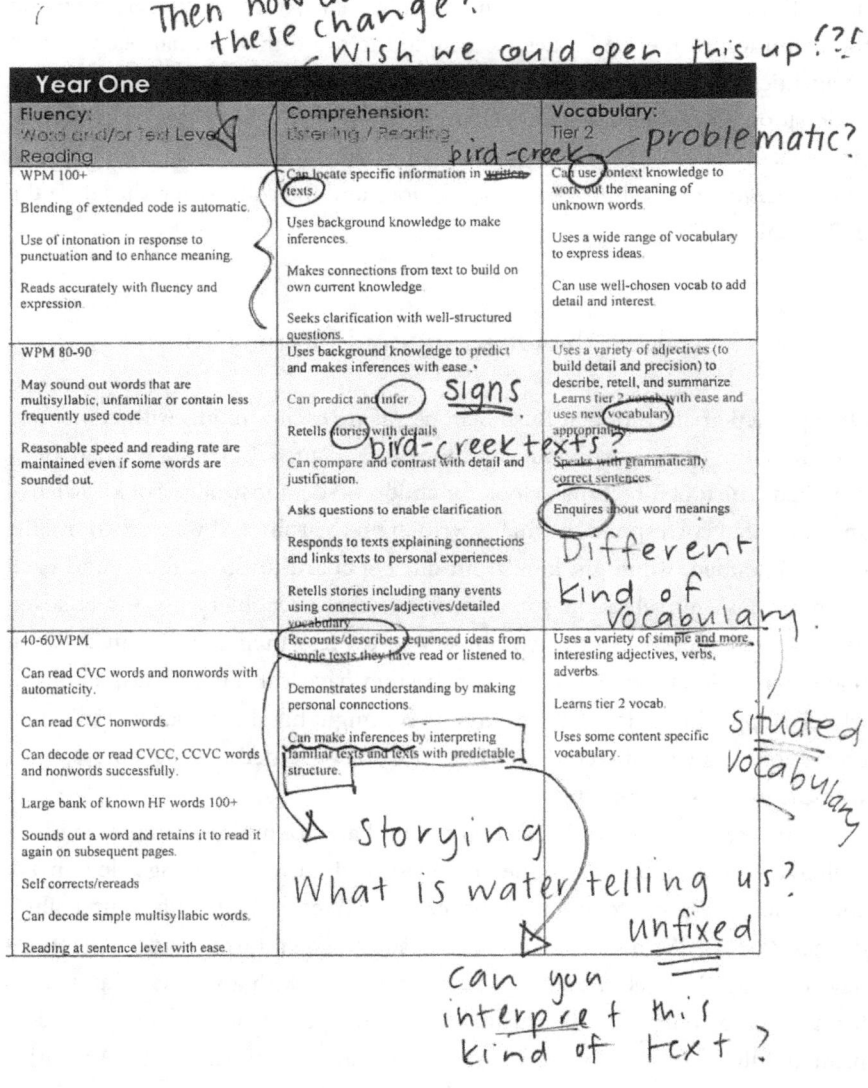

Figure 4.3 A section of the messed-up observational literacy tool.

its traditional form, then it would be easy to see how some children can make connections between what they have learnt about the word erosion from the text read in class and the eroded banks of the creek that they are now seeing at Bush School. This narrow conceptualization of *text* limits the observer to focus solely on children's demonstrations of knowledge in very specific ways. Looking up from our clipboards, we can see how the language used in the tool draws us away from attending to the creek water, creek bank and weathering times with children. Sensing this limitation, we engage our first hacking tactic.

Hacking Tactic #1: Messing-With

Curious about what might happen if we troubled the language used on the tool, we began crossing out, underlining and circling words. Instead of highlighting words and phrases that indicated childrens' achievements, we were intentionally drawing attention to certain words that by their very definition, immediately close off ways in which literacy is understood in early childhood education. Not unlike Kuby, Gutshall Rucker and Kirchofer's experimentations with 'opening up' limited curricular definitions of writing, we considered what might happen if we unbound definitions of words such as text, vocabulary and reading (2015). Drawing from their observations of a second-grade writing workshop, Kuby and colleagues propose that more expansive definitions of writing create possibilities for children to enact new relations with time, space and materials (2015). We see these experimentations of opening up and troubling bound definitions of certain words on the tool as essential to messing-with tactics. Messing-with the language challenged the ways in which the tool could be used and consequently messed-with how we saw Place, children and literacies during the walk.

The tool quickly became messy and chaotic as we circled, crossed out, made links and wrote down questions. Similar to the ways in which post-it notes were used to hack a gallery space in the Feminist Museum Hack, this tactic directly challenged the linear and hierarchical layout of the tool and almost immediately it became a space for critique, speculation and experimentation (Clover & Williamson, 2019). We were tentative with some of our wonderings, aware that we were shifting into unchartered territory and that this always comes with risks. Mindy, along with Veronica Pacini-Ketchabaw and Affrica Taylor, is well versed in working with the risks involved in de-centring taken-for-granted human knowledge (Pacini-Ketchabaw et al., 2016). Rather than avoiding an unknown outcome, we found the unpredictable nature of this tactic generative in helping us to think otherwise about the literacy tool. While walking, we wondered what would happen if the meanings of words such as *text* and *vocabulary* were expanded so that they would become more inclusive of Place? And, what might this look like? Together, we grappled:

If Place was understood to be a type of text, then how does Place generate texts?

I guess the flowing Creek water could be a text . . . remember how the current moved the boats? Those currents are telling us something . . .

Would the flowing creek water be a text? What would a flowing creek water text look like and sound like? How would you read this type of text? I suppose you would need to know specific knowledge about this Place, about the season and how the season relates to the movement of the currents. Then I don't think Place texts can be read in isolation, flowing-creek-water text would have to be read with the season, with wind.

What vocabulary might be needed to be able to talk about and create *with* Place texts?

I think you would need a different type of vocabulary to be able to do this. It would have to be situated and specific to this Place. I also think that Noongar names are important. The vocabulary that the children learn in class is important but it is not enough for talking about and creating with Place in this way. I think vocabulary would have to emerge in-the-moment. It could be invented in response to noticing a Place text . . . maybe we don't have human words to talk about every kind of Place text.

If Place has its own vocabulary that is not made up of human words then how do we recognize this?

Is it through movements, rhythms? Maybe different sounds . . . like the sound of the creek water bubbling as it moves? Or the sound of the wind rustling leaves in the trees? Is it a different language that we would have to learn? Maybe we don't need to learn the language . . . as in, it's not our language to learn. Maybe you would get to know a Place's languages by visiting the Place multiple times, then you would get to know the subtle changes in its language in response to the seasons. That would mean a different type of listening and noticing.

Generated from messing-with tactics these questions open up the literacy tool to make space for Place.

Hacking Tactic #2: Reading-With

'Jaarnnitt' comes from across the creek. We turn our heads away from the children who are testing out their boats in the creek, distracted by the sound. Wardong caws, perched on a low hanging tree branch. Creek is in constant motion, bubbling and making ripples as it flows beneath the bridge. Wardong waits and watches us, children and creek. 'Jaarnnitt' echoes through the trees above. Looking up, there are more Wardongs in the trees.

One Wardong hops down from the branch onto the creek's edge, then hops again, and again, into the still shallows of the creek. Bending their neck down, they take a drink. Wardong stays for a while, bathing in the tannin coloured water. Every now and again, they will bend their neck, dipping their beak into the creek. Perhaps they are feeding on the tiny fish that dart in and out of the tree roots and the loose, fallen branches that rest in creeks' shallow waters.

Figure 4.4 Wardong and creek.

Suddenly, Wardong hops out of the creek and onto the sloping banks, wings flapping in rapid succession. After a moment's pause, with head bent forward, Wardong strides quickly across the grass towards the trees. Then, fluttering its wings, Wardong jumps from branch to branch, finally resting on a low hanging limb. Another Wardong lands on the same branch, causing it to rock up and down from the weight of the two birds. Perched together on the branch, there seems to be a reason for their meeting here.

We sense that Wardong, creek and trees are communicating something, but what? (taken from field notes, 16th August 2021)

Reading-with Aboriginal authorship is an intentional hacking tactic that opens up possibilities for experimenting with ways in which the observational literacy tool might make space for thinking-with Aboriginal ways of knowing Place. In the vignette earlier, instead of returning to look at the children and boats or at the observational literacy tool, we allow ourselves to be distracted by Wardong's call and the changing rhythms of the creek. Shifting the focus away from the children and their literacy learning makes room for us to notice the liveliness of Place at this moment. Noticing and allowing ourselves to be distracted by Wardong and creek is only one part of this hack. Reading-with tactics began *prior to* the walks when we read-with the prose of Aboriginal author Ambelin Kwaymullina. We then employed tactics of thinking and walking-with Kwaymullina *during* the walking event as a way to orientate our thinking and attention towards other ways of knowing Place. For example, in her book, *Living on Stolen Land*, Kwaymullina invites us to think-with the concept of holism. Kwaymullina, an Aboriginal writer from the Palyku people, describes holism as thinking about Place as a 'pattern made up of many threads', all of which connect with one another across time and space (Kwaymullina, 2020, p. 21). Holism reminds us that we are all connected, with Wardong and with creek. In other words, Wardong and creek are not a backdrop to the human activities happening during Bush School, but they are all part of Place literacies.

Reading-with Kwaymullina, as opposed to reading about or from her work is intentional in that it 'requires us to pay attention to who else is speaking alongside us' (Liboiron, 2020, p. 98). Reading-with challenges extractivist methods of reading that are common to Western research practices by acknowledging Indigenous contributions to world-making (Todd, 2016). With this in mind, we do not seek to apply Kwaymullina's concept of holism to what we do on the walks or in how we use the observational tool. Instead, this hacking method is an orientation towards thinking, listening and doing in ways that respectfully engage with other knowledge systems (Sundberg, 2014). For example, if we think of Wardong, creek and branch as connected, then we begin to notice how Wardong relies on creek for both food and water while trees' roots uptake life-giving water from creek. Wardong also works with creek to soften tough food that has been foraged from trees (van Dooren, n.d.). Tree is also where Wardong sleeps as she gathers with other Wardong at sunset to roost for the night (van Dooren, n.d.). The trees above the creek are filled with the sounds of Wardong, these trees are an important place for Wardong, who use their call to make a claim for territory and alert others of danger. Perhaps we are the potential danger to Wardong or at least a source of interaction in their environment (van Dooren, n.d.).

Thinking-with holism orientates our attention away from only noticing the individual elements of Place and towards connections, including our own relations with Wardong, creek, trees and so much more. When we think-with Place in this way, then the orientation of the literacy tool towards an *individuals'* knowledge and development becomes problematic. If we think-with holism, then we must also think of literacies as collective and relational. Thinking about literacies in this way challenges the rigidity of the tool and prompts us to speculate about what would happen if we took away the lines on the tool to allow for Aboriginal knowledges to seep through.

Listening to our colleague, Noongar researcher and educator Libby Jackson-Barrett, we are attentive to the ways in which non-Indigenous attempts to foreground Aboriginal knowledges can lead to further separation of different knowledge systems. Often used in curriculum and policy, terms such as *implement* and *foreground* imply Aboriginal knowledges to be an 'add on' to the curriculum (Australian Curriculum, Assessment and Reporting Authority, [ACARA], 2014). We find Jackson-Barrett's (2021) idea of *infusion* insightful in the way that it challenges us to think beyond merely embedding Aboriginal knowledges in curriculum and practice. The tactic of reading-with Kwaymullina, is a way of opening up possibilities for thinking about how we might begin to infuse Aboriginal knowledges with and from within our walks-with Place and children. Furthermore, if the literacies generated from Place relations were privileged in the observational literacy tool, then we would be on the lookout for Place literacies, opening up further opportunities for understanding how literacies produce new relations and new ways of being with the world.

Hacking Tactic #3 – Blogging-With

Following each walk, blogging-with tactics were used as our third hack of the observational literacy tool. Composed by Karen after each walking event, the blog was shared with the children, families and teachers involved in the walks. The blog was also made visible to members of the public and outside academia who were interested in the project. We see the collective and generative nature of the blog as what characterizes it as a process of blogging-*with*. In other words, we acknowledge that the blog is never composed in isolation and that we are always blogging-*with* Place, children, teachers, theory, histories and much more. The public visibility of the blog was critical to this tactic as it directly challenges the ways in which the observational tool focuses on fixed outcomes for the individual child. The observational literacy tool is used to communicate where a child's learning is situated along a fixed continuum of development. Teachers and parents then use this information to plan for ways to move the child along to the next stage of development. By always focusing on ways to improve or fix a child's development, the tool is grounded in a deficit view of children and learning (Burman, 2017). In contrast, the blog stories Place-child(ren) encounters that foreground Place–children *relations*. This means that rather than providing answers or plans for 'where to next' for learning, the blog opens up spaces for sustaining the grappling of and with ideas that emerged from the walks. This means that the blog is not a fixed end product but always emerging as new and otherwise perspectives are generated from shared thinking and dialogue.

We see blogging-with tactics as having similar characteristics to the ways in which archiving is used as a hacking tactic in *Hacking the Anthropocene* (Hamilton et al., 2021). For example, like archiving, blogging-with ensures that Place stories are told from otherwise perspectives and keeps us accountable for acknowledging our own partiality in any event (Neimanis, 2021). Teachers are trained to use literacy tools, such as the one we were provided, to observe the literacy competencies of children. When literacy development is front and centre of observations, it is easy to overlook the possibilities that arise when considering Place literacies. The blog enabled us to revisit and rework Place–children encounters by bringing Place to the foreground of each story. This intentional tactic became an invitation for the teachers involved in the walks to reconsider each walking event from the perspective of Place literacies. The following reflection from one of the teachers involved in the project highlights the ways in which the blog redirected one teacher's thinking towards more expansive conceptualizations of literacies and Place.

After reading the blog I was reminded . . . that different languages have increasing complexity of words which are increasingly specific in relation to things of importance for that society . . . I found that it (the blog) got me thinking more deeply about literacies in relation to our Bush School and what we can do in this space with the children. I think this is definitely a space that could be explored further. (Shona, teacher who participated in the project.)

The intent of blogging-with tactics was to create these types of openings for sustained dialogue and thinking about how Place and literacies might be approached differently in early childhood education. In contrast to more traditional teacher resources such as teaching guides, the blogs do not outline a formula or description of what or how to teach. Rather, they provided a space for sitting with the complexity and tension that arises when grappling with ideas that challenge normative approaches (Nxumalo & Cira Rubin, 2019). For example, the blog has prompted the teacher to think more expansively about what counts as vocabulary knowledge and the ways in which vocabulary emerges from Place relations. Blogging-with tactics have exposed to the teacher the constraints of the language used on the observational literacy tool by inviting this tension.

Conclusion

Our encounters with Wardong, creek, children and so much more brought to light the limitations of the observational literacy tool that we were provided. By its very design and due to its grounding in developmental logic, the tool privileges specific types of literacies and literate bodies. While these literacies are important for certain purposes, they are not adequate for understanding the ways in which Place contributes to the generation of literacies. Place literacies are necessary for creating spaces for children and teachers to generate literacies *with* Place. Learning to think, live and learn with Place is essential if education is to make a significant contribution to a sustainable future (Common Worlds Research Collective, 2020). This chapter has shown how through a process of hacking, we were able to make space on the tool for Place literacies. The intentional tactics of messing-with the language on the rubric, reading-with Aboriginal authorship and blogging-with Place and more, created openings for thinking about Place and literacies in more expansive ways. The narrow constraints of the observational literacy tool were unbound as we grappled with the idea of Place as a type of text and the vocabulary that is necessary for reading, thinking and creating with Place texts.

At the beginning of our hack, we asked how Place literacies might be understood if the observational literacy tool was reconfigured to also include the more-than-human elements of Place. Reconfiguring the tool to include Place shifts the observer's attention away from an individual's development of literacy skills and knowledge and towards the literacies emerging from and with Place. The encounters with Wardong, creek, children, weather and more demonstrate how the generation of Place literacies is a collective endeavour, emerging from the relations between both human and more-than-human. This means that learning and thinking-with Wardong-creek-tree texts require that we notice our own entanglement in Wardong-creek-tree worlds. Noticing the literacies that we generate *with* Wardong, creek, trees and more has the potential to make a difference to Place-making.

Notes

1. An Acknowledgement of Country is a demonstration of respect for the custodians of Australian Country, Aboriginal and Torres Strait Islander peoples. It can be carried out by a non-Aboriginal person and usually occurs at the beginning of an event (Australian Curriculum, Assessment and Reporting Authority [ACARA], 2014).
2. Capitalizing Place is an intentional move that makes the distinction between place as it is commonly conceptualized in early childhood education and Place that is recognized as agentic in the making of worlds and realities (Watts, 2013). This practice draws on the scholarship of Vanessa Watts, a Mohawk and Anishinaabe woman, who works with the Indigenous concept of Place-Thought to demonstrate the impossibility of separating Place from thought in Indigenous ontologies. Central to this work is acknowledging that colonial ontologies limit agency to only the human by separating knowing (human) from world-making (nature) (Watts, 2013).
3. In situating ourselves in a place that has been invaded and colonized, we do not use the term settler in this chapter as our presence seems so much more implicated and violent than the act of settling. We acknowledge that using the term non-Indigenous can also be problematic due to the fact that it implies a distinction that cannot be widely applied. The local Noongar people refer to non-Indigenous people as wedjela.

References

Andrzejewski, C. E., Baker-Doyle, K. J., Glazier, J. A., & Reimer, K. E. (2019). (Re) framing vulnerability as social justice work: Lessons from hacking our teacher education practices. *Review of Education, Pedagogy, and Cultural Studies, 41*(4–5), 317–351.

Australian Curriculum, Assessment and Reporting Authority (ACARA). (2014). *The Australian Curriculum*. http://www.australiancurriculum.edu.au

Barrable, A., & Booth, D. (2020). Nature connection in early childhood: A quantitative cross-sectional study. *Sustainability*, *12*(1), 375.

Barad, K. (2007). *Meeting the universe halfway: Quantum physics and the entanglement of matter and meaning*. Duke University Press.

Bennett, J. (2010). *Vibrant matter: A political ecology of things*. Duke University Press.

Burman, E. (2017). *Deconstructing developmental psychology* (3rd ed.). Routledge.

City of Melville. (n.d.). *Whadjuk boodja: Aboriginal land*. https://www.melvillecity.com.au/our-city/publications-and-forms/community-development/sites-of-aboriginal-cultural-significance

Clay, M. M. (1991). *Becoming literate: The construction of inner control*. Heinemann Education.

Clover, D. E., & Williamson, S. (2019). The Feminist Museum Hack as an aesthetic practice of possibility. *European journal for Research on the Education and Learning of Adults*, *10*(2), 143–159.

Common Worlds Research Collective. (2020). Learning to become with the world: Education for future survival. Paper commissioned for the UNESCO Futures of Education report (forthcoming, 2021).

Ehri, L. C., Nunes, S. R., Stahl, S. A., & Willows, D. M. (2001). Systematic phonics instruction helps students learn to read: Evidence from the national reading panel's meta-analysis. *Review of Educational Research*, *71*(3), 393–447.

Elliot, S., & Chancellor, B. (2014). From forest school to bush kinder: An inspirational approach to preschool provision in Australia. *Australasian Journal of Early Childhood*, *39*(4), 45–53. https://doi.org/10.1177/183693911403900407

Hackett, A., MacLure, M., & Pahl, K. (2020). Literacy and language as material practices: Re-thinking social inequality in young children's literacies. *Journal of Early Childhood Literacy*, *20*(1), 3–12. https://doi.org/10.1177/1468798420904909

Hackett, A., & Somerville, M. (2017). Posthuman literacies: Young children in time, place and more-than-human worlds. *Journal of Early Childhood Literacy*, *17*(3), 374–391. https://doi.org/10.1177/1468798417704031

Hamilton, R., Reid, S., van Gelder, P., & Neimanis, A. (Eds.). (2021). *Hacking the anthropocene: Archive*. Open Humanities Press. http://www.openhumanitiespress.org/books/titles/feminist-queer-anticolonial-propositions-for-hacking-the-anthropocene/

Hamm, C. (2015). Walking with place: Storying reconciliation pedagogies in early childhood education. *Journal of the Canadian Association for Young Children*, *40*(2), 56–66. https://doi.org/10.18357/jcs.v40i2.15179

Jackson-Barrett, L. (2021). *Learning on Country*. Curtin University, Western Australia. Unpublished PhD.

Kuby, C., & Rowsell, J. (2017). Early literacy and the posthuman: Pedagogies and methodologies. *Journal of Early Childhood Literacy*, *17*(3), 285–296. https://doi.org/10.1177/1468798417715720

Kuby, C., Spector, K., & Thiel, J. (Eds.). (2019a). *Posthumanism and literacy education*. Routledge.

Kuby, C., Zapata, A., & Fontanella-Nothom, O. (2019b). Teaching and learning literacy in early childhood education. In C. Brown, M. McMullen, & N. File (Eds.), *The Wiley handbook of early childhood care and education* (pp. 301–28). John Wiley & Sons, Inc.

Kuby, C. R., Rucker, T. G., & Kirchhofer, J. M. (2015). 'Go be a writer': Intra-activity with materials, time and space in literacy learning. *Journal of Early Childhood Literacy, 15*(3), 394–419.

Kwaymullina, A. (2020). *Living on stolen land*. Magabala Books.

Liboiron, M. (2020). Exchanging. In K. Jungnickel (Ed.), *Transmissions: Critical tactics for making and communicating research* (pp. 89–108). MIT Press.

Merriam-Webster. (n.d.). Grapple definition and meaning. *In Merriam-Webster.com dictionary*. Retrieved November 15, 2021, from https://www.merriam-webster.com/dictionary/grapple

Merriam-Webster. (n.d.). Tactic definition and meaning. *In Merriam-Webster.com dictionary*. Retrieved November 15, 2021, from https://www.merriam-webster.com/dictionary/tactic

Neimanis, A. (2021). An archive of an epoch that almost was. In R. Hamilton, S. Reid, P. van Gelder, & A. Neimanis (Eds.), *Hacking the anthropocene: Archive* (pp. 7–16). Open Humanities Press. http://www.openhumanitiespress.org/books/titles/feminist-queer-anticolonial-propositions-for-hacking-the-anthropocene/

Nxumalo, F., & Cira Rubin, J. (2019). Encountering waste landscapes: More-than-human place literacies in early childhood education. In C. Kuby, K. Spector, & J. Thiel (Eds.), *Posthumanism and literacy education* (pp. 201–213). Routledge.

Pacini-Ketchabaw, V., Taylor, A., & Blaise, M. (2016). Decentring the human in multispecies ethnographies. In Carol A. Taylor & Christina Hughes (Eds.), *Posthuman research practices in education* (pp. 149–167). Palgrave Macmillan.

Rees, D., Shortland-Jones, B., & Western Australia Education Department. (1997). *Reading: Developmental continuum*. Rigby Heinemann.

School Curriculum and Standards Authority. (2014). *Curriculum and assessment outline*. https://k10outline.scsa.wa.edu.au/home/p-10-curriculum/curriculum-browser/english-v8/overview/glossary/text

Snow, E. (2006). What counts as literacy in early childhood? In K. McCartney & D. Phillips (Eds.), *Blackwell handbook of early childhood development*. Blackwell Publishing Ltd. http://nrs.harvard.edu/urn-3:HUL.InstRepos:34785388

Somerville, M. (2007). Place literacies. *Australian Journal of Language and Literacy, 30*(2), 149–164. https://www.researchgate.net

Sundberg, J. (2014). Decolonizing posthumanist geographies. *Cultural geographies, 21*(1), 33–47. https://doi.org/10.1177/1474474013486067

Taylor, A. (2013). *Reconfiguring the natures of childhood*. Routledge.

Todd, Z. (2016). An Indigenous feminist's take on the ontological turn: Ontology is just another word for colonialism. *Journal of Historical Sociology, 29*(1), 4–22.

Truman, S. E., Hackett, A., Pahl, K., McLean Davies, L., & Escott, H. (2020). The capaciousness of no: Affective refusals as literacy practices. *Reading Research Quarterly*, 1–14. https://doi.org/10.1002/rrq.306

van Dooren, T. (n.d.). *The urban field naturalist guide to crow appreciation (with an Australian focus)*. https://urbanfieldnaturalist.org/resources/guide-to-crow-appreciation

Watts, V. (2013). Indigenous place-thought and agency amongst humans and non humans (first woman and sky woman go on a European world tour!). *Decolonization: Indigeneity, Education & Society, 2*(1), 20–34.

5

Reconceptualizing Observations with Infants and Toddlers

Perspectives from Aotearoa, New Zealand

Kiri Gould, *The University of Auckland*
Marek Tesar, *The University of Auckland*
Jen Boyd, *The University of Auckland*

In this chapter we will analyse and discuss the notion of 'observation' and what it means for infants and toddlers in early childhood settings in Aotearoa New Zealand. We theorize what observation means in our context, how it is conceptualized and understood in the Antipodes and feature and analyse a series of vignettes from the early childhood education and care settings in Aotearoa New Zealand. Furthermore, this chapter develops methodological thinking about what observation is and how it is performed drawing on both a post qualitative and Indigenous lenses (Lenz Taguchi, 2010; Malone et al., 2020; Mika, 2017). In doing so it challenges traditional developmental thinking and the way observation is used in documentation and learning stories. The chapter explores the range of approaches that teachers utilize – gaze, visibilities, cameras, written documentation and other methods – to capture and describe the experiences, development and learning of children in their early childhood education settings. These approaches stem from the various philosophies and methodologies developed among the teaching profession to address pedagogical and policy initiatives and changes and to meet the goals of the curriculum framework. Alongside this teacher perspective, the chapter also explores infants and toddlers' ecological sense-making and their relationality with materials and objects, human and non-human entities and narratives and traditions (Taylor & Pacini-Ketchabaw, 2019; Malone et al., 2020). These encounters with teachers' and children's perspectives should not be viewed as in opposition but rather woven together as a *Whāriki*, which calls for complex engagement and reciprocal relationality between adults and young children to discuss learning as *ako* in the anthropocene.

Histories of Present

Aotearoa New Zealand has a unique history and distinct practice when it comes to the idea of 'observation' as part of early childhood practice. Many ideas are part of a result of weaving influences from Europe and the United States, and following local responses to issues of colonization, equity, cultural identities and self-determination (tino rangatiratanga) for Māori (Malone et al., 2020). The complexities of the sociopolitical landscape – including responses to Aotearoa New Zealand's colonial past present, increasing diversity in the population, and market-driven and neoliberal policy shifts – further shape how ideas about observation have been received, adapted or resisted. *Te Whāriki: He Whāriki Mātauranga mō ngā Mokopuna o Aotearoa*, Aotearoa's early childhood curriculum is underpinned by Māori understandings of development and pedagogy and sociocultural theories. It brings together Māori and Western understandings of the child, and young children's learning (Ministry of Education [MoE], 2017). Learning stories are the predominant form of observational assessment linked to *Te Whāriki*; they are formative, narrative and credit-based (Carr, 2001). The non-prescriptive nature of both *Te Whāriki* and learning stories promotes reciprocal and responsive relationships, inclusivity and multiple perspectives (Arndt & Tesar, 2015). Learning stories have been embraced by early childhood teachers in Aotearoa, to such an extent that other observational and assessment practices are rarely found in early childhood settings. They are a powerful tool in shaping views of children and pedagogical practice offering opportunities for teachers to resist developmental, normalizing and marginalizing understandings of the child and what is considered valuable learning. However, the practice of learning stories can be understood in multiple ways. There are significant tensions and contradictions as learning stories intersect with the rise of neoliberal, managerial and performative discourse in policy. Further issues arise as the best practice of learning stories is translated for the sector and co-opted by digital platforms designed for sharing and archiving them. The first section of this chapter overviews the journey to learning stories as the key form of observational assessment in Aotearoa and engages with some of the complexities of learning stories in contemporary early childhood settings.

Early childhood education and care (ECEC) in Aotearoa has emerged from an early history of middle-class charitable and philanthropic endeavours, focused initially on poor settler children in cities, and later educational endeavours aligned with the benefits of preschool education (May, 2019). These were, early on at least, strongly influenced by the ideas of Fröebel (Fröebel & Lilley, 1967; Wells & May, 2019). May (2019) traces the ways that early education in this country has been framed by shifting and overlapping 'political gazes' which she describes as 'cumulative and broad rationales for framing pedagogical and political understanding ... about the rearing and education of young children and the changing role of the state' (p. 18). Early in the colonial history of Aotearoa, political interest was mostly on settler children, the potential of early education to influence their moral life, and a focus on healthy infants as the foundation for a secure nation (May, 2019). From the 1940s, a psychological gaze, strongly influenced by child development studies coming out of Europe and the United States, began to shape pedagogical understanding and decisions in the Antipodes. The works of G. Stanley Hall, Arnold Gessel, Susan Isaacs, Piaget and Freud all expounded the importance of objective and systematic child observation during a time when key early childhood services were emerging and government interest was increasing (May, 2019). By the 1950s and 1960s, child observation, including infant observation, was an important and innovative part of teacher education programmes (Podmore & Luff, 2012). Educational programmes for mothers involved in the newly emerging, family led, Playcentre service were also using the ideas of Piaget to understand child development and how to support it. Teachers and mothers were observing, recording and analysing children's physical, social, emotional and cognitive behaviours against established developmental norms and were using the observational information to structure educational environments and provide developmentally appropriate experiences for children (Podmore & Luff, 2012). These practices asserted positivist and individualist world views in which only knowledge about children that had been objectively and quantifiably verified counted. Sellers (2013) point out the resultant conflation of ECEC with child development as well as the exclusion of other world views and knowledges. Later, ECEC was also impacted by social movements demanding rights and equity for children, women and minority groups. However, Western developmental paradigms continued to dominate ECEC practice well into the 1990s. These perspectives can be linked to broader debates about methodologies associated with young children, including New Zealand, Western, Indigenous and global views, and what it means to be a child and what childhood is (Tesar, Duhn et al., 2021; Tesar, Guerrero et al., 2021).

The advent of *Te Whāriki* provided a significant disruption to pervasive developmental approaches to curriculum; it also called for reconceptualized ways of observing and assessing children. *Te Whāriki* is a non-prescriptive, bicultural and sociocultural curriculum statement deeply embedded in the history and politics of Aotearoa. It posits a collective and relational view of the child immersed in their local cultural context. The story of the development of *Te Whāriki*, including the partnership between the government-contracted writers and Te Kohanga Reo (a movement focused on revitalizing and sustaining the Indigenous Māori language and culture through family participation in early education) has been told in detail elsewhere (Reedy, 2019; Te One, 2013). The foundations of the curriculum are the four principles: whakamana (empowerment), kotahitanga (holistic development), whānau tangata (family and community) and hononga (relationships). These are intended to be interwoven in unique and localized ways with the five strands of mana atua (well-being), mana whenua (belonging), mana tangata (contribution), mana reo (communication) and mana aturoa (exploration). As outlined in the document:

> Kaiako [teachers] in ECE settings weave together the principles and strands, in collaboration with children, parents, whānau and communities, to create a local curriculum for their setting. Understood in this way, the curriculum or whāriki is a 'mat for all to stand on'. (MoE, 2017, p. 12)

Te Whāriki then is open to multiple perspectives about children and important learning and resists a universalized and individualized view of the child, acknowledging that each child has a 'unique learning journey' shaped through and in their relationships with 'people, places and things' (MoE, 2017, p. 21).

Rethinking Learning Stories

Learning stories are a key pedagogical expression of *Te Whāriki*. As Arndt and Tesar (2015) note, learning stories perform the conceptual framework and underpinning principles of the curriculum. Learning stories are narrative records of teachers' observations of children in which storied interpretations of valued learning are documented and reinterpreted to contribute to a shared conversation about the child as a learner. They focus on representing a child's learning over time through a collection of stories contributed by the community of people engaged with the child, including the child themselves. They are intended to illuminate attributes important to learning but difficult to measure such as curiosity, trust and confidence (Carr, 2001). Learning stories 'make learning visible' to children and their families, are credit-based and are open to reinterpretation and multiple perspectives. Complex and holistic learner identities are formed through the contribution of different voices and the accumulation of stories. These are not fixed, but formative and uncertain, understood to be evolving, interrelated with the learning environment (people, places and things). Learning stories counter the notions of objective observation, universal and linear trajectories of development that fail to recognize the complexity and relationality of learning and to acknowledge other world views and knowledges.

However, the understanding and practice of learning stories is also shaped by additional discourses including the human capital and economic discourses shaping the sector. Teachers in Aotearoa are subject to increasing expectations of accountability and performativity; the practices and purposes of their work are subject to increasing external definitions and measurements (Gould, 2021). Teachers are often subject to workplace expectations around the production of learning stories including being responsible for particular children and the number of stories produced for each child over a set period of time. The best practice of learning stories is explicated for teachers through the additional resources and professional development available to them including in *Kei Tua o Te Pae*, a twenty-book resource that theorizes the practice of learning stories and provides exemplars (MoE, 2004). Strongly associated with 'quality' teaching practice, learning stories are an approved pedagogy through which to transform human capital, and teachers' performance of them has become a key measure of professionalism (Gould, 2021). White et al. (2021) research shows how the production of learning stories can be,

> part of complex webs of accountability that also mediate educators' work, including to (some but not all) parents, children, other members of staff, centre leaders who check documentation against organisational priorities and, in some cases, simultaneous use as a source of data for staff appraisals and teacher registration. (p. 15)

Further research by Knauf (2020) shows how teachers balance expectations for producing learning stories for all children with other teaching tasks, revealing how organizational arrangements, values and work conditions impact on how, why and what learning stories are published. A repeated idea in relation to learning stories is that that they 'make learning visible'. The use of photos, photo sequences and videos are normalized best practices (MoE, 2004). Indeed, the framing, taking, curating, managing and archiving of photographs take up substantial amounts of teacher time in Aotearoa.

The pervasiveness of visual evidence and its impact on meaning-making in relation to learning has been problematized in recent scholarship. Hopkins

(2019) questions the ability of the photograph to provide evidence of learning, countering that what isn't visible also matters but may go unrecognized if teachers 'hold too tightly' (p. 220) to photographic evidence. Raising issues of privacy, consent, surveillance and control, Hopkins argues that photographs should be used to open situations and provoke possibilities, rather than define them. The introduction of commercially produced digital platforms to share learning stories adds layers of complexity to these concerns. White et al. (2021) also question the way teachers '"see" and do not "see" learning through digitally enabled means' (p. 7) by examining teachers' use of these digital tools to craft and upload learning stories. Digital platforms, such as Storypark and Educa, are an increasingly common part of observation and assessment practice in Aotearoa. They include the affordance of applying the pre-populated tags built into the tool.

These tags are usually the principles and strands of *Te Whāriki* but can also be customized towards the specific learning priorities of each ECEC setting. Families (those with the right technologies at least) can access and share them and contribute via the associated application software (app). White et al. (2021) argue that when learning stories are retold and reinterpreted via digital platforms, the learning that is 'seen' and valuable is understood through implicit parameters that are a part of the functionality of the tool. These include learning that 'is tag-able, trackable, complete and co-constituted' and results in 'new types of decisions, opportunities, and emerging tensions' (p. 15) for teachers choosing how and which stories to tell. While the subjectivity of learning stories is celebrated, the ways that knowledge is produced through the visual and digital elements of learning stories are not well understood or contested by ECEC teachers and policymakers who may see them as neutral teaching tools.

Engaging with the Multiplicity

Learning stories have justifiably been the focus of critical inquiry that raises performative and political questions about how they shape and are shaped by practice in ECEC settings. Despite this, Sellers (2013) points out that '*Te Whāriki* opens a multiplicity, stating that everything surrounding learners and learning matters, simultaneously avoiding specifics of what and how' (p. 40). Engaging with the multiplicity of *Te Whāriki*, Tesar and Arndt (2019) argue for a wider range of theories and philosophies to be included in ECEC theorizing and practice, including a re-reading of *Te Whāriki* using a posthuman childhood studies lens. The lens 'offers more specific articulations and understandings of children and their childhoods interdependent and intra-related with more-than-human worlds, things, and beings' (Tesar & Arndt, 2019, p. 181). Drawing on Braidotti (2013), Barad (2015), Bennett (2010) and others, Tesar and Arndt (2019) argue that a posthuman reading of *Te Whāriki* elevates 'the messiness of Aotearoa New Zealand childhoods as entangled not only human, but also material, temporal, and worldly interconnected matter, determinations, and forces' (p. 182). In learning stories, teachers notice, recognize and respond to the learning they see occurring (Carr, 2001). Given the non-prescriptive nature of learning stories, they also provide opportunities to engage with children's learning in more generative, uncertain and worldly ways. The challenge posed by Tesar and Arndt (2019) and others (Hopkins, 2019) is for teachers to attune to what does not get or cannot be 'observed', to notice and recognize what might usually be over-looked or discounted, and to be open to the more than just human actors in a learning story scenario. Posthuman pedagogies challenge teachers to expand what they notice, recognize and respond to, and to be open to other knowledges and truths rendered invisible in traditional understandings of early childhood education. Challenging human-centric perceptions, posthuman pedagogies advocate a collective approach, in which children are viewed as always in relation to and interdependent with human and more-than-human matter, energies and things (Cedar, 2018). Malone et al. (2020, p. 111) explain that 'Posthuman pedagogies always come back to relationality, how we come to be together in the world with others, a host of others in awkward uneasy encounters that help us understand our own humanness, while pressing us to look outside our own humanness.' This is particularly evident through the vignettes that follow which call attention to children's relational encounters with the non-human world.

Moving beyond a humanistic approach to observation invites us to consider the potentialities of place and space in both a local and global sense (Yelland et al., 2021). The environment becomes an assemblage of embodied and intra-active matter, and observation is reconceptualized as a multi-sensorial force between infants, adults and the early childhood setting. Social worlds are accompanied, experienced, and formulated through a range of non-human (or more-than-human) things and flows (Nairn & Kraftl, 2016). The following vignettes unravel the act of observation as it transforms from an adult-centric interpretation, becoming one of relational complexity. Raindrops fall on an upturned metal bowl as an infant connects to land and sky. A cat introduces a new way of being within the infant and toddler room, and a toddler builds a cartography between their mother's place of work and the ECEC setting. What might occur if teachers considered posthuman pedagogies beyond traditionally documented observation?

Movement between Sky and Earth

Within Māori mythology, Papatūānuku (the earth mother) and Ranginui (the sky father) were joined together in darkness, their children (tamariki) born into the space between them. The children decided to separate them – bringing light to the world. All cultures have stories explaining the world, yet Western ways of knowing have taken precedence (Hall, 2018; Mika, 2017). If we strip back layers of cultural constructs and teacher identities as guardians and holders of knowledge, how might one approach the following observation?

The rain makes a familiar pattering sound as it lands on the veranda in the infant-toddler room. However, this time there is an overturned metal bowl that makes a different, trill sound. As the rain continues, the vibrations hit the bowl, and it slowly begins to move towards an eighteen-month-old child. The child moves towards the bowl and picks it up; the sounds and movement stop. The child looks to the sky and looks at the bowl, placing it back again. They hold both hands up to the sky, listening and waiting. For a week, the child carried this bowl, placing it in various spaces and places indoors and outside. Are we tempted to interpret the meaning of this narrative? Would we write notes about cause and effect? Would we extend the 'learning' to introduce more bowls of differing shapes and sizes? Would we take some photos or a video and share it with their family and other teachers? These are the bricolage of outcome-based results in which observation is at risk of being siloed into a developmental narrative of appropriate pedagogical and curriculum approaches. In Aotearoa, the curriculum *Te Whāriki* (MoE, 2017), states:

> Children construct knowledge as they make meaning of their world. Knowledge is cultural, social and material. It draws on cultural, aesthetic, historical, social, scientific, technological, mathematical and geographical information. Skills are what children can do; they are what make interaction in and with the world possible. (pp. 22–5)

This framing is problematic from a posthumanist, postdevelopmental conceptualization, as it remains bound in the anthropocentric world view. If we replace interaction with intra-action when thinking about the child with the bowl, the rain, the surfaces and the sounds expand the theoretical underpinnings of observation.

Intra-action can be described as an entanglement of co-existing bodies and activities in practice. To think-with the Baradian term intra-action (Barad, 2007), teachers can think beyond the child's individual agency and come to see it as creating a new merged agency between child, rain, bowl, surface and indeed teacher as an observer. The rain created a musicality with the bowl, a chiming sound, producing a vibration causing movement, causing the child to notice and connect with the phenomena. The observer then intra-acts with this in a way that can either diminish or empower a child's agency. Static images (photographs) only create partial understanding. Words tailored to fit into a learning story create one way of knowing. Conversation provokes new perspectives. Did the child separate the earth from the sky or feel a simultaneous connection to both?

It can be argued that this brief moment can be reconceptualized as a matter of sound and movement, not bound by the nature/culture binary of brain vs. bodily knowing (Matthews, 2017). The young child was embodied in that space, feeling the rain touch their skin, listening and seeing the effect of the rain on the bowl. There was a sense of trust and bodily autonomy for this eighteen-month-old to be 'out in the rain' and able to guide their experiential narrative. Via a purely developmental lens, a young toddler would not have the agency to determine their actions at that moment – a regulatory gaze. The teacher did not ask questions to guide the conversation. They did not immediately plan to extrapolate evidence of appropriate learning. Nor did the teacher usher the child inside to avoid the 'bad' weather, with potentially behaviouralist pseudoscience about 'catching a cold'. Aotearoa New Zealand's health and safety regulations in ECEC (Moe, 2008) have a broad and necessary selection of criteria to ensure children's environments and the materials available are safe and protect children from harm. However, these regulations are still subject to nuance and conjecture when unscored by years of sedimented developmental theory (Giroux, 1997).

In a postdevelopmental approach, a teacher's observation is non-linear and non-invasive. If a postdevelopmental approach perspective were assumed within this vignette, the teacher's figuration of the child would have been measured in terms of the collective aspects of that moment, the child's competency and connection with place and space and the elements entangled in it (Murris, 2018). There would have been no hierarchical approach to learning and teaching – because 'at its core, post-development thinking is focused on an examination or challenge of power dynamics' (Johnson, 2014, para. 4). Instead, observation would be a two-way dance between child and teacher, with the teacher touching the rain, feeling the vibrations of the bowl. The teacher sat beside the child, making eye contact and engaging with the moment rather than the human-centric expectation of the adult 'making learning visible'. While a video was taken, it was from a camera placed on the ground indoors, being non-invasive and a non-judgemental conduit to the experience. There was no timeframe or tick box documentation, but rather an intra-active mattering of child, sky, earth and all the elements and materialities in between.

When examined from a postdevelopmental perspective, the observation 'method' in this vignette was diffracted out into a multimodal way of sensing and being in mind and body (Enriquez, 2016). There was no method, no handbook or ascribed dynamic of child and teacher because postdevelopmental thinking eschews convention and instead seeks to challenge the agency of subject/object (Johnson, 2014). The blueprint is that there is no blueprint but rather an ongoing entwining of fluid theorizing and practice in action (Ziai, 2004).

A Cat on the Window Ledge

What happens when non-human geographies mesh with an infant-toddler space and broader community? It was a sunny morning inside the infant-toddler room, with the children engaged in quiet acts of play until there was an exclamation of 'ooh ca . . . ooh cat!' from a thirteen-month-old child pointing towards the window still. There, stretched out and seemingly oblivious, was a small brown cat. After this first encounter, the cat returned again and again to different parts of the centre, and parents and older children remarked that they saw it out and about in the wider community. Then one day, the cat stopped visiting, having tried in vain to cross a busy main road.

The earlier vignette challenges the concept of human hierarchy while grappling with a topic distasteful to infant-toddler pedagogy – the death of a beloved animal. Within this postdevelopmental examination, it is necessary to dive into the complexities of common world theorizing (Haraway, 2016; Taylor & Pacnini-Ketchabaw, 2019) and childhood geographies (Kraftl, 2016) as they become tangled. Increasingly in the vignette, infants and toddlers grapple with coexistence and difference. Ultimately humans and non-human are thrown together in a precarious world (Taylor & Giugni, 2012): a local geography in which children are exposed to the dangers of a busy traffic route outside their centre gates – and they experience a loss so often minimized as 'just the way it is'.

The cat, whose name we do not know, showed no fear of humans. It was the infants and toddlers who were unsure of this new visitor in their space. Yet over time, the children began to mimic some of the fluid movements and positions of the cat – finding sunshine to stretch together in, playfully balance on seats or for toddlers to make daring jumps as they had witnessed their non-human friend do. This symbiosis of space was at odds with a developmental narrative of observation. Instead of adults recording and then planning for learning and next steps as per a learning story, the infants and toddlers observed and responded autonomously to the cat. In re-situating, the children with the animal teachers could promote a logic of connection. This relational logic is necessary for establishing postdevelopmental pedagogies, which decentre the individualistic exceptionalism of humans' separation from the non-human and more-than-human world (Blaise & Hamm, 2020). The cat influenced the children to move differently, slowing and noticing where the sun streamed in or how much they could stretch out or curl up. In turn, this challenged the construct that teachers should enact developmentally appropriate challenges for the children's fine and gross motor development. Instead, there was a collective joy organically sprung up in co-existing together with their non-human visitor.

However, there is a darker aspect to this vignette in which the human geography of busy roads and cars was at odds with the non-human geography of the cat. Long has it been 'common knowledge' that animals take risks when interacting with the human-centric world. Often the death of a beloved pet or seeing the remains of a wild animal or any non-human life on the road are suburban children's youngest experience with death. In a developmental narrative of learning, this friction is often unobserved and not part of an early childhood narrative unless it's curated and narrated in psychosocial terms (Shonfeld, 2021).

Within common worlds scholarship, the geographies of childhood entangle to unsettle notions of neighbourhood and community. The road outside the centre became a source of danger within the adult's eyes – with older children at the centre understanding that the cat had been 'run over'. Yet, the infants and toddlers still looked towards the busy road with its colourful trucks, cars and buses having already been enculturated into the acceptance of noise, pollution and the inevitable grind of the morning commute. Taylor and Pacini-Ketchabaw (2015) trouble the simplistic definitions of nurture/culture, human and non-human noting that the power struggles of life and death survival still exist and need to be addressed pedagogically. In reconceptualizing the impact of the cat's death on infants and toddlers, it is critical to address the question of understanding and impact on very young children. Their daily visitor no longer came, but the busy road continued with its congestion, noise and relentless forward movement. Eventually, the children stopped their previous cat-like moments and resumed a humanistic approach to their space. Yet, who is to say for certain the memories are fleeting and bound to mind rather imbued in the children's bodily connection with that animal?

There is never just one story to be told – and teachers must look beyond the easier developmental narratives or cute cat-child relations. A postdevelopmental approach allows for the complex cautionary existence of humans sharing worlds with animals. In worlding this event, teachers can stay with the trouble of human geographies, intra-acting with the place and spaces of the more-than-human, causing rippling effects with community, without dismissing or rationalizing them into tidy learning narratives.

Can You See the City?

Every morning, soon after the child arrived, he would climb to the loft space and look out the window, visually tearful and anxious. 'Can you see the city?' asks a teacher. 'Mummy there' replies the twenty-month-old toddler, pointing out the window and across the harbour to the city.

This vignette explores how a toddler builds a relational ecology of belonging, by creating a cartography of the early childhood setting and their mother's place of work. Over time, having explored the standardized ways of promoting belonging, the teachers supported the child and their mother in a paradigm of postdevelopmental observation. By utilizing the scholarship of childhood geographies and Delaune's (2020) Murdocian perspective on love, a toddler's separation anxiety is reimagined.

The concept of belonging is intrinsic to infant and toddler pedagogy, and within *Te Whāriki* (MoE, 2017) it states, 'belonging is nurtured through social interaction with kaiako (teachers) and other children and by respecting the achievements and aspirations of each child's family and community' (p. 31). *Te Whāriki* (MoE, 2017) highlights the importance of social relationships within 'developmentally appropriate' age categories. While relational connections to others form an important part of any pedagogical approach, postdevelopmentalism can also take into account posthumanist perspectives in which more-than-human connections also foster belonging. The toddler within this vignette was not seeking a relational connection bounded by human to human, but also seeking a connection from place to place.

Kraftl (2016) acknowledges that the majority of children's geographies take place in urban contexts. These geographies are not just related to children's physical presence, but also the emotional spaces that they inhabit. The window which the child looked out of was a window into his world, in which he was embodied in the space between himself and his mother – a space separated by physical kilometres and emotional milliseconds. At first the teachers had tried techniques such as distraction (removing the child to another place in the room) and other forms of connection via his cuddly toy, books or singing the child's favourite songs. However torn the teachers were to see the child upset, there was a veil of professional problem-solving that emerged. There were conversations between teachers, all with differing solutions to the child's daily sadness after he farewelled his mother. Then, when speaking to the child's mother, a conversation arose about how he liked to trace his steps to signpost from place to place, 'He knows my building is next door to the Sky Tower' (in Auckland's CBD).

From a Murdochian conceptualization of attention (Murdoch, 1998), the teachers found they needed to step back from observational governance – monitoring and 'fixing' the child's distress and embrace what Delaune (2020) describes as a 'moral imagination' to support deep thinking about ethical concepts and ideas (p.22). A reimagining occurred in which teachers sought to resist institutionalization of the child's emotions as a phase of 'separation anxiety'. Instead, they embraced an embodied pedagogy of the spaces in between.

Over time, a cartographic mapping of the infant and toddler room occurred between the toddler and his teachers. Instead of moving straight to the window every day, the child selected one thing from the room to give to his mother to take to work. However, this only mapped their connection one way. So, the mother suggested she take her son to her office to explore and map out the objects in the space that he liked and recognized. A reciprocal exchange of matter and materials began to take place between the child's ECEC setting and his mother's place of work with items returned and swapped out. A new ecology of belonging had unfolded outside of the usual developmental approaches to transition and settling in.

Via a mapping with matter, the child forged an active role in his sense of place and space, no longer leaving it in the hands of his teachers. This vignette, and its reimagining, uncover a postdevelopmental approach to observation and subsequent action. Rather than the classical Newtonian distinction between the observer and the 'object' we observed (Lenz Taguchi, 2010), a reframing occurred. The child agentically built a bridge of love between himself and his mother empowered by everyday matter. Thus, subverting the psychological and behavioural practices found within the hierarchy between teachers and children. By giving attention and love to the spaces in between and empowering a new ecology of belonging, observation was not passive but a vital agentic force – mattering matter.

Reconceptualizing Observations with Infants and Toddlers

Concluding themes from this section of the chapter serve to act as a launching point to continue to explore infants' and toddlers' ecological sense-making and their relationality with materials and objects, human and non-human entities, and narratives and traditions. It is also clear that it is not only education but care that matters in the early years and for our youngest citizens (Ailwood et al., 2022). The conceptualizing of the vignettes from a postdevelopmental and posthumanist perspective trouble the notion of passivity within the observed. Adult-centric acts of documenting learning were disrupted by the agency of infants and toddlers and their connection with the more-than-human. From Papatūānuku and Ranginui, the earth to the sky and all that is in between, nothing is merely observed but is an ever-evolving state of being and becoming together.

References

Ailwood, J. et al. (2022). Communities of care: A collective writing project on philosophies, politics, and pedagogies of care and education in the early years. *Policy Futures in Education*. https://doi.org/10.1177/14782103211064440

Arndt, S., & Tesar, M. (2015). Early childhood assessment in Aotearoa New Zealand: Critical perspectives and fresh openings. *Journal of Pedagogy*, 6(2), 71–86. https://doi.org/10.1515/jped-2015-0014

Barad, K. (2007). *Meeting the universe halfway: Quantum physics and the entanglement of matter and meaning*. Duke University Press.

Barad, K. (2015). Transmaterialities: Trans*/matter/realities and queer political imaginings. *GLQ: A Journal of Lesbian and Gay Studies*, 21(2–3), 387–422. https://doi.org/10.1215/10642684-2843239

Bennett, J. (2010). *Vibrant matter: A political ecology of things*. Duke University Press.

Blaise, M., & Hamm, C. (2020). Lively emu dialogues: Activating feminist common worlding pedagogies. *Pedagogy, Culture & Society*. https://doi.org/10.1080/14681366.2020.1817137

Braidotti, R. (2013). *The posthuman*. Polity Press.
Carr, M. (2001). *Assessment in early childhood education: Learning stories*. Paul Chapman Publishing.
Ceder, S. (2018). *Towards a posthuman theory of educational relationality*. Routledge.
Delaune, A. (2020). Love and infants: A Murdochian perspective. *The First Years: Ngā Tau Tautahi. New Zealand Journal of Infant and Toddler Education, 22*(2), 19–23.
Enriquez, G. (Ed.). (2016). *Literacies, learning and the body: Putting theory and research into pedagogical practice*. Routledge.
Fröbel, F., & Lilley, I. M. (1967). *Friedrich Froebel: A selection from his writings*. Cambridge U.P.
Giroux, H. (1997). *Pedagogy and the politics of hope: Theory, culture, and schooling. A critical reader*. Westview Press.
Gould, K. (2021). *Early childhood teacher identities and the complex business of early childhood education and care in Aotearoa*. Unpublished Doctoral Thesis. https://hdl.handle.net/2292/57644
Hall, S. (2018). The west and the rest: Discourse and power [1992]. In D. Morley (Ed.), *Essential essays, volume 2: Identity and diaspora* (pp. 141–184). Duke University Press. https://doi.org/10.1215/9781478002710-009
Haraway, D. (2016). *Staying with the trouble: Making Kin in the Chthulucene*. Duke University Press.
Hopkins, R. (2019). *The photograph, Flusser and early childhood education*. Unpublished Doctoral Thesis. http://hdl.handle.net/2292/49684
Johnson, C. K. (2014). *Post development and the practitioner*. E-International Relations. https://www.e-ir.info/2014/01/08/post-development-and-the-practitioner
Knauf, H. (2020). Learning stories, pedagogical work and early childhood education: A perspective from German preschools. *Education Inquiry, 11*(2), 94–109. https://doi.org/10.1080/20004508.2019.1591845
Kraftl, P. (2016). The force of habit: Channelling young bodies at alternative education spaces. *Critical Studies in Education, 57*(1), 116–130. https://doi.org/10.1080/17508487.2016.1102753
Lenz Taguchi, H. (2010). *Going beyond the theory/practice divide in early childhood education: Introducing an intra-active pedagogy*. Routledge.
Malone, K., Tesar, M., & Arndt, S. (2020). *Theorising posthuman childhood studies*. Springer.
Matthews, S. J. (2017). Postdevelopment theory. In *Oxford Research Encyclopedia of International Studies*. https://doi.org/10.1093/acrefore/9780190846626.013.39
May, H. (2019). *Politics in the playground: The world of early childhood in Aotearoa New Zealand* (Rev. ed.). Otago University Press.
Mika, C. (2017). *Indigenous education and the metaphysics of presence: A worlded philosophy* (1st ed.). Routledge.

Ministry of Education. (2008). *Starting a centre based ECE service*. Ministry of Education. https://www.education.govt.nz/early-childhood/running-a-service/starting-a-service/starting-a-centre-based-ece-service/redownloadpdf/#page39

Ministry of Education. (2004). *Kei Tua o Te Pae: Assessment for learning: Early childhood Exemplars*. Learning Media.

Ministry of Education. (2017). *Te Whāriki. He Whāriki Mātauranga mō ngā Cokopuna o Aotearoa: Early childhood curriculum*. NZCER Press.

Murdoch, I. (1998). *Existential Jets and Mystics: Writings on philosophy and literature*. Penguin.

Murris, K. (2018). Posthuman child and the diffractive teacher: Decolonizing the nature/culture binary. In A. Cutter-Mackenzie, K. Malone, & E. Barratt Hacking (Eds.), *Research handbook on childhoodnature*. Springer. https://doi.org/10.1007/978-3-319-51949-4_7-2

Nairn, K., & Kraftl, P. (2016). Introduction to children and young people, space, place and environment. In T. Skelton, K. Nairn, & P. Kraftl (Eds.), *Space, place and environment* (pp. 1–24). Springer.

Podmore, V., & Luff, P. (2012). *Observation: Origins and approaches in early childhood education*. Open University Press.

Reedy, T. (2019). Tōku Rangatiratanga nā Te Mana-Mātauranga: "Knowledge and power set me free …". In J. Nuttal (Ed.), *Weaving Te Whāriki. Aotearoa New Zealand's early childhood curriculum framework in theory and practice* (pp. 25–44). NZCER Press.

Sellers, M. (2013). *Young children becoming curriculum Deleuze, Te Whāriki and curricular understandings*. Routledge.

Shonfeld, D. (2021). How early childhood can explain death to children. *Teaching Young Children, 13*(3).

Taylor, A., & Giugni, M. (2012). Common worlds: Reconceptualising inclusion in early childhood communities. *Contemporary Issues in Early Childhood, 13*(2), 108–119. https://doi.org/10.2304/ciec.2012.13.2.108

Taylor, A., & Pacini-Ketchabaw, V. (2015). Learning with children, ants, and worms in the anthropocene: Towards a common world pedagogy of multispecies vulnerability. *Pedagogy, Culture, & Society, 23*(4), 507–529. https://doi.org/10.1080/14681366.2015.1039050

Taylor, A., & Pacini-Ketchabaw, V. (2019). *The common worlds of children and animals: Relational ethics for entangled lives*. Taylor and Francis.

Te One, S. (2013). Te Whāriki. Historical accounts and contemporary influences. In J. Nuttal (Ed.), *Weaving Te Whāriki. Aotearoa New Zealand's early childhood curriculum framework in theory and practice* (pp. 7–34). New Zealand Council for Educational Research.

Tesar, M., & Arndt, S. (2019). Re-reading and re-activating Te Whāriki through a posthuman childhood studies lens. In A. Gunn & J. Nuttall (Eds.), *Weaving Te Whāriki: Aotearoa New Zealand's early childhood curriculum document in theory and practice* (pp. 181–194). NZCER Press.

Tesar, M., Duhn, I., Nordstrom, S. N., Koro, M., Sparrman, A., Orrmalm, A., Boycott-Garnett, R., MacRae, C., Hackett, A., Kuntz, A. M., Trafí-Prats, L, Boldt, G., Rautio, P., Ulmer, J. B., Taguchi, H. L., Murris, K., Kohan, W. O., Gibbons, A., Arndt, S., & Malone, K. (2021). Infantmethodologies. *Educational Philosophy and Theory*. https://doi.org/10.1080/00131857.2021.2009340

Tesar, M., Guerrero, M. R., Anttila, E., Newberry, J., Hellman, A., Wall, J., Santiago-Saamong, C. R., Bodén, L., Yu, H., Nanakida, A., Diaz-Diaz, C., Xu, Y., Trnka, S., Pacini-Ketchabaw, V., Nxumalo, F., Millei, Z., Malone, K., & Arndt, S. (2021). Infantographies. *Educational Philosophy and Theory*. https://doi.org/10.1080/00131857.2021.2009341

Wells, C., & May, H. (2018). Advocacy and collaboration in the kindergarten movement of New Zealand. In T. Bruce, P. Elfer, S. Powell, & L. Werth (Eds.), *The Routledge international handbook of Froebel and early childhood practice. Rearticulating research and policy*. Routledge. https://doi-org./10.4324/9781315562421

White, E. J., Rooney, T., Gunn, A. C., & Nuttal, J. (2021). Understanding how early childhood educators 'see' learning through digitally cast eyes: Some preliminary concepts concerning the use of digital documentation platforms. *Australian Journal of Early Childhood*, 66(1), 6–18. https://doi.org/10.1177/1836939120979066

Yelland, N. J., Peters, L., Fairchild, N., Tesar, M., & Pérez, M. S. (2021). *The SAGE handbook of global childhoods*. SAGE.

Ziai, A. (2004). The ambivalence of post-development: Between reactionary populism and radical democracy. *Third World Quarterly*, 25(6), 1045–1060.

'What's Happening *Here*?'

Speculative Routes to Observation in Early Art Teacher Education

Christopher M. Schulte, *University of Arkansas*

Introduction

As early artist-educators, rarely is it the case that we are *just* observing children and their art. What we observe, the way we observe, and the rationales we use to justify this observational work are always tangled in force and desire and intent. Or rather, as art historian James Elkins might say, our observational practices are 'heated' (1997, p. 21). In other words, observation is always a process that is connected to, directed towards and/or guided by something else. But what is this something else? What are the conditions, tendencies, and attachments that so effectively shape our observational practices in early art teacher education? In this chapter, I consider these questions with great care to attend to the idea that we never *just* observe children and their art. As Elkins (1997) says 'There is no such moment' (p. 21). I attend to this recognition to gesture towards something else, a way of observing that is more open, less assured. To do this, I introduce three specific turns of phrase, each purposed to illustrate a certain set of complexities and their relations to observation in early art teacher education.

The first turn of phrase, 'Nothing's happening here', is structured to capture the passive, often inattentive ways that observation unfolds in early art teacher education, specifically within the context of early fieldwork experiences. To explore the particularities of how this turn of phrase functions, I draw on Lauren Berlant's (2011) work on optimism and its objects, specifically her thinking related to the object of desire. For Berlant, an object of desire is ultimately 'a cluster of promises we want someone or something to make to us and make possible for us' (Berlant, 2011, p. 23). For many pre-service early artist-educators, the feeling that 'Nothing's happening' is not entirely uncommon, especially when being asked to observe children and their art, only to realize that the *something* they had expected – that cluster of promises – is unlikely or unwilling to appear. This experience, of not observing what one expects to observe – or more pointedly, of children and their art not being quite what the pre-service early artist-educator had in mind – is critical to understanding how and why certain discourses are able to prevail in early art teacher education.

Second, and relatedly, the phrase '*Here*, it's happening' is used to illustrate the assumptive, near prescriptive contours of observation, especially when tethered to normative and normalizing discourses in early art teacher education, for example, the discourse of development. Whereas the first turn of phrase 'Nothing's happening *here*' underscores an observational experience in which the object of desire is absent or perhaps present in a way that did not immediately register as intelligible, whereby children and their art do not quite materialize as expected, the turn of phrase '*Here*, it's happening' is focused on the object of desire itself (e.g. Berlant, 2011; Love, 2012). Specifically, this part of the chapter centres on how the discourse of development, as an example, functions as a dominant object of desire in early art teacher education, one that routinely shapes observation as a process of looking *at* something, looking *for* something and in many cases looking *away* from the *something else* that is also present.

Third, and as a response to these initial turns of phrase, I introduce another phrase, though situated as a question: 'What's happening *here*?' I do this to complicate how early artist-educators conceptualize, approach and experience observation in early art teacher education, specifically to orientate themselves to children's engagements with the visual arts. It is a question that stretches the frames of reference we have become accustomed to using and also troubles the interpretive values we lean on most to rationalize this use. To ask this question is to commit to contingency and the iterative act of wondering how, why and in what ways, right *here*, children's making is inviting us – at times nudging us – into a 'wormhole' (Sakr, 2021) of difference.

Specifically, in this chapter I contemplate the conceptual and pedagogical relationship of this question to early art teacher education, including the ideas presented in prior sections, but especially the way in which this question stands to refigure observation as a speculative act. In doing so, I argue that 'What is happening *here*?' as a speculative point of entry to observation makes it possible to generate new, different and unsettling relations to children and their art. Of course, this isn't to suggest that by asking this question we will somehow manage to omit from consideration the matter of our attachments, their creation and the tenacity of faith we bequeath to our inclinations and the familiarity they provide. Rather, my point is to begin to curate a picture of observation, one that may well be committed to fostering observational routes that are speculative in their capacities to orientate us to early art teacher education, but that also acknowledges the influence of our commitments and convictions, no matter how conflicting or contradictory they may be.

'Nothing's Happening *Here*'

While discussing observations from the week prior – what I typically refer to as fieldwork – there is inevitably one student who declares, 'Nothing happened' during their observation. I've come to expect this response. While I don't agree with it, of course, I do understand that it will happen. In fact, over the years, responses like this have proven to be a near-omnipotent presence within my work as an early art teacher educator, especially as it relates to students' observational practices toward children and their art. I must admit that when I am faced with a student who feels this way, I often think to myself, incredulously: 'How can a student be in this setting, with young people who are incessantly doing, being, thinking, sharing, exchanging, learning, exploring, etc., and somehow – despite all of this – be left with the impression that nothing has happened?' But despite how frustrating or discouraging it may be, I understand that this response is often about much more than the person who is delivering it. Most important, for me, is the fact that responses like this are ultimately occasions to think with students about how the act of observing 'nothing' may in fact be 'something' very important to observe more closely. (Schulte, 2019, Teaching Reflection)

The Challenge of Observation

For many pre-service early artist-educators, the process of observing children and their art can be a strange and sometimes challenged-riddled experience. Aside from some of the usual difficulties, for example, one's uncertainties about how best to enter the social, cultural and aesthetic worlds of children (Schulte, 2018) (see also, e.g. Corsaro & Molinari, 2008; Corsaro, 1985, 2003) and the impulse to make sense of children's work through the lens and experience of adulthood (Lee, 2001) (see also, e.g. Schulte, 2021; Qvortrup et al., 1994), pre-service artist-educators are often hesitant to get involved and equally uncertain about their own presence when they do. And when you consider that pre-service artist-educators are being asked – perhaps for the first time – to actively account for the social milieus and cultural marginalia that surrounds and supplements children's making (Thompson, 1995; McClure, 2007), the subtle albeit complex work of building an attentive presence in the lives of children is, understandably, a complicated process. It is also not something that we (adults) can simply do, nor is it a practice that is easily sustained.

Additionally, there is the expectation that children be recognized and approached as experts of their own lives and practices (e.g. Graue et al., 1998; Greene & Hogan, 2004; James, 1998: James & Prout, 2003; Thompson, 2009), a request that may prove difficult for many students to accept, even entertain. Too, and perhaps most importantly, is the hope that students' daily efforts to learn more about young people and their art will also move them to uncover their own attitudes and assumptions about who children are, how they work and create and learn, and what they may need or benefit from.

Allison James (1996), a noted childhood studies scholar, does especially well to capture this tension. She writes, 'Fieldwork made me relearn what it is to be a child through witnessing children learning how to be children in the same moment they were learning to be themselves' (James, 1996, p. 315). This very same dynamic is at play when pre-service artist-educators are asked to observe children and their art, particularly in early childhood settings. Like James, pre-service early artist-educators' experiences of observing children learning to be children in the same moment they are learning to be themselves is an occasion that moves them to relearn – or at least invites them to consider differently – what it is to be a child. The same can be said about children, their art and the matter of what it might mean to be a child artist. Importantly though, and this is a key addition, pre-service artist-educators are also being made to face and potentially relearn what it is to be a good art teacher (Moore, 2004) – an elusive and change-inclined project, one that evolves because it is a practice, like children's art, that varies considerably from site-to-site, from child-to-child and setting-to-setting and from one community and educative ecology to another.

Children and Their Art: A Cluster of Promises

It is for this reason that we can never *just* observe children and their art. There are simply too many degrees of complication to temper our presence and too many layers of investment to remain neutral or somehow think that we can be objective. Indeed, just below the surface of our observational work there exists an always-evolving network of interests, values and norms, a set of personal, social, cultural, political and historical dynamics that can never quite be spoken or accounted for but that nonetheless manage to twist and turn and toggle their way into our thoughts and into our ways of seeing and being with children and their art. This is the *something else* I alluded to previously, what Berlant describes as a cluster of promises.

There is no shortage of possibilities regarding what this cluster of promises may be or entail. That said, there are certain clusters which always seem to prevail in early art teacher education, especially in relation to pre-service early artist-educators' observational fieldwork. For example, there are those clusters which relate to how pre-service early artist-educators conceptualize the child, and children and childhood more broadly (e.g. Moss et al., 2000; James & James, 2017), but there are also clusters reflected in their thinking about art and aesthetics (e.g. Leeds, 1989; Wilson, 1997), and those ways of knowing that are indebted to a particular set of conceptual frames as it pertains to teaching and teachers, especially when presumed to be emblematic of what some would consider to be *good teaching* (e.g. Moore, 2004, 2012; Rudduck, 1985). And of course, there are many other clusters too, which cut across and intersect with those outlined here (e.g. gender, race, ethnicity). The point is that each cluster of promises – while always contingent, always variable, always differentially shaped and assembled – has a direct and discursive effect on how we talk to the child, how we ask the child questions, how we manage to listen to the child's ideas, and the extent to which we can ever fairly and adequately account for or manage to express the child's work, life, and experience as an artist (e.g. Malaguzzi, 1993; Rinaldi, 2006; Thompson, 2009).

In this way, the relations we have to a particular cluster of promises are always a matter of aspiration, a desiring for a story that will turn out in a particular way. It is for this reason that I turn to the work of Lauren Berlant, a cultural theorist who has written extensively on the concept of desire (1998, 2012), especially as it pertains to domains of intimacy (2005) and normative and radical practices of social belonging (2011). Berlant's work around desire has been instructive to my thinking about how and why pre-service artist-educators stay attached to certain fantasies, even when said fantasies – whatever they might be – have proven to be problematic or continue to be patterned in ways that bring about and/or reproduce limiting, unhelpful, distortive, even painful effects or outcomes. The point being that what we desire to be promised isn't always delivered and what we believe a particular promise will deliver is not always possible, or even helpful.

'Nothing's happening here' is about staying in proximity to a particular set of fantasies related to children and their art, and to early art teacher education more generally. Such fantasies are desirable because what they promise enables pre-service early artist-educators to either preserve a certain set of personal and professional realities or convert the scenes and materials of their experience into props for a particular reality, one that is more familiar or perhaps preferable to what they have just encountered or been made to face. In this way, 'Nothing's happening here' is a form of observational shorthand, a habit that enables pre-service early artist-educators to not have to observe at all (Schulte, 2016) (see also, e.g. Colebrook, 2002). This experience, of understanding observation as optional or of not observing what one expects to observe – and to be more direct, of children and their art not reflecting the fantasies that pre-service early artist-educators have in mind or hold allegiance to – is essential to understanding how a certain cluster of promises manages to prevail in early art teacher education.

Of importance then is not only the matter of how this cluster of promises attenuates our observational scope to the point that we believe the very assumptions we have manufactured, notably that 'Nothing's happening here'. Also of importance is the matter of considering how this same cluster of promises comes to direct us to take up observation as a practice of locating and confirming those specific instances in which *right here*, 'It's happening.' This too is a form of observational shorthand, a habit that Elkins (1986) does well to analogize to hunting and the everyday experience of shopping. To further illustrate this point and the relationship of these practices to looking, Elkins writes:

> After all, I am the one who decides to go shopping, and normally I'm on the lookout for something in particular: I'm hunting for it and trying to pick it out of the thousands of objects that I do not want. If I can find the one perfect watch, it's because I know what I'm looking for, and I can tell a good watch from imitations and distinguish styles that are very close to one another. In this way of looking at things, the watches are all camouflaged: each is almost identical to the next, and the one I want is somewhere among them. Like a leopard hunting in the jungle, I can look at the tangle of leaves, vines, and flickering lights and pick out just half of the pupil of a frightened deer. (Elkins, 1997, p. 20)

Of crucial importance for pre-service early artist-educators is the process of cultivating an awareness for what this *something* might be and how it manages to direct them to observe children and their art – that is, to hunt and shop for it. Here, I'm reminded of what Berlant (2011) writes about the object of desire, that ultimately a cluster of promises refers to what we want someone or something to make to us and make possible for us. Continuing with this line of thinking, Berlant describes how a cluster of promises could be 'embedded in a person, a thing, an institution, a text, a norm, a bunch of cells, smells, a good idea – whatever' (p. 23). In this way, to hunt and shop for children and their art is to attempt to observe through a particular set of proximities, which of course enable us to maintain the very cluster of things (i.e. desires and affects) that have been promised to us or made possible for us. For example, a version of the child that we have come to expect, that we know and trust, and that we readily use to relate to and sustain a way of thinking about the child's work, life and experience. The same can be said about our versions of art, aesthetics and the materiality and scenes of this work in early childhood. These versions of childhood art, what Berlant might refer to as the objects of childhood art, make to us certain promises about who the child is or will be and how they should and can engage in art-making. We hunt and shop for these objects, these versions of the child and art because what they allow us to maintain is what we already know – that is, the ideas, histories, values and practices that we are most familiar with and that permit us a certain level of comfort or confidence in our relations to children and their art. Perhaps too much.

'*Here*, It's Happening.'

The kids I observed were 'just' scribbling. Nothing really happened. (Schulte, 2019, Teaching Reflection)

In early art teacher education, the cluster of promises that has most effectively constituted our time and relations to children as well as their art is that of development and the developmental discourse, also referred to as the developmental psychology approach (e.g. James et al., 1998), developmentalism (e.g. Woodhead, 2009), and more broadly as the developmental paradigm (e.g. Burman, 2016). The developmental discourse, which first emerged in the nineteenth century, was based on an evolutionary model (Jenks, 1996, 2005; Moss, 1990). The model, which emphasizes a natural conception of the child – that is, a figure whose progression to adulthood is structured around a series of predetermined, biologically oriented stages – also forces art and its making to assume a similarly restricted form. In other words, the developmental psychology approach figures art as a neutral practice for a natural child (Schulte, 2021).

When pre-service artist-educators' observations and understandings of childhood art only ever get to be imagined, experienced or expressed relative to optimizing discourses like development (McClure, 2011), too often they end up restricting themselves to the role of plotting time – that is, to an accountancy of where children have been, where they are now, and where they should have gone or will go next (Sakr et al., 2018). To take this approach – that is, to become a manager of milestones – is to assume that you know the child in advance and to acquiesce to a frame of reference that fails to take seriously the matter of how, right here, in a particular moment and place, children and their art are in the making.

Just Scribbling

At the onset of this section, I shared a comment from a student which summarized their first day of field experience. Recounting the unremarkable nature of his observational experience and the specific encounters he had while visiting the childcare centre, the student stated: 'The kids I observed were just scribbling. Nothing really happened.' This comment has always managed to stay with me. It is a statement that reflects a more general sentiment about children and their art, one that is commonly expressed in the courses I teach. What I find intriguing about this statement – and others like it – is the level of contradiction, assumption and ambivalence embedded within it. On the one hand, it is a statement that reflects very clearly the complexities outlined in the first phrase, 'Nothing's happening here.' For the student, nothing *is* happening. This is because what the student is observing, the scribbling, is a process that aligns with what he may already count as intelligible from a childhood art standpoint. Meaning, that the student is already accustomed to thinking with and observing through a certain cluster of promises; in this case, that young children's drawing, and perhaps other like processes of art-making, take the form of scribbling. While scribbling is indeed common for children at this age, an observation that has been widely discussed by researchers of childhood art (e.g. Kellogg, 1959; Kindler & Darras, 1998; Mathews, 1984; Tarr, 1990; Thompson, 1990), it is a cluster of promises that enables the student to convert the scenes and materials of his experience into a prop that stabilizes a particular set of understandings about children and their art, and about observation too. In this way, the student's suggestion that 'Nothing really happened' is a form of observational shorthand, a habit that legitimates for him the belief that nothing *is* happening because everything he has observed was already understood and thus, the subject of his anticipation. In this view, the child is merely an object, a determinable figure that no longer requires or even permits interpretation, and whose context and work are either scrubbed clean from view or regarded as unnecessary to consider in the first place. The result? Nothing happened because *here*, in this moment of observing children scribbling, *it* was happening, which is to say the scribbling, the very thing that the student was expecting to witness as part of this observational experience.

Forceful Seeing

But this is about more than scribbling. It is also about how the student has come to understand the child and children, art and aesthetics and observation too, particularly as a process centred on the art-making experiences of children. But specifically, the focus on scribbling reveals how in relation to each of these things the student has come to embody the developmental discourse. Specifically, how the student is moved by this discourse to think about children, to talk to children, to listen to children, to observe and take note of their work, to question children, and to inquire about their ideas and experiences. Or rather, and perhaps more to the point, to have done very little of this. I don't render this assessment to be critical of the student. After all, thinking and acting against such discourses is difficult and enduring work, a reality that is shared by many, including myself. I share this example because it highlights a disposition that I think we can all recognize to some extent, that way of being oriented to something that is difficult to think or act contrary to. Clearly, if it were an easy relation to subtend, the developmental discourse would long ago have been forced to relinquish its status as 'dominant' (Sakr et al., 2018), an outcome that would no doubt have blunted its power and appeal but also circumvented perhaps the need for volumes like this and chapters like mine. But this isn't the case, nor is it really the point.

The point, following Elkins (1996), is that 'the more forcefully [we] try to see, the more blind [we] become' (p. 210). What Elkins suggests here resonates with what Berlant says about fantasies, specifically that when something has become normalized – for example, when our ideas about children's art have become accepted in form and thus a matter of opinion and expectation – these same norms promise to us certain fantasies that we agree to, that we accept and come to believe in, and that we end up becoming attached to (see Berlant, 2012, p. 7). As it relates to the student in my class, as one such example, there are three specific norms at play: *the child, art-making in childhood* and *observation*. Addressing what these norms are and how they operate is important to understand how the student – and perhaps other students too – come to the realization that nothing really happened. It is also an important step in understanding that the student's response, which posited that the kids were '*just* scribbling' was really a way of saying, '*Here*, it's happening.' Because in saying this, what the student is ultimately telling us is that his experience of observation, his *seeing*, is *forced*, rooted in assumption and supported by an enduring grid of normalcy.

Development and Childhood Art: A Grid of Normalcy

Individualized in focus (McClure, 2011), the developmental discourse is structured around the normalizing idea that children's proficiency as artists is best demonstrated by how they manage to progress towards an increasingly realistic ideal in their drawing and art-making. In other words, what matters most is that children's art takes a form that is recognizable by adults, which is to say that a tree looks like a tree, a person looks like a person, and so on (Schulte, 2021, p. 9). As you might imagine, this puts younger children in a rather precarious and unfavourable position, where the scope and specificity of their work is not only misunderstood but so too is the child as an artist, figured instead as a 'failed realist' (Matthews, 1984, p. 3) – that is, as the less skilled, less competent version of their older, more realistically inclined peers.

Like other developmental accounts of children's growth and learning, undergirding this perceived maturation process is a clear and predetermined relationship between age and competence (Duncum, 2002; Schulte, 2021). The result of this relationship, when funnelled through the aesthetic filters of visual realism, is an emphasis on *what* children draw, with little to no regard for *how* or *why* they have come to draw it. Moreover, by favouring a semiotic analysis of children's art that focuses entirely on the drawing itself, what Pearson (2001) calls the 'artifactual residues' (p. 348), and specifically its fervour for realism, the developmental discourse is able to facilitate the fantasy that children's drawings act effectively as a 'print-out of the child's mind' (Golomb, 1992, p. 7).

In fact, the study of children's drawing has long been dominated by such interests and assumptions (e.g. Gardner & Winner, 1982; Kerschensteiner, 1905; Lowenfeld, 1957 [1987]). These stage-based and quasi-predictive accounts, which result in what Sakr (2017) calls 'developmental tick lists' (p. 2), rarely hold space for the 'conversations and play that surrounds and supplements' (Thompson, 1995, p. 8) children's art, nor does it account for the personal rationales and social wrinkles that mediate children's interests and their encounters and engagements with art-making. Instead, such complexities tend to be omitted from consideration or reduced entirely to the role of background noise (e.g. Atkinson, 2002; Matthews, 1999; Thompson & Schulte, 2019).

This isn't to suggest that the *what* of children's drawing should not be prioritized or understood as important. Rather, the point is to highlight how the dominance of the developmental discourse, which tends to favour the residues of children's practice (Pearson, 2001) (see also, e.g. Dyson, 2013; Ivashkevich, 2009; Rech Penn, 2019; Schulte, 2011; Sunday, 2015), actually risks marginalizing children and young people whose orientations to drawing and art-making are sometimes quite different from the patterns and parameters of normalcy that come to define it (e.g. Knight, 2013; Osgood & Sakr, 2019; Pearson, 2001; Schulte, 2021), and especially the people (adults) who are positioned to make decisions about what these patterns and parameters ought to be.

To make this discourse and its normalizing powers the singular story of childhood art (Atkinson, 2016; Thompson, 2021) is to subtract from view a vast network of child-situated interests, values and events, ignoring too the complicated and often conflicted sociopolitical spaces that materialize children's bodies, lives and ecologies (e.g. Trafí-Prats, 2014, 2017, 2019), including how adults come to experience and participate in this work. From an observational standpoint, the acceptance of this discourse readies in early artist-educators and other interested adults the tendency to focus their perceptions of children's art in ways that are reductive, predetermined and often devoid of context.

When I think about the student from class and his comments about the children he observed, this is precisely what comes to mind. It is quite literally the embodiment of forceful seeing – a lesson that reveals the material effects of how something like development can become 'the norm, the given, the unstated, and true' (St. Pierre, 2016, p. 27), a cluster of promises to which we are so emotionally entangled and so intellectually attached that we actually elide our own capacity to sense the work of fantasy as it washes over us. But it doesn't have to be this way. There is always room to manoeuvre, time to forget, time to ask of ourselves, of others, and the events to which we have committed to our time and attention, 'What's happening, *here*?'

'What Is Happening *Here*?'

While subtle, it is a question that stands both to broaden and complicate how we orientate ourselves to children's engagements with the visual arts. It stretches the frames of reference we have become accustomed to using and troubles too the interpretive values we lean on most to rationalize this use. In short, it is a question that moves us to consider differently our attachments to existing knowledge and to further explore the matter of how, why and in what ways, right *here*, children and their art are in the making. Of particular importance to this question is the extent to which it refigures observation as an act of inquiry that is situated and specific, and a result is speculative in its orientation to children and their art.

Key to this refiguring is the idea that observation be understood foremost as a process of attention that unfolds in relation to 'the situations' (Sakr et al., 2016, p. 294) (see also Cox, 2005; Frisch, 2006) of childhood art. Meaning, that our observational experiences are attuned to the 'here-and-now' (Massey & Massey, 2005, p. 140) of children's work, even when we fail to recognize this to be the case or resist it as a possibility. The here-and-now, as Massey and Massey (2005) write, is special precisely because it captures the 'throwntogetherness' of place and the 'unavoidable challenge' of having to negotiate current circumstances and 'the history and geography of thens and theres', that, in this moment of situatedness, have managed to gather and accumulate (p. 140). While the uncertainty and flux of such encounters is no doubt daunting to consider, in part because what is minimized in the process is the inevitability of an account that is general and universal in character, it is ultimately – and importantly – a reminder that 'place is always specific' and this specificity is a necessity to thinking differently the matter of how and why children make art.

In circling back to the student from class, let's consider again his experience of observation. The student, when asked to provide an account of his time at the centre, specifically his experience of drawing with the children, stated, 'The children I observed were *just* scribbling. Nothing really happened.' While it may well be true that the children observed were indeed scribbling, little else was revealed about this event or about the student's efforts to relate to it, and even less was provided about the context of this encounter, what was referred to earlier as *the situation* of children's art. The absence of consideration for how this scribbling was *situated* is important, in part because it underscores how omissions such as these make ready a dramatically reduced radius of care, an ambit of attention so narrow that it tends only to render that of generality and platitude. But the other part, which is a residual effect of decontextualizing children and their art (e.g. Tarr, 2003; Schulte, 2021), is the defection and demise of *specificity*, exclusions that reinforce existing developmental norms and further chance 'the marginalization and alienation of children' whose thinking, doing and being do not align with 'the standard account' (Sakr, 2021, p. 12).

A Shift in Attention

The result is a form of observational shorthand, what Colebrook (2002) describes as 'habit' (p. 15), a way of being with and attending to children's work, whereby we are either unable to get beyond our own interests and those we side with or simply unwilling to do so. The question then, is how do we get beyond these interests? How can we begin to work against those inbuilt and socially affianced tendencies for thought to settle with what is already known and obvious? To what extent can we trouble this impulse, which aims to prioritize and reinforce what Boundas (1991) calls 'common and good sense' (p. 4)? Questions like these are important because, as Tarr (2004) writes, 'Our histories blind us to other possibilities and we must continue to negotiate new possibilities, becoming cognizant of those underlying assumptions that are maintained despite evidence to the contrary' (p. 119). Take for example the student from class. Following the initial remarks made about his experience of observing the children drawing, the conversation between us took a slightly different turn, where the process of *becoming cognizant*, as Tarr says, began to emerge:

Student: *'The children I observed were "just" scribbling. Nothing really happened.'*

Me: *'So, out of curiosity, were you sitting with the children at the drawing table during this time?'*

Student: *'Yes. It was me and then three kids, three boys.'*

Me: *'Okay. Did the boys choose to draw together or did they just happen to be there at the same time?'*

Student: *'I think it was their choice. I think they were friends. I mean, it seemed like they were friends. They were really talkative.'*

Me: *'Oh, okay, well that's helpful. What were they talking about?'*

Student: *'They were talking about Paw Patrol. It's a television show, I think.'*

Me: *'That's correct, it is a television show. Do you recall what they were saying about the show? About Paw Patrol?'*

Student: *'No, I don't remember. I think they were talking about a rescue mission, or something like that. I wasn't really paying attention to what they were saying.'*

Me: *'Okay. But all this talking was happening while they were drawing together, correct?'*

Student: *'Yeah, that's right. . . . But they were also talking about it before they*

> *came to the drawing table.'*
>
> Me: *'What do you mean?'*
>
> Student: *'Well, they were playing with blocks before they came to the drawing table. And they were talking about it then too.'*
>
> Me: *'Oh, okay. So Paw Patrol had been a focus of their discussion for a while.'*
>
> Student: *'Yeah. I think so . . .'*
>
> *. . . Short pause (maybe 30-seconds or so . . .*
>
> Student: *'Oh wait, okay, I think I see what you are getting at. Their drawing might be about Paw Patrol? Like, maybe the scribbles are like a story or something?'*
>
> (Schulte, 2019, Teaching Reflection)

While brief, this follow-up conversation does well to illustrate how even a subtle shift in attention, in this case the addition of a few probing questions, stands to animate a circuit of intrigue that unsettles existing and perhaps already accepted relations to children and their art. It is by way of moments like this, where the distinctiveness of what *was* and what *is* suddenly becomes muddled, what Sakr (2021) describes as 'unsettled' (p. 16), that I am reminded of what Thompson (2021) has always been so clear to express:

> Very little of what I have learned – in years of looking, listening, and lingering among young children – is explained by or related to developmental processes or stages. In fact, it has always been specific children chasing lines of flight that, in their ubiquity, deny the very existence of a normal path. This is where art making happens, in these idiosyncratic and unpredictable moments when children resist categorization, where they exceed and challenge all expectations. (p. 167)

What Thompson does well to capture, beyond the specificity and situatedness of children's art, is the need for an 'attentiveness of a different order' (Manning & Massumi, 2014, p. 11), an observational practice that not only values the gathering and contextualization of insights about children's interests and experiences, but that also holds space for the 'gestural, lived, bodied, haptic, choreographic, affective, and enacted speculations and propositions' (Kind, 2020, p. 53) that emerge with and among children as they make art. To conceptualize observation in this way is to reframe observation as a speculative act, one that produces 'generative and interruptive' routes to encountering children and their art, and to the 'situated places and spaces' (Nxumalo, 2018, p. 18) in which this work materializes. This also includes the post-observational settings where pre-service artist-educators (such as the students from class) are moved to reflect on and re-engage their experience – that is, to continually ask, 'What's happening *here?*'

Speculative Routes to Observation

As an educator, I made the decision to ask the student some additional questions. I did this because I felt it was an opportunity to model how demanding more of the information we have, or that we think we have, puts into question the stability of our thinking, and helps us as well to interrupt the practices that we use to normalize this thought. It isn't easy though, nor is it a natural inclination, that capacity to ask, 'What's happening *here?*' My hope is that this chapter has been helpful in clarifying this point. Certainly, it is far easier to walk the already-established pathways of prior thought. Even more challenging is the work of admitting that what we think we know about children and their art (Leeds, 1981) isn't always what it seems and that perhaps it never really was (Duncum, 2002). It isn't easy after all to work against our objects of desire, especially when those objects have a dominant presence in the work that we do with children, an attendance that shapes observation as a matter of looking *at* something, looking *for* something and in many cases looking *away* from the *something else* that is also present.

If we can manage to catch ourselves in the act, thwarting the inclinations we have to give in to the fantasy of what we think we know about children and their art, difference and possibility can begin to emerge. You see this in the teaching reflection that was shared previously, most notably in the student's final comment:

> *Student: Oh wait, okay, I think I see what you are getting at. Their drawing might be about Paw Patrol? Like, maybe the scribbles are like a story or something?"*

What's important about this comment isn't so much that the student managed to see what I was 'getting at', though there is certainly some evidence of this connection. Rather, what is important about the student's comment is that it reveals the moment in which he begins to sense the 'other dimensions' (Sakr et al., 2018, p. 11) of children's art – those place-based relations of complexity that often go unnoticed and that tend to be overlooked or minimized by traditional perspectives such as development. This is what Kind (2020) had in mind when she described observation as the enactment of speculations and propositions, a 'refusal space' (Lather & St. Pierre, 2013, p. 629) (see also, Sakr & Osgood, 2019) in which the student, to stay with this example, re-encounters his own experience in relation to his – and other(s)' – dominant objects of desire.

It is not imperative that the student determine or be certain about the potential connection between the children's scribbling and expressed interest in and playing of Paw Patrol? What matters is that such connections are possible and that we make a point to cultivate the type of attentive presences that are necessary to make them possible. *This* is the work of thinking observation as a speculative act – that is, as an observational gesture that is connection-inclined, situated and specific, and intensely committed to the possibility of differencing how art is understood in children's lives. Though indirectly, I shared this sentiment with the students in class:

> Me: *There is an important lesson here about what gets to count as drawing and art making more generally in childhood. Meaning, when we observe children making art or playing in some way, are there parameters in place that predefine what art and play is or will become? Parameters, for example, that tell us in advance how this work is important or meaningful? Do these same parameters have an impact on what we attend to and how we go about attending to it? Is it only about what see or what a child draws on the paper, for example? Or is there more to consider, other details perhaps that might also be important to contemplate? So yes, it is possible that the scribbles are in fact a story of some kind, maybe even a story about Paw Patrol, but it could also be that there is something else at play, something more difficult to apprehend or understand. It is also possible that the scribbles you've witnessed are part of a larger event of art making and play, and that by attending only to what was drawn on the paper, we've removed from consideration entire networks of information. What do you all think (I ask to the class)?*

My comments were not intended to provide clarity or somehow better surmise what was thought to be absent from the student's initial impression. Rather, it was an attempt to fashion what Manning and Massumi (2014) described as attentiveness of a different order, a speculative gesture that makes possible the generation of new, different and interruptive routes to observing children and their art.

References

Atkinson, D. (2002). *Art in education: Identity and practice.* Springer Science & Business Media.

Atkinson, K. (2016). A touch of paint: Transgressing unspoken boundaries. *Journal of Childhood Studies, 41*(2), 60–65.
Berlant, L. (1998). Intimacy: A special issue. *Critical inquiry, 24*(2), 281–288.
Berlant, L. (2011). *Cruel optimism.* Duke University Press.
Berlant, L. (2012). *Desire/love.* Punctum.
Berlant, L. G. (2005). Unfeeling Kerry. *Theory & Event, 8*(2), doi:10.1353/tae.2005.0021.
Burman, E. (2016). *Deconstructing developmental psychology.* Routledge.
Boundas, C. (1991). Translator's introduction: Deleuze, empiricism, and the struggle for subjectivity. In G. Deleuze (Ed.), Constantin V. Boundas (trans.), *Empiricism and subjectivity: An essay on hume's theory of human nature* (pp. 1–19). Columbia University Press.
Corsaro, W. (1985). *Friendship and peer culture in the early years.* Ablex.
Corsaro, W. (2003). *We're friends right?: Inside kid's culture.* Jospeh Henry Press.
Corsaro, W., & Molinari, L. (2008). Entering and observing in children's worlds: Reflections on a longitudinal ethnography of early education in Italy. In P. Christensen & A. James (Eds.), *Research with children: Perspectives and practices* (pp. 239–258). Routledge.
Colebrook, C. (2002). *Gilles Deleuze.* Routledge.
Cox, S. (2005). Intention and meaning in young children's drawing. *International Journal of Art and Design Education, 24,* 115–125.
Duncum, P. (2002). Children never were what they were: Perspectives on childhood. In Gaudelius & P. Spiers (Eds.), *Contemporary Issues in Art Education* (pp. 97–107), Pearson.
Dyson, A. H. (2013). *Rewriting the basics: Literacy learning in children's cultures.* Teachers College Press.
Elkins, J. (1997). *The object stares back.* Houghton Mifflin Harcourt.
Frisch, N. S. (2006). Drawing in preschools: A didactic experience. *International Journal of Art and Design Education, 25,* 74–85.
Gardner, H., & Winner, E. (1982). First intimations of artistry. In S. Strauss (Ed.), *U-shaped behavioral growth* (pp. 147–168). Academic Press.
Golomb, C. (1992). *Art and the young child: Another look at the developmental question.*
Graue, M. E., Walsh, D. J., & Graue, E. M. (1998). *Studying children in context: Theories, methods, and ethics.* Sage.
Greene, S., & Hogan, D. (Eds.). (2004). *Researching children' s experience: Approaches and methods.* Sage.
Ivashkevich, O. (2009). Children's drawing as a sociocultural practice: Remaking gender and popular culture. *Studies in Art Education, 51*(1), 50–63.
James, A. (1996). Learning to be friends: Methodological lessons from participant observation among English schoolchildren. *Childhood, 3*(3), 313–330.
James, A. (1998). Confections, concoctions, and conceptions. In *The children's culture reader* (pp. 394–405). New York University Press.

James, A., Jenks, C., & Prout, A. (1998). *Theorizing childhood*. Routledge.

James, A., & Prout, A. (2003). *Constructing and reconstructing childhood: Contemporary issues in the sociological study of childhood*. Routledge.

James, A., & James, A. (2017). *Constructing childhood: Theory, policy and social practice*. Macmillan International Higher Education.

Jenks, C. (1996). *Childhood*. Psychology Press.

Jenks, C. (2005). Childhood and transgression. In J. Qvortrup (Ed.), *Studies in modern childhood* (pp. 115–127). Palgrave Macmillan.

Kellogg, R. (1959). The sense of scribbles. *Design*, *61*(2), 64–67.

Kerschensteiner, G. (1905). *Die entwickelung der zeichnerischen begabung*. Рипол Классик.

Kind, S. (2020). Wool Works, Cat's Cradle, and the art of playing attention. In C. M. Schulte (Ed.), *Ethics and research with young children: New Perspectives* (pp. 49–62). Bloomsbury.

Kindler, A. M., & Darras, B. (1998). Culture and development of pictorial repertoires. *Studies in Art Education*, *39*(2), 147–167.

Knight, L. (2013). Not as it seems: Using Deleuzian concepts of the imaginary to rethink children's drawings. *Global Studies of Childhood*, *3*(3), 254–264.

Lather, P., & St. Pierre, E. A. (2013). Post-qualitative research. *International Journal of Qualitative Studies in Education*, *26*(6), 629–633.

Lee, N. (2001). *Childhood and society: Growing up in an age of uncertainty*. McGraw-Hill Education.

Leeds, J. A. (1989). The history of attitudes toward children's art. *Studies in Art Education*, *30*(2), 93–103.

Love, H. (2012). What does Lauren Berlant teach us about X? *Communication and Critical/Cultural Studies*, *9*(4), 320–336.

Lowenfeld, V. (1957 [1987]). *Creative and mental growth*. Prentice Hall.

Malaguzzi, L. (1993). Your image of the child: Where teaching begins. In *Child care information exchange* (pp. 52–52).

Manning, E., & Massumi, B. (2014). *Thought in the act: Passages in the ecology of experience*. University of Minnesota Press.

Massey, D., & Massey, D. B. (2005). *For space*. Sage.

Matthews, J. (1984). Children drawing: Are young children really scribbling? *Early Child Development and Care*, *18*(1–2), 1–39.

Matthews, J. (1999). *Helping children to draw and paint in early childhood*. Hodder and Stoughton.

McClure, M. (2007). Play as process: Choice, translation, reconfiguration, and the process of culture. *Visual Arts Research*, *65*, 63–70.

McClure, M. (2011). Child as totem: Redressing the myth of inherent creativity in early childhood. *Studies in Art Education*, *52*(2), 127–141.

Moore, A. (2004). *The good teacher: Dominant discourses in teaching and teacher education*. Routledge.

Moore, A. (2012). *Teaching and learning: Pedagogy, curriculum, and culture*. Routledge.
Moss, P. (1990). Work, family, and the care of children: Issues of equality and responsibility. *Children & Society, 4*(2), 145–166.
Moss, P., Dillon, J., & Statham, J. (2000). The 'child in need' and 'the rich child': Discourses, constructions and practice. *Critical Social Policy, 20*(2), 233–254.
Nxumalo, F. (2018). Situating indigenous and black childhoods in the anthropocene. In A. Cutter-Mackenzie et al. (Eds.), *Research handbook on childhoodnature* (pp. 1–22). Springer.
Osgood, J., & Sakr, M. (Eds.). (2019). *Postdevelopmental approaches to childhood art*. Bloomsbury Publishing.
Pearson, P. (2001). Towards a theory of children's drawing as social practice. *Studies in Art Education, 42*(4), 348–365.
Qvortrup, J., Bardy, M., Sgritta, G., & Wintersberger, H. (1994). *Childhood matters: Social theory, practice and politics*. Avebury.
Rech Penn, L. (2019). Drawing, bodies, and difference: Heterocorporeal dialogs and other intra-actions in Children's classroom drawing. *Studies in Art Education, 60*(2), 103–119.
Rinaldi, C. (2006). *In dialogue with Reggio Emilia: Listening, researching, and learning*. Routledge.
Rudduck, J. (1985). Teacher research and research-based teacher education. *Journal of Education for Teaching, 11*(3), 281–289.
Sakr, M. (2017). *Digital technologies in early childhood art: Enabling playful experiences*. Bloomsbury Publishing.
Sakr, M. (2021). Reconceptualizing early childhood art as entanglement: Playing with chalk in the home. In H. Park & C. M. Schulte (Eds.), *Visual arts with young children: Practices, pedagogies, and learning* (pp. 11–23). Routledge.
Sakr, M., Connelly, V., & Wild, M. (2016). Narrative in young children's digital art making *Journal of Early Childhood Literacy, 16*(3), 289–310.
Sakr, M., Federici, R., Hall, N., Trivedy, B., & O'Brien, L. (2018). *Creativity and making in early childhood: Challenging practitioner perspectives*. Bloomsbury Publishing.
Sakr, M., & Osgood, J. (2019). Introduction. In *Postdevelopmental approaches to childhood art* (pp. 1–11). Bloomsbury.
Schulte, C. M. (2011). Verbalization in children's drawing performances: Toward a metaphorical continuum of inscription, extension, and re-inscription. *Studies in Art Education, 53*(1), 20–34.
Schulte, C. M. (2016). Deleuze, concept formation, and the habit of shorthand inquiry. *Qualitative Inquiry, 24*(3), 1–9.
Schulte, C. M. (2018). Entering the milieus of children's drawing: Complicated proximities. *International Journal of Education & the Arts, 19*, 1–11.

Schulte, C. M. (2019). *Teaching reflection*. University Park: The Pennsylvania State University.

Schulte, C. M. (2021). The making of a deficit aesthetic. *Global Studies of Childhood*, *11*(1), 54–68.

St. Pierre, E. A. (2016). The long reach of logical positivism/logical empiricism. In N. Denzin & M. Giardina (Eds.), *Qualitative inquiry through a critical lens* (pp. 27–38). Routledge.

Sunday, K. E. (2015). Relational making: Re/imagining theories of child art. *Studies in Art Education*, *56*(3), 228–240.

Tarr, P. (1990). More than movement: Scribbling reassessed. *Visual Arts Research*, *1*(31), 83–89.

Tarr, P. (2004). Consider the walls. *Young children*, *59*(3), 88–92.

Tarr, P. (2003). Reflections on the image of the child: Reproducer or creator of culture. *Art Education*, *56*(4), 6–11.

Thompson, C. M. (1990). "I make a mark": The significance of talk in young children's artistic development. *Early Childhood Research Quarterly*, *5*(2), 215–232.

Thompson, C. M. (1995). "What should I draw today?" Sketchbooks in early childhood. *Art Education*, *48*(5), 6–11.

Thompson, C. M. (2009). Mira! Looking, listening, and lingering in research with children. *Visual Arts Research*, *35*(1), 24–34.

Thompson, C. M. (2021). Beyond the single story of childhood: Recognizing childism in art education practice. In H. Park & C. M. Schulte (Eds.), *Visual arts with young children: Practices, pedagogies, and learning* (pp. 159–168). Routledge.

Thompson, C. M., & Schulte, C. M. (2019). Repositioning the visual arts: Continuing reconsideration. In O. Saracho (Ed.), *Handbook of research on the education of young children* (pp. 1–5). Routledge.

Trafí-Prats, L. (2014). The existential territories of global childhoods: Resingularizing subjectivity through ecologies. *Occasional Paper Series*, *2014*(31), 5.

Trafí-Prats, L. (2017). Learning with children, trees, and art: For a compositionist visual art-based research. *Studies in Art Education*, *58*(4), 325–334.

Trafí-Prats, L. (2019). Thinking childhood art with care in an ecology of practices. In J. Osgood & M. Sakr (Eds.), *Postdevelopmental approaches to childhood art* (pp. 191–210). Bloomsbury.

Qvortrup, J., Bardy, M., Sgritta, G., & Wintersberger, H. (1994). *Childhood matters: Social theory, practice and politics*. Avebury Press.

Wilson, B. (1997). Types of child art and alternative developmental accounts: Interpreting the interpreters. *Human Development*, *40*(3), 155–168.

Woodhead, M. (2009). Child development and the development of childhood. In J. Qvortrup, W. A. Corsaro, & M. S. Honig (Eds.), *The Palgrave handbook of childhood studies* (pp. 46–61). Palgrave Macmillan.

7

Alone-Together

Exploring Children's Material/Digital/Analogue Engagements through Intergenerational Research

Mark Shillitoe, *International School Delft, the Netherlands*
Harriet Hand, Scarlett Shepherd and William Squire, *University of Bristol*
Jennifer Rowsell, *University of Sheffield*

Introduction

In December 2020, three researchers began a study that traversed ages, spaces and theories to map the movements, interactions, learning, teaching and life they experienced during Covid-19. Our observations identified meanderings across and between the kind of online/offline, home/nature, human/more-than-human experiences that need greater exploration and articulation. Getting stuck in the middle of these movements seemed the best place to be in order to make sense of Covid life and learning. What is more, we recognized differences and similarities: between Gen Xers' (forties and fifties) observations contrasted with millennials; and between Gen Zers' (twenties) observations of Covid-19 contrasted with nine and ten-year-old children's pandemic lives and experiences. To imbue order and discipline into unordered and unscripted research, there were certain guiding principles: (1) it would apply post-qualitative, emergent methods (Springgay & Truman, 2017); (2) it would focus on younger to older generations (i.e. how older people can learn with younger people); and (3) it would move across our everyday digital/analogue, home/school, inside/outside spaces. Beyond these three directives, the research design and how it came to fruition was organic, played out in the spirit of a dérive (Debord, 1958) where our research journey unfolded in the moment, guided by our encounters.

This chapter recounts the four-month research study that took place in two cities, Bristol in the UK and Delft in the Netherlands, with a research team made up of twenty children who are nine and ten-year-old, two undergraduates in their twenties and three middle-aged researchers. The span was deliberate in that we hoped to capture a spectrum of ages and stages and their lived literacies (Pahl & Rowsell, 2020) during the lockdown. The research team adopted arts-based methods to conduct exploratory research between undergraduates and children who completed parallel mapping and multimodal activities, and who shared their thoughts and artefacts with each other. The structure of the chapter begins with post-structural and socio-material theories that informed the research design, followed by a framing of the different moving parts of the study and then a drawing out of intergenerational observations across geographies of the artefacts that matter to us and the ways that we slowly felt alone-together during our research journey.

The chapter fits into this volume on postdevelopmental approaches to childhood observations by spotlighting a research study where multimodal mapping experiments were rich alternatives to more traditional approaches to documenting and assessing how children moved into online learning during the pandemic. A developmental, 'learning loss' script that has been attached to lockdown learning is thereby challenged, even pushed against by showing how a group of children observe and attune to the world around them through their objects, maps, sensory wayfinding and artwork, *not* by Mark observing and assessing them as students. That is, children, twenty-somethings and fifty-somethings all observed reflectively and made sense of their Covid lives through the things, sounds, senses and modes that matter to them. In this way, the chapter is in good company with other chapters in a book that attempts to orient children's worlds within 'post' approaches to childhood, redressing an emphasis on accountability and deficit framings that all-too-often frame early childhood discourses, especially around the global pandemic and lockdown learning.

Applying Posthuman and Feminist New Materialist Theory

Relying on the comfort of things (Miller, 2008), the sticky viscosity of objects and modal work combined with human contact, the research reported explores digital, analogue, artefactual and multimodal encounters during different degrees of lockdown over four months in a primary classroom in the Netherlands (Mark) and with two undergraduates, Will and Scarlett, in Bristol (Jennifer and Harriet). This chapter focuses on children and their natural, often articulate ways of valuing objects big, small, invisible and ephemeral.

In devising the research design, and interpreting data, we leaned heavily on the notion of *becoming with matter*, focusing on intra-actions (Barad, 2007) between matter and humans during the 2020–1 pandemic. This is not to say that we are authorities on posthuman and post-structural theory, but rather that new materialist theories really helped us to identify interconnections across spaces with children and adults in the research. Without doubt, a posthumanist and new materialist lens were generative for us to draw out pandemic experiences. The rationale for posthuman, feminist new material theory (Barad, 2007; Braidotti, 2013) rests on their strength to push against binary ways of separating humans from matter or more-than-humans. Importantly, posthumanism and new materialism problematize a privileging of certain types of knowledge and ways of being over others (Niccolini & Ringrose, 2019; Truman, 2021). Another key point here is the intra-actions (Barad, 2007) that took place during the alone-together research involving people and their treasured artefacts, like a Mary Berry cookbook, a skateboard and a bed, that pointed to some important qualities of being and learning for children and adults during the pandemic. Barad (2007) describes moments when matter is deeply meaningful but equally opaque/invisible in human-oriented knowledge disciplines like quantum physics. Barad describes a meeting up of humans with non-humans as 'an assemblage of individual events, entities, and sets of practices' (Barad, 2007, p. 389). These assemblages are not only productive but they also carry human and non-human agency. For people during lockdown, screens, trees, birds, faces, bodies and beds are not separate or *less than* during events and practices, but instead co-constitute each other, move together, assemble and entangle. They imbue meaning and life into everyday practices like looking at a screen. They are objects that matter and that have agency. Feminist scholars like Barad (2007) and Haraway (2016) have made this point abundantly clear in their writings over the years and their theorizing of the anthropocene (i.e. the current historical period when humans dominate) has made a substantial contribution to offset a human focus on research inquiries (Truman, 2021). Post-qualitative methods provide ways to identify and draw out the micro, meso and macro intra-actions that we observed during Covid-19. So many strands of this project involved a process of becoming (Mazzei, 2020) within our individual spaces while being joined together by screens.

Starting from a contention that the world is a continual, intra-active process of becoming (Barad, 2007) gave us room as researchers to listen carefully to everything shared, said, drawn and felt: it all counted as 'knowledge' (St. Pierre, 2019). The natural world and its curative force during Covid-19, and the inescapable presence of screens during online learning and teaching, are two examples of humans intra-acting with non-humans in entangled, assembled and co-constitutive ways. As co-researchers, this meant that everything comes to matter in relation to acknowledgement and interpretation (Davies, 2014). Barad offered the notion of *response-ability* as an ethical responsibility to look at everything, seen or unseen, as agentive. Children involved in this research had little issue with this contention – in fact, they reinforced its authenticity during the research process. Of course a bed is agentive and it goes without saying that a teddy has a voice (see the following data examples). Researchers like Rautio (2013) have applied socio-materiality and intra-action to research with young children to disrupt developmental explanations of children's engagements with matter (Rautio, 2014) by concentrating instead on what gets animated, felt and learned as a child intra-acts with objects. By shifting focus away from knowledge acquisition and cognitive stages for children and turning attention more to what knowledge is produced *through* children and matter intra-acting, early childhood researchers have recognized the complex negotiations of meanings that take place (Collier & Harwood, 2017; Kuby et al., 2018; Hackett & Somerville, 2017; Hultman & Lenz Taguchi, 2010; Lenz Taguchi, 2011; Rautio, 2013, 2014). The intergenerational research study, *alone-together*, consolidated ways of knowing, relating, feeling and thinking together listening carefully to intra-active spaces of meaning.

So it is, throughout the chapter, that we share moments as acts of meaning, knowledge and research-creation. The research applies more-than-human, arts-based methods to observe and document how the whole team (adult-child alike) related through affective, human and more-than-human connections. In this way, participatory and creative methods (Springgay & Truman, 2017) that involved making maps, artefact boxes and alone-together walks consider experiencing and ways of knowing as emergent through intra-actions and entanglements. Becoming with alone-together shaped our research time. As Stewart expresses it, these relational and object-led practices acted as an assemblage that threw themselves 'together into something recognizable as a thing' (p. 119).

The Alone-Together Intergenerational Research Study[1]

Setting the Scene

In Bristol, Harriet and Jennifer met Scarlett and Will as a part of an optional placement unit offered for undergraduates in the Educational Studies programme at the University of Bristol. Scarlett and Will joined the research team as volunteers who wanted to learn about and engage in creative research methods. This was a time of lockdown and the four met, and continued to meet, via online video meetings or through exchanges of materials delivered by hand to their homes. In Delft, Mark and the nine- and ten-year-old children were also in lockdown for the start of the project but returned to school over the course of the research, with restrictions to movement and mixing that continued to shape their learning experiences.

We conceptualized the research as a series of encounters to be enacted alone-together. For the majority of the encounters, we were alone in our homes during periods of lockdown in our respective countries, but we were together online as we experienced each encounter. Mark, Harriet and Jennifer followed the movement of these events and remained in the middle of what emerged through staging regular walks, mappings and dialogues that mirrored the research encounters for the intergenerational participants. In this space we shared wayfinding prompts to help us navigate our individual and collective ways through the research as it unfolded. Influenced by the notion of the score, and within the spirit of the art movement fluxus (Higgins, 2002), we used instructions as an 'enabling constraint' (Miles & Springgay, 2020, p. 1010) to productively disrupt and open-up space for new ways of observing, and to activate a dialogue between our practice and theory (Springgay & Truman, 2017) as the project played out. Adopting post-qualitative inquiry gave us a way to engage with critical qualitative methodologies (Mayes, 2019), focusing on connections with posthumanist and feminist new materialist orientations to co-researching. Mayes (2019) encourages researchers to explore how matter connects with voices that are collected as data. By highlighting the entanglements of objects, spaces, bodies, discourses and so on, our attention shifted onto processes, practices and ontologies.

Research Design

The research started from the question: What can mapping teach us about experiences of lockdown and Covid-19 across generations? Mark, Harriet and Jennifer determined a loose design of co-research encounters for our two locations and co-researching groups: (1) Harriet, Jennifer and undergraduate interns Will and Scarlett; (2) Mark with twenty, nine- to ten-year-old children. We planned synchronous and asynchronous events using multimodal and multisensory mapping as a method of engaging with the enriched layers of analogue and digital spaces of self. These encounters continued from late January until May 2021.

At the centre of our activities were two synchronous mapping encounters that ran in parallel in both locations. First, in Delft, sound notation was developed to plot inside and outside spaces as personal sound scores. While, in Bristol, visual sketch maps (Gieseking, 2013; Lynch, 1960) of outside, inside, physical and digital spaces, before and during the pandemic, were created. Second, in both locations, children and adults mapped while listening to layers of a soundscape composed of remixed sounds taken from pre-lockdown spaces woven into a lockdown walk. We responded to the question: Where does the soundscape take you?

The research began to take shape at the very start during three separate walks by Mark, Harriet and Jennifer around their respective neighbourhoods while they spoke and shared images of the places they traversed on Microsoft Teams. In total, more than twenty different encounters played out in the twin contexts: the design of each one emerged through our joint reflections and in response to new questions that were activated by the events. Punctuating the succession of these events were further walks that brought us together in different groups. Jennifer walked with Will; Harriet walked with Scarlett; Mark and the children walked together.

In Delft, Mark had already began mapping with children in his class in the autumn of 2020 and their work together continued as we began the research. Mapping and arts-based activities with the children played out as a series of encounters that spanned a period of lockdown and times when schools opened up for learning. Using methods of sketch mapping (Lynch, 1960), maps were constructed online as well as collectively when the class were together. Other events were inspired by the performances of fluxus artists (Ono, 2015), like a synchronous and identical brunch where Mark and the children responded to instructions to prepare, eat and clear away food while maintaining a video link online that allowed them to be alone-together.

In Bristol the mapping encounters untangled our sense of self to consider different spaces separately: inside and outside, digital and analogue, before and during the pandemic. We then used layering as a technique that extended this mapping to augment the generative and emergent qualities of space (Corner, 1999). In superimposing one map on top of another, we brought our spaces together where a 'stratified amalgam of relationships' emerged (1999, p. 235). Understanding the way mapping unfolded in playful ways (Kitchin et al., 2012), and the possibilities of the 'chance of space' (Massey, 2005, p.116), these techniques of layering continued to be used throughout the project to augment the affordances of mapping as a site of continuous production and as a means of constructing dialogues between the artefacts and across generations.

Bristol encounters included three sessions that were devoted to readings: the first was Corner (1999); the second was Lefebvre (2004), and the third from Springgay and Truman (2017). In this last session, Harriet, Jennifer, Will, and Scarlett thought with the ideas within the text to engage with the children's artefacts as a means of exchange and method of analysis.

In Table 7.1 we have selected from the larger range of arts-based and dialogue-based events examples of mapping encounters that form the focus for our discussion here.

Mapping in the research became 'a material movement of becoming *other* that, in addition to the production of new signs, mutually constitutes emergent understandings of self as materially embodied through encounters with both human and non-human objects' (Powell, 2016, p.4, italic in original). In this way, mapping was a type of self-portraiture. A kind of selfie that is not only focused on our physical selves but also one that brings us closer to the entangled interrelations that constitute our world. Mapping, in this sense, offered adults and children another way of seeing their world through active practices of describing, making associations, envisaging and possibility thinking (Corner, 1999). Mapping using sound, word, image, object and mark-making is a way of participating 'within the very contours and fabric' of the world around us (1999, p. 235). Many of the mapping encounters comprised the event itself as well as reflections from the children and adults recorded after the event as an audio or video file. This layering of spoken word onto the maps revealed another layer of understanding and a way of inhabiting and mobilizing spaces that emerged from the mapping. Mapping became a common terrain for adults and children. We shared our maps and photographs with Mark's class to reflect on and analyse as a group.

As a coda to the research, in May 2021, we shared data from the Bristol study with Mark's class. As well, Will, Scarlett, Harriet and Jennifer sent 'burning' questions in a letter to the children:

1. Was it strange to ask your room questions?
2. What are the best and worst parts of the pandemic?
3. How would you describe mapping to someone who hasn't mapped before?
4. Did you learn anything about yourself during these activities?
5. Would you map your experiences or walks that you do again?
6. Which activity or mapping task was your favourite, and why?

Table 7.1 Selected Mapping Encounters

Intergenerational mapping encounters (we explore the highlighted encounters in more detail in this chapter)	
Title	Description
Mapping sound: list poem	*Children & Adults:* Synchronously in separate online sessions, the class in Delft and adults in Bristol listed sounds they could hear in their homes during ten minutes. A notation was created and used for each sound.
Inside/Outside spatial sound map	*Children:* Synchronously online, the class in Delft digitally mapped the sounds they heard from their home-learning spaces. The map invited them to consider the spatial arrangement of the sounds inside and outside. A key was added, this often included symbols for feelings, volume or importance.
Soundscape performance score	*Children & Adults*: A soundscape was listened to synchronously (for some, on personal devices). Children drew digital soundscapes; in Bristol, we drew on paper while on an online video call. Both groups drew in silence with microphones on.
Favourite part of the room	*Children*: Engaging with their personal spaces, children created a sketch map of the favourite part of the room and asked three questions.
50 sounds of me	*Children & Adults:* A parallel encounter where children and adults listed '50 sounds of me'. Some children chose to write on paper, others digitally.
Mapping the magical story box	*Children:* A curated arrangement of objects in a box was shared with the group. They were invited to imagine it is a birds-eye view (i.e. looking down from the sky like a drone). They were told that all the objects had a connection. The instructions were: Can you see the connections? Take a walk through the streets and draw your journey. What do you see when you are walking around? Think about the people, places and things.
Where we were	*Children:* Mapping the locations of each member of the class during lockdown. The location map was layered with personal images of the place by each of the children.
What can we learn from sewing a circle?	*Children:* Children sewed a circle onto an off-cut of tie-dye fabric. The class asked themselves: What can we learn by sewing a circle? Children added the route of their walk onto the sewn fabric.

The children met with Mark and they answered all of the questions together and shared their recordings with us. Then, Harriet met with Will and Jennifer met with Scarlett and they shared their own 'burning' questions.

The repository of data are: photographs, maps, drawings, Seesaw texts, sound recordings, written texts, recorded conversations/reflective circles, Teams recordings and observational field notes. As a result, there were many moving

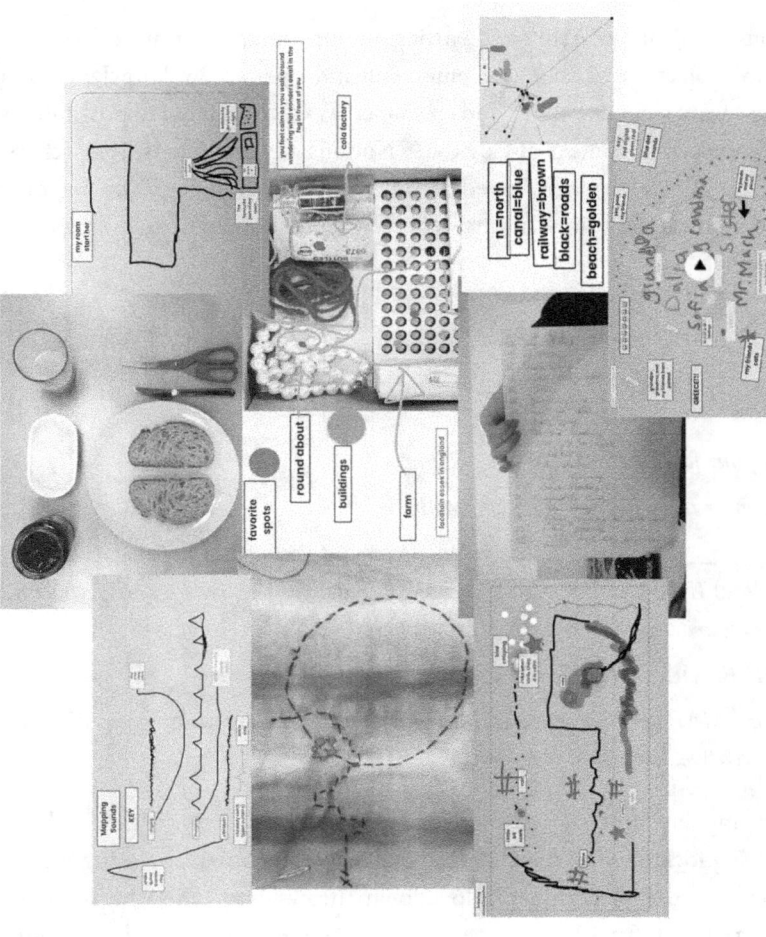

Figure 7.1 Clockwise from top left: Mapping sound, Identical brunch; Favourite part of the room; Mapping the magical story box; Where we were; Inside/Outside spatial sound map; 50 sounds of me; Soundscape performance score; Sewing circle reflection.

parts during the research process, but the simple message of the project was the kaleidoscopic ways of relating through matter across generations.

Exploring Children's Mapped, Sensory, Sonic and Sewn Entanglements

The various layers of researcher and participant mapping, over time, constituted a dynamic project space that was emergent and open. New knowledge and experiences were shared and methods reshaped as we responded to possibilities within the uncertain context of Covid-19. Notions of participants, researchers, children and adults became blurred as the entire group engaged in mapping and made multimodal compositions, reflecting upon them and analysing them alone-together.

Exploration #1: Favourite Part of the Room

//*What is your favourite part of your room?*

//*Write a letter to it. Begin your letter with:*

Dear _____ *(write the favourite part of your room here e.g. First shelf near window) INCLUDE in your letter all at least THREE reasons why you find this your favourite part.*

//*ASK THREE QUESTIONS to your favourite part of the room.*

//*CREATE a MAP to show where your favourite part fits in relation to the WHOLE room. Be creative, have fun!*

This mapping encounter engaged closely and inquisitively with children's spaces during lockdown. Returning to our discussion earlier, analysing visuals of children's home worlds during lockdown throws into relief the merging, overlapping and shifting that happens when children reflect on intra-actions (Barad, 2007) with matter around them.

Making use of sketch mapping (Lynch, 1960), a method of visually constructing a mental image of a place or space, children's maps became a way of inhabiting their personal spaces. The maps acted not as representations of their space but as a means of uncovering more-than-human relations (Giesking, 2013) and acknowledging the agency of objects (Powell, 2016).

Figure 7.2 Map: Favourite part of the room.

The mapping in Figure 7.2 spatially places the important objects within the room. Use of colour for books, details such as hanging clothes and the consistency of drawing suggest an intimate engagement with the objects. Depicting other rooms hints at a sensitivity to the spatial relations of personal space to family space. The questions: Why are you my favourite? Do you like to be my favourite? Did you try to be my favourite? personify the object but seem to be simultaneously reflexive. By inhabiting the map, an exchange plays out that brings relations between the child and the world around them into being.

In other maps, questions appear initially as simple curiosity, a kind of noticing that activates sensemaking of the world around us: Is the pilo part of you? In contrast, with the question, Does it hurt for me to lie on you every night? The relations of self and object are thrown closer together: imbued with empathy, the question shifts feeling and thought to the notion of becoming with the world around us. There are questions that reveal a sensitivity to time and history. Books have lives before entering their home, mapping and thinking with the toys activates care and tenderness. The question, Dear toys did other people love you before me? brings into being an awareness of the limits of relations with our objects, and many questions represent similar nuanced, felt responses to matter, like: Who is your favourite YouTuber? Who is your best friend, pillow? Why is my blanket always too short? Did I crush you teddy?

Throughout the maps, scale and detail bring emphasis to the importance of the children's toys. Toys, for example, often have features – colour, recognizable form, detail – where, in contrast, furniture and architecture are often reduced to symbols, even punctuation. The encounter brought to life ways that children value and care about objects around them and expressed a deep attention to personal lived spaces. Attending to matter in their rooms allowed Mark's class to see themselves in relation to their intimate spaces. Shedding a new light, mapping was a way of making something new out of the familiar (Rautio, 2013). The material-discursive visuals drew out affective flows, showing remarkable empathy for objects/matter, it is clear that children became within this space.

Exploration #2: Inside/Outside Spatial Sound Map

//SIT comfortably in your bedroom (be sure to tell everyone at home that you do not want disturbing because you want to write. Do this for at least 10 minutes, use a timer)

//DO NOT make a sound and carefully listen to all the sounds around you. Make sure you notice whether the sounds are inside or outside your room and which direction they are coming from. NOTE down all the different sounds in the part of the space they occur.

//Think about showing where the sound is happening around you.

To unpack the smallness and seemingly quiet nature of lockdown, this encounter compelled the children to be aware of cascading sounds around them over a brief period of time. Kress argues that children's pathway into writing derives from an unbiased modal interest in what best suits a composition (Kress, 1997). Drawing from this insight, what we recognized in children's inside/outside spatial maps are thoughts, feelings, people and objects bubbling up into the map. Driven by interests, memories and felt sensibilities, children responded to sounds based on gut instincts, motivated by affect and sentiments.

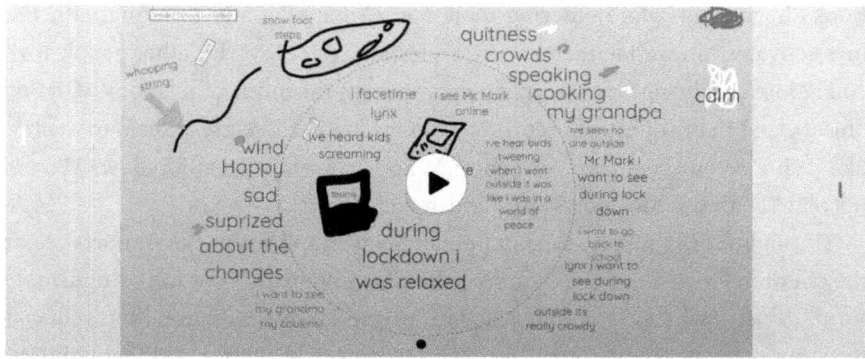

Figure 7.3 Inside/outside spatial map.

In Figure 7.3, the mapping engages with the enmeshed nature of the big and small, the subtle sounds of cooking and the interruptions of louder noises that might only be evoked by the listing of wind, crowds, etc. The exercise of quiet listening also dislodged metaphoric thoughts like: 'I hear birds tweeting when I am outside and it was like a world of peace.' Drawing relations between inside and outside sparked an engagement with anticipation of futures for the child who drew the map. In many other maps outside became 'after lockdown', this map is an example of how the entanglement of hopes, for example to see family, and concern for the unexpected, the things that the child says are 'not calm' are made visible. What unfolds as they describe the surprise reaction to changes, with this they refer to Covid-19 restrictions, as not their own surprise but their lived and felt experience of the unsettling sound of adults' discussions. Here we made note that the act of mapping worked to mobilize thoughts and feelings that are often hidden as they are so enmeshed in past, present and future.

Throughout these experimental mappings, we were attuned to how the event engaged children with often unacknowledged sounds like: 'yawning', 'giny pig drinking', or 'owles singing'. The resulting mappings and the children's reflections were rich with multisensory animations of their home-learning worlds. What was animated was also the embodied and felt intra-actions with this space: 'I heard rain which is like crying.' Another child added to their inside space: 'hearing myself think' helping us see the mapping as an affirmative method of activating multisensory experiences of spaces (Powell, 2010).

Exploration #3: Mapping Soundscapes

//LISTEN to the Soundscape. Just listen.

//It is around 4 minutes long.

//Mark an X on your paper – this is where the journey starts and ends.

//Now we are going to listen to the soundscape again.

//This time you need to draw the map of the soundscape journey.

//It is a circular journey! Therefore it ends at the start.

//Where does the soundscape that you listened to take you?

Our third exploration is the parallel mapping of soundscapes in Bristol and Delft. Mark had recorded the sounds of our first walk alone-together. In the cycle of listening-editing-relistening he realized how repetitive and seemingly unimaginative the soundscape of immediate lockdown appeared. To create the soundscape for the workshop, Mark remixed this original recording and layered onto it pre-lockdown sounds from his personal archives, including recordings from Berlin, Potsdam, Geneva and the Swiss Jura. This created an experience which was outside of our present rhythms and routines. The recording became a compilation of disparate routine sounds that inspired him: a dog's lead; birds; a football crowd; a tram passing by; partiers in the street.

For Mark's class, the children listened to the recording together online while within the confines of their own personal space. Many used their own personal devices to play the sounds, ensuring they were (almost) synchronized. As they listened, the children mapped the soundscape digitally, drawing alone but together. They mapped the sequence of sounds, but also the associations, the relations between places, people and objects that were activated by what they heard. At the suggestion of the children, everyone posted their map at the same time, making the sharing of the event into a ritual.

In Bristol, Scarlett analysed the children's maps. There was a spectrum of responses given to the recordings, in curating their visuals, Scarlett identified some key conceptual strands: (1) relationships and relational moments that sounds evoke; (2) design and semiotic practices in transmodal and transductive work through sounds, lines, dots, colours and symbols; (3) sounds resurrecting place and associating place with emotions; and, (4) sounds associated with emotions and affective experiences.

For Scarlett, Figure 7.4 offers an example of the relational qualities of mapping, where sound forms connections with people, memories, emotions, places and objects of the child's world. Scarlett observed this as another manifestation of the intergenerational research theme. In this image, the child connects the sound

Figure 7.4 What can we learn from sewing a circle?

of tram whistles to his grandparents which materializes a fluid movement from sound to image with resonances of Kress' notion of a motivated sign (Kress, 1997). The sound motivates the child to draw a picture of his grandparents – one mode igniting a modal, semiotic response. Kress (1997) refers to a *motivated sign* as a process when people decide which modes to privilege in sign-making. A sign-maker's interest strongly informs the creation of an image. Subjectivities thereby fold or sediment themselves into a text (Pahl & Rowsell 2006). Kress builds on these ideas when he talks about sign-making as a metaphor for the ways that meanings are multiplied in texts.

Also, on prominent display within the sound map is synaesthetic activity. Synaesthesia involves the crossing of senses in a meaning-making moment. An example is when a colour is deliberately linked to a sound or a noise is linked to an emotion which then links to a colour. Scarlett documented these sensory connections and found it surprising in one map that the key was emotions rather than descriptions of sounds. She said: 'this was not an association I found myself making when we did the sound mapping with Harriet'. Admittedly, Mark's planning deliberately activates synaesthetic responses and mixing of senses because it invites and sparks active responses across modal chains. In response, the depth this added to the maps, Scarlett commented 'It's helpful to view as an outsider because you can see the relationship between noise/sounds and emotion. There are so many layers to this by including how they associate this to experience.'

The maps materialized a *sense of home* in response to the soundscape for some of the children. A child listened to Mark's compilation of sounds which evoked memories of his home in Poland. Another wrote: 'The people at the party sound like they are in India.' This particular mapping activity drew on the children's transductive capacities to move across modes with fluency and ease. Transduction refers to moving from one mode to another which represents a key strand of all of the exploratory activities. In certain places, a quiet but profound glimpse of the children's responses and sensemaking of lockdown emerged from the movement of sounds: 'I like it when people shout because it shows they are together and that is important.'

Exploratory #4: What Can We Learn from Sewing a Circle?

The final engagement we have chosen to share involved Mark's class sewing a circle onto an off-cut of tie-dye fabric. The question: What can we learn by

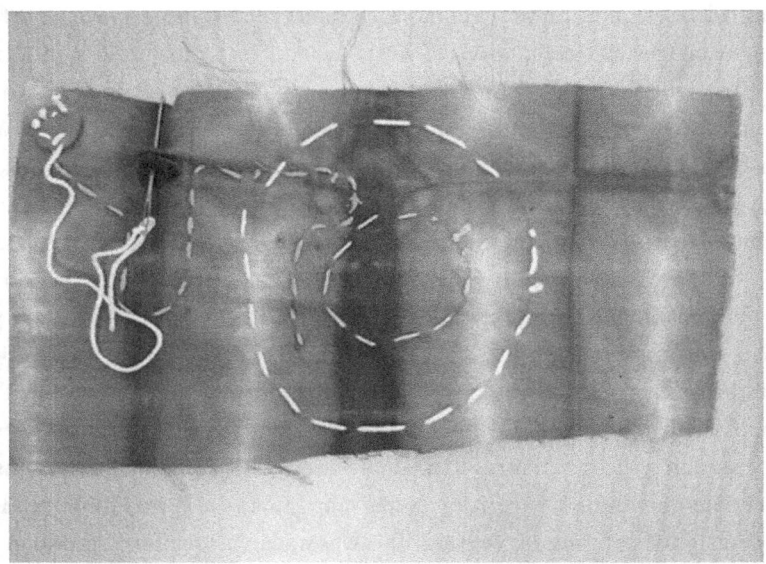

Figure 7.5 Soundscape performance score.

sewing a circle? was posted to the group and during the engagement they were asked to consider relations of self and the group, through rhythms, emotions, feelings and discussion. Once the circle was complete another trail was stitched carefully over the circle: this was a path drawn from the *Mapping the magical story box*: the imaginary journey through a cityscape of objects and embodied through a walk. The map was layered over the circle of stitches.

This reflective inquiry was a slowing down the rhythms of the day to ask: What can we learn about ourselves? Making use of the craft of sewing as a thoughtful and mindful practice that offers space for contemplation of our self and the world around us (Corbett, 2013), children reflected during the event. Their personal discoveries emerged from their engagement with the material, the needle, the thread and the lines and shapes of their stitches:

> *Child:* 'I need to unpick things. I always doubt myself . . . I am a perfectionist.'
>
> *Mr. Mark:* Is there such a thing as perfect? Do your Mums and Dads expect something as perfection?
>
> *Children:* Nooooo!
>
> *Child:* My Mum says, 'Perfect is not a thing. Practice makes progress. NOT practice makes perfect.'
>
> *Mr. Mark:* Your Mum is always sending me wise words. She said to me that gardening is the first ever job that people had and how important it is

that we are doing a community garden. We are learning the way that our ancestors learned thousands of years ago.

A multitude of connections emerged through rhythms, emotions, feelings and discussion. Sitting sometimes silently, sometimes in dialogue, the sewing of paths and circles invited children to craft, think and feel together. There was a strong sense of *becoming* through the intra-actions between children and materials. As one of the few encounters that played out face-to-face, the group were afforded time and space for reflections to emerge as they worked with the thread and the thread worked to mobilize their thoughts:

'I learned about other people in a calm way.'
'I learned about patience because my friend helped me find a path'
'When we are impatient, we get angry with ourselves.'

Conclusion

When we debriefed about the *alone-together* research in July 2021, all of us across the ages and stages of life agreed that the project brought light and inspiration after feeling beleaguered by Zoom meetings and Teams seminars. As Will expressed it,

> All I can say, is the creative multimodal spectrum of the research design including the creation of maps and interaction or engagement with other participants maps through post analysis and discussion, allowed for a collaborative connection between participants and researchers. It entirely blurred the lines of generations. It was a collaborative effort to explore rather than research expectations. (July 2021)

The 2020 pandemic is a historical moment. It changed everything not least of which the ways that people of all ages teach and learn. The encounters and observations shared in this chapter depart from more traditional pedagogies because they called on learners and researchers to actively listen to and participate in their worlds to learn. As bell hooks says about transgressive teaching: 'we communicate best by choosing that way of speaking that is informed by particularity and uniqueness of whom we are speaking to and with' (hooks, 1994, p. 11). There are inflexions of transgressive teaching in this research and of hook's sense of *an engaged voice* that is never fixed, but always moving with ears, eyes and senses open to what unfolds. Maps, mapping and derives were fitting ways to move learning and keep conversations going. We don't want to claim that our intergenerational research was transformative, but instead that the research provided a healing space for everyone involved and as such, there is a lesson to be learned.

One fundamental resonance in the research that continues to be felt, has been the comfort of digital spaces when they became fluid spaces to map quietly alone and spaces to share thoughts and dialogue. Allowing silence to be part of the online space evoked a trust and deep(er) connection between us. Children in Mark's class felt the most at ease within the silence, drawing with microphones on, small sounds of keyboards, sniffs and background noises forming a backdrop to their thinking. Concentrating on a piece of paper, drawing lines, nodes, and stars where things (people, objects, modes, etc.) mattered to us and that drew a meaningful, collaborative circle around our experiences. A number of the children in Mark's class talked about the togetherness that they felt in thinking with us about mapping, multimodal compositions and reflective conversations. The intergenerational sharing activated new ways for all of us to observe the strange world of lockdowns, masks, screen fatigue and online learning and teaching. In many ways, *community* was central to the project – a community that spanned ages, genders, cultures, nationalities and interests – that found ways to share ideas around events like a virtual brunch; sharing objects; home spa with homemade masks; and neighbourhood walks. These encounters gave us a listening space which allowed everyone to feel more connected to who they are and to share experiences during a lonely time.

There is a research implication for this project too. Certainly, for long-time researchers like Jennifer, the research-creation element was novel and insightful. Drawing inspiration from scholars like Truman (Springgay & Truman, 2017; Truman, 2021) and co-researching with Harriet, Will, Scarlett and Mark moved Jennifer into a new phase of her research and scholarship. The open and responsive quality of the research inquiry permitted us to engage in the rich, multilayered, multidimensional experiences of young people. These were more-than-human, felt and, crucially, sensory-led encounters that could certainly be described, but more than this *observed and experienced together*. It reminded Jennifer of her early days of reading Kress' *Before Writing* (1997) and the sea change in her thinking. What is more, the sequence of research encounters was not linear and without doubt layered on top of each other strengthening connections across people, things/stuff, time and space.

Looking ahead and thinking about this collection on observations about children, we consider what lessons can be learned from such exploratory research? There is great potential in pursuing the layering of pedagogical and research methods that this project generated. There were many moving parts to the research design from co-researcher mapping; parallel mapping; making and sharing multimodal compositions; talking to our objects; walking the same spaces; and, sending questions across time, space and ages. These layers built up into a rich and tapestried portrait of experiencing lockdown life. We were responsive to what emerged, permitting these layers to do their work in enlivening entangled relations of human and non-human intra-actions. There were so many layers to the project that we turned to geological terminology to unpack the porosity and density of the corpus of data. Enmeshed in this layering is a noticing and attuning to the details of life which gave texture to documenting our research, alone-together.

Note

1 Prior to data collection, we secured ethical clearance through University of Bristol. All participants have signed consent forms and agreed to share their artefacts and artwork.

References

Barad, K. (2007). *Meeting the universe halfway: Quantum physics and the entanglement of matter and meaning.* Duke University Press.

Braidotti, R. (2013). *The posthuman.* Cambridge: Polity Press.

Collier, D., & Harwood, D. (2017). The matter of the stick: Storying/(re)storying children's literacies in the forest. *Journal of Early Childhood Literacy, 17*(3), 336–352.

Corbett, S. (2013). *A little book of craftivism.* Cicada.

Corner, J. (1999). The agency of mapping: Speculation, critique and invention. In D. E. Cosgrove (Ed.), *Mappings* (pp. 213–252). Reaktion Books.

Davies, B. (2014). *Listening to children: Being and becoming.* Routledge, Taylor & Francis Group.

Debord, G. (1958). Theory of the dérive. In K. Knabb (Ed.), *Situationist international: Anthology* (pp. 50–54). Bureau of Public Secrets.

Gieseking, J. J. (2013). Where we go from here: The mental sketch mapping method and its analytic components. *Qualitative Inquiry, 19*(9), 712–724. https://doi.org/10.1177/1077800413500926

Hackett, A., & Somerville, M. (2017). Posthuman literacies: Young children moving in time, place and more-than-human worlds. *Journal of Early Childhood Literacy, 17*(3), 374–391.

Haraway, D. J. (2016). *Staying with the trouble: making kin in the Chthulucene*. Duke University Press.

Higgins, H. (2002). *Fluxus experience*. University of California Press.

Hultman, K., & Lenz Taguchi, H. (2010). Challenging anthropocentric analysis of visual data: A relational materialist methodological approach to educational research. *International Journal of Qualitative Studies in Education, 23*(5), 525–542. https://doi.org/10.1080/09518398.2010.500628

hooks, b. (1994). *Teaching to transgress: Education as practice of freedom*. Routledge.

Kitchin, R., Gleeson, J., & Dodge, M. (2012). Unfolding mapping practices: A new epistemology for cartography. *Transactions – Institute of British Geographers, 38*(3), 480–496.

Kress, G. (1997). *Before writing: Rethinking the paths to literacy*. Routledge.

Kuby, C. R., Spector, K., & Thiel, J. J. (Eds.) (2018). *Posthumanism and literacy education: Knowing/becoming/doing literacies*. Routledge.

Lefebvre, H. (2004). *Rhythmanalysis: Space, time, and everyday life*. Continuum.

Lenz Taguchi, H. (2011). Investigating learning, participation and becoming in early childhood practices with a relational materialist approach. *Global Studies of Childhood, 1*(1), 36–50.

Lynch, K. (1960). *The image of the city*. MIT Press.

Massey, D. (2005). *For space*. SAGE Publications Ltd.

Mayes, E. (2019). The mis/uses of 'voice' in (post)qualitative research with children and young people: Histories, politics and ethics. *International Journal of Qualitative Studies in Education, 32*, 1191–1209.

Mazzei, L. A. (2020). Speculative inquiry: Thinking with whitehead. *Qualitative Inquiry, 27*(5), 554–566.

Miles, J., & Springgay, S. (2020). The indeterminate influence of Fluxus on contemporary curriculum and pedagogy. *International Journal of Qualitative Studies in Education, 33*, 1007–1021.

Miller, D. (2008). *The comfort of things*. Polity Press.

Niccolini, A., & Ringrose, J. (2019). Feminist posthumanism. In P. Atkinson, S. Delamont, A. Cernat, J. Sakshaug, & R. Williams (Eds.), *The SAGE encyclopedia of research methods*. SAGE. https://methods.sagepub.com/foundations/feminist-posthumanism

Ono, Y. (2015). *Grapefruit*. Reprint. Museum of Modern Art.

Pahl, K., & Rowsell, J. (Eds.) (2006). *Travel Notes from The New Literacy Studies: Instances of Practice*. Multilingual Matters.

Pahl, K., & Rowsell, J. with D. Collier, S. Pool, Z. Rasool and T. Trzecak. (2020). *Living Literacies: Literacy for Social Change*. MIT Press.

Powell, K. (2010). Making sense of place: Mapping as a multisensory research method. *Qualitative Inquiry, 16*(7), 539–555.

Powell, K. (2016). Multimodal mapmaking: Working toward an entangled methodology of place. *Anthropology & Education Quarterly, 47*(4), 402–420. https://doi.org/10.1111/aeq.12168

Rautio, P. (2013). Children who carry stones in their pockets: On autotelic material practices in everyday life. *Children's Geographies, 11*(4), 394–408. https://doi.org/10.1080/14733285.2013.812278

Rautio, P. (2014). Mingling and imitating in producing spaces for knowing and being: Insights from a Finnish study of child–matter intra-action. *Childhood, 21*(4), 461–474.

Springgay, S., & Truman, S. E. (2017). A transmaterial approach to walking methodologies: Embodiment, affect, and a sonic art performance. *Body & Society, 23*(4), 27–58.

St. Pierre, E. A. (2019). Post qualitative inquiry in an ontology of immanence. *Qualitative Inquiry, 25,* 3–16.

Truman, S. E. (2021). *Feminist speculations and the practice of research-creation: Writing pedagogies and intertextual affects.* Routledge.

8

Hidden Mothering and Mutated Modest Witnessing with Hop(scotch) Studio

Marissa McClure *Indiana University of Pennsylvania*

'Painting, drawing and cutting', my son Robert, now age six, shares his thoughts on Hopscotch Studio – our shared home art studio space – that I should include in this book chapter. He's cuddled up to me under a blanket on the sofa in the early morning darkness as I write. He continues, 'I think there might be just one more thing. Let me think of something that's kind of messy in there. Remember that machine where we put paint in it and then we start stirring it at the top. Let's just call it the sticky machine. I can call it the sticky machine because what it does is that it sticks paint to paper in there' (Figure 8.1).

I hadn't thought very often about the sticky machine. I noticed the old salad spinner serving bowl in the corner of the studio floor week or two ago and wondered if I should try to clean it up. I thought that maybe it had been discarded or misplaced but I was simply too tired to deal with it. I hadn't considered stickiness as part of its identity as an object or its role as an actor in my children's art-making play. In our studio space, it was no longer just the old salad bowl but rather the sticky machine. Its purpose was hidden from my perspective, even though I spent a sizeable portion of almost every day with my three young children in our shared studio space: Hop(scotch) Studio.

In this chapter, I consider how I have engaged in hidden mothering as an artist/mother/scholar. I consider hidden mothering in my curating of art-making space for my children, my initial selection of materials, and my first observations of my young children's time in our shared studio space. Hidden mothering scrubs material agency as it (re)produces exclusive and falsely neutral representations of children and childhoods. In contrast, Osgood's framework of 'mutated modest witnessing' holds rich potentials to directly challenge hidden mothering and its manifestations in observations of young children. Osgood

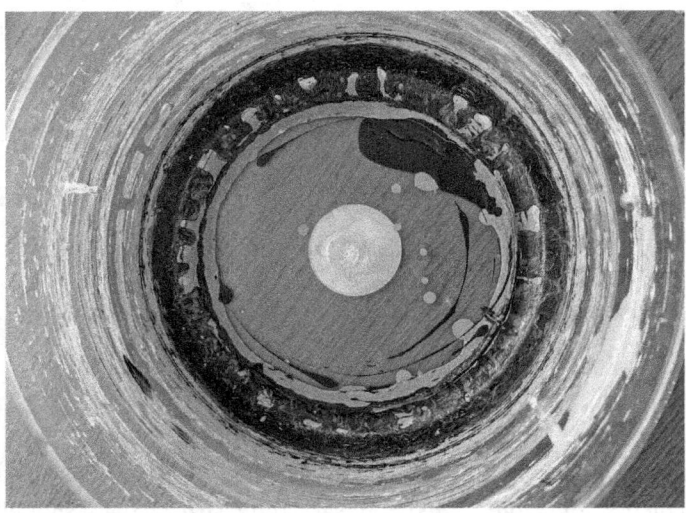

Figure 8.1 The sticky machine.

describes mutating modest witnessing as a contradiction to the objectivity of early scientific research that is 'open to the queerness that resides in spaces where habits, magic, and fantasy comingle with regulation, containment, and surveillance' (p. 124). Following Haraway, she explains that this *feminist* objectivity is 'characterized by situated knowledge' that embraces partiality (p. 118, original emphasis).

Osgood applies Haraway's figure of the mutated modest witness as a practical guide for researching with young children differently in her work with young children in a multicultural nursery. She explains, 'The mutated modest witness is not an innocent bystander gathering representational accounts of the world out there, rather she is implicated and invested.' She continues 'early childhood contexts are extraordinarily ordinary, excessive and affectively charged' (p. 126).

Following this, I consider how my hidden mothering embodies a 'desired face' of artist/mother/scholar that (re)produces privilege even as I assumed an objectivity or lack of agency in the materials that I initially offered my children. The year that I spent with my three young children ages five, three and one in a shared studio space as a participant in artist Lenka Clayton's Artist Residency in Motherhood (ARIM) revealed these tensions within myself as I regularly observed and documented my work with my children in our studio. I will provide an orientation to ARIM further within this chapter.

Osgood's concept opened and held space for me to newly encounter myself, the materials that I had selected for my children to use in our shared space, and even the contours of my own childhood experiences through the expectations that they generated for how I embodied a future mother-self. This revelation has charged experimentation with the consequences and potentials of more fully and honestly admitting my own embedded and situated perspective. Sakr's (2021) proposal to reconceptualize the 'shadow work' of observations in work with young children further provided me with the inspiration and the courage to reveal myself within this work. Using Carl Jung's idea of the shadow self, she theorizes the promise in our doing the shadow work of uncovering the shadow self who appears during observational moments that are uncomfortable for adults, such as messes that occur.

Hidden Mothering

Throughout this chapter, I mobilize the idea of hidden mothering as a dual practice in which an artist/mother/scholar is not only hidden but complicit in her hiding. This is in direct contrast to mutated modest witnessing which is a practice of disclosure and of lingering in the unknowing and unknowable. It is the opposite of masculine modesty and masculine objectivity in which access to knowledge was restricted by class, race and gender and the boundaries of scientific theatre. Victorian-era modest witnessing and 'Hidden Mother' images might be seen as cultural cognates.

'Hidden Mother' images were practical. Early cameras required long exposure times that posed the expected challenge of remaining still for young children. Mothers and studio assistants stepped in to hold children while the images were being produced. Often, they are shrouded by a blanket or furniture. Occasionally, a hand or forearm slips through the artifice. Here, I draw relationships between hidden mothering as management of children's movements in observations and the potential of mutated modest witnessing. The experiences that I share would often remain private in accounts of observation with young children as would my deeply personal intent. The strangeness of 'Hidden Mother' photographs troubled me long before I became a mother. Now, they evoke sadness in my recognition of the daily experiences of motherhood in which I often feel unseen and disease in my realization of being complicit in my own erasure. This is especially true as I enter a third year of pandemic isolation with my three very young children, in which our daily emotional and material lives are restricted and shared with few others in-person outside of ourselves.

Contemporary artist Jennifer Combe, who interrogates the concept of biological motherhood in her work *Nurture/Nature*, has created a series of *Hidden Mother* photographs with her two young children in which her hands, which do a lot of the unseen work of motherhood, remain visible. Her hands confront the viewer of the images, making seen and emphasizing the hidden labour of motherhood, even when the image is fixed upon her children (Figure 8.2). Her (un)Hidden Mother images are an example of mutated modest witnessing in which she directly confronts the structures that expect her to remain hidden.

Figure 8.2 Hidden Mother, *2016*, 37" x 27," archival pigment print, by Jennifer Combe (Image courtesy of the artist). She explains, 'Responding to Linda Fregni Nagler's book *Hidden Mother*, I pose holding my daughter, yet with my hands visible. Her book documents a collection of 1000 (and growing) "hidden mother" portraits from the turn of the 19th century. Historically, small children were held by adults to account for long exposure times, due to the mechanical limits of the time. These people, usually mothers, were obstructed from view, rendered invisible. The visibility of a mother's working hands suggests all domestic modern labor that is poured into child rearing: in addition to actual work there is also the task of organizing and planning, what feminists term "the mental load."'

Her work references a continued interest in Hidden Mother photography within US popular culture. In a recent *New Yorker* article, culture writer Lauren Collins recounts a Twitter feed in which mothers counted how many family photographs that they appeared in comparison to fathers. The implication was that the mothers were behind the lens. As she explains, 'There's a certain power, of course, in being the orchestrator of the family tableau, in choosing the frame to which the image of your world conforms.' Throughout this work, I am interested in not only this oft-unforgiving choreography but also in the possibilities that are created when hands, forearms and shadow selves bleed through and resist the trick.

The Artist Residency in Motherhood

I create an intersection of these theories and apply this confluence to my analysis of representations of my participation with three of my children ages three, five and one in artist Lenka Clayton's *Artist Residency in Motherhood (ARIM)*. Clayton is a UK-born, Pittsburgh-based interdisciplinary artist whose work engages with everyday situations, extending the familiar into the realms of the poetic and absurd (2012). On 1 January 2021, I began my own ARIM, an open-source, self-defined and self-determined residency using Clayton's DIY Residency Kit. I became one of 1,200 artists in residence who represent all fifty US states and seventy-three countries and committed to a regular weekly art-making routine with my three young children. My intention was to make unfamiliar the achingly mundane cadence of domestic life and to re-enter the processes of arts-based research with young children that had been on hiatus since the concurrent birth of my youngest child and the arrival of the Covid-19 pandemic.

In describing why she created ARIM in 2012, Clayton writes that before having children she had often attended artist residencies and was inspired by the unfamiliarity of each new environment and used this as material to make my work with (. . .) I wondered how I might instead apply the framework of an artist residency to the wild new world that was unfolding at home, one that I usually felt entirely too tired to notice. I will undergo this self-imposed artist residency in order to fully experience and explore (. . .) limited movement and general upheaval that parenthood brings and allow it to shape the direction of my work rather than to work 'despite it'.

Following Clayton's provided template, I wrote my manifesto and the children and I began to convert an unused darkroom in our basement into a shared

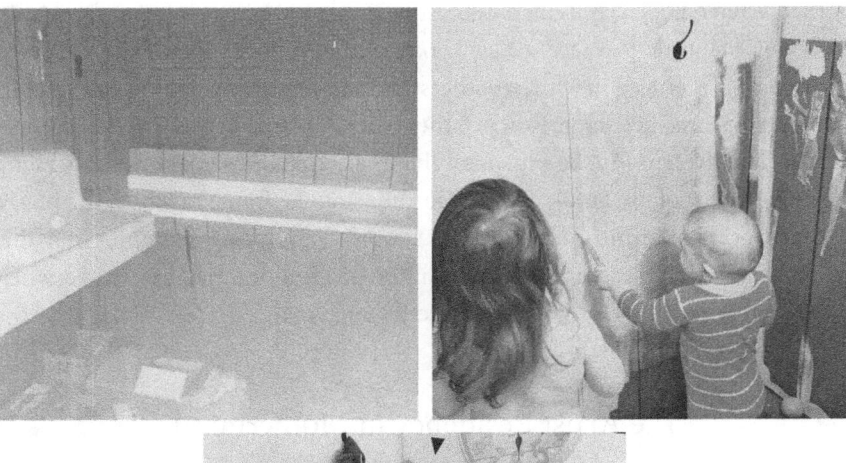
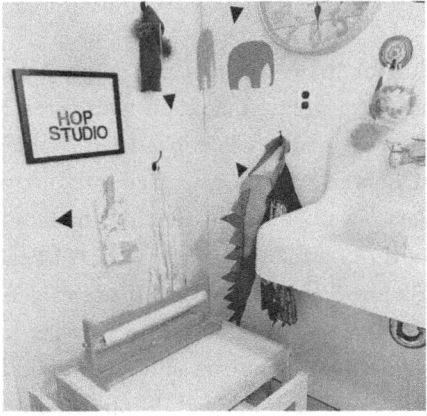

Figure 8.3 Views of Hopscotch Studio, before, at the beginning and throughout the first year of ARIM.

studio space (Figure 8.3). They chose the name Hopscotch Studio. We did not have enough vinyl letters to create the studio signage that Clayton recommends so we call our space Hop Studio instead. I answered the questions that Clayton proposed in my written submission. I answered question two, **Describe as specifically as possible, anything about your current situation that makes your creative life difficult** (original emphasis), as follows:

Time, sleep, lack of social and emotional support, conflict and cohesion between my personal and professional lives. And, of course, the little fingers playing on this keyboard right now. I have been working full-time as an art education professor and a full-time parent, mostly without childcare. So, therefore I am juggling all the children home with me. This has become an even more profound experience during the current pandemic, as my social support system has significantly weakened and even the small access that I had to childcare is gone. My two older children have been home with me without preschool since December 2019, when my infant son was born. His entire baby year was spent in quarantine and isolation (. . .) I am struggling to rebuild both my sense of self and of belonging.

And question six: **Write a manifesto for yourself:**

I want to work with my children. I see our work as collaborative: as a shared life's work, a series of films and installations that we make together daily. A living document, a testimony to strength, fragility, vulnerability and an affront to containment and shame. I see our shared artistic practice as bringing more presence and more intention to my parenting practice and the converse, too.

I committed to working ten hours per week on the residency, and to sharing our work together through audio recordings, a podcast and on social media using the hashtags #artistresidencyinmotherhood and #ARIM. I began in earnest but quickly realized that the ambitious pace that I had set was not sustainable for me.

Hiding Myself

Since giving birth to my first child during my first year in a new tenure-track position at a regional teaching university in the United States, I have struggled like most new parents with the seismic impact of motherhood upon every plane of my life, including my professional identity. Prior to becoming a parent, I was an artist/educator/researcher who worked with young children in a variety of pedagogical settings including classrooms and museums. Inspired by the young children with whom I worked in these spaces I emphasized my research upon ameliorating impoverished images of vulnerable groups of young children by sharing my research agency with them. I presented our initial work together through digital photography and video. I wrote most vignettes to accompany these images to draw attention towards the themes present in the children's pieces and in the playscapes and landscapes that surrounded them. I wanted to try to capture the feelings of young children's art-making more accurately in as much of the complexity that we had experienced. I saw the work as affective, multimodal, and embodied but I was frustrated by my continued inability to convey this through traditional approaches to qualitative and arts-based research. I was most eagerly interested in the seepage between the inside and the outside of the frame of children's art-making. I saw this work as instrumental in positing a richer image of the complexity in young children's lives. I created much of this work before having my own children. During my encounters with young children I dreamt often about the kinds of artistic experiences that I might provide as a mother. Having often worked with young children experiencing trauma and having adopted the role of a responsive educator, I never questioned my ability to be a good mother: one I saw not only as child-centred, emotionally available and unconditionally supportive but also as well-presented and composed.

My path to parenthood was less than straightforward: paved with infertility, pregnancy and adoption loss and haunted by ever-present grief. I still encounter the physical effects of IVF treatment and adoption that included years of hormonal upheaval culminating in my hospitalization with ovarian hyperstimulation syndrome and my subsequent diagnosis of anxiety and depression. Even as a traditionally accomplished researcher, as an educator who spent much of her time in intimate contexts with very young children, and as a stepmother to two school-age children through my marriage, I struggled to define myself outside of my learned perception of 'good' motherhood. That included becoming a biological parent easily and naturally to children who would allow me to perform my desired identity (DeGroot & Vik, p. 44).

On the heels of a final failed adoption attempt and an eighth IVF cycle, my first child thundered into the world after a forty-two-hour labour on the Sunday evening before Monday's semester began. He attended his first academic conference with me at six weeks. I changed his diaper on a hotel bathroom floor before my presentation while still wearing disposable underwear myself. Reality leaked through my blouse. Yet, I continued to try to hide myself in my outward work, living what the women in DeGroot & Vik's study called 'living two lives. The presented life and the lived life' (p. 51). I did a passing job of performing face even as my second child arrived mid-semester on a Monday. I returned to teaching on Tuesday, too worried to press for parental leave as my application for promotion was due three weeks after her birth. My image of 'good' academic coalesced with my image of a 'good' mother. Burdened by guilt and shame as an infertility survivor and buoyed by the treachery of the 'flawless double bind' (DeGroot & Vik, 2021), I assumed I should be able to be both. Like many dual-academic couples, my partner and I live in a small university town, away from family and without childcare and community support.

Days, nights and months melted together as I wore myself through attempting to keep pace with publishing and research while presenting myself and my children through the particularly peaceful and muted aesthetic that signified the kind of thoughtful and considered approach to the material culture of childhood that I felt compelled to stage: lots of natural materials, wooden toys, highly textured papers and pastel paints. My relentless schedule of caretaking and teaching without break from either left almost no time for the pleasures of reading, writing and art-making with my own children that I had imagined. Instead, I often found myself overwhelmed: cleaning up spills and mourning broken heirlooms while the children continued to make so much of everything at a frenzied pace punctuated by sudden cat naps on a dirty floor. Yearning for those experiences that I had so craved and aching with isolation, I founded a community-based art programme for young children that summer. This became yet something else to be curated and to be managed: a public extension of my private ambitions. By the time my third child arrived along with a global pandemic, my face was all but lost. We waded through those months of lockdown, all together, in an alternate reality: an Overton Window in which what was previously unimaginable became reasonable. I emerged reluctantly radicalized.

Becoming Mutated

It is perhaps telling that while I intended ARIM to be a shared experience, the emphasis was decidedly upon me at the beginning and upon my desire for an impossibly fulfilling external validation that never arrived. As sequestered as I was in still-new motherhood, I was eager to share a neatly curated space that brimmed with the kinds of art-making supplies that excited me to my imaginary audience. This included many materials that were imbued with the kinds of sensibilities that I had acquired before I had children. Some of these objects were too painful for me to look at during my experiences with infertility and loss and so had remained preciously tucked away for years. They largely represent the objects and materials that I associated with good mothering and good researching as a Montessori-trained and Reggio-inspired early art educator: wooden stairs and towers in groups of ten; a handmade Grimm's rainbow; leaves, sticks and rocks collected on our many hikes together; all arranged in faceted glass jars; their muted earth-tones sorted chromatically. There are very few primary colours, only a few necessary plastic tools and no remnants of popular culture.

At first, as the children and I worked together in Hop Studio, they followed my lead into this new aspect of our relationship. Following the teaching/research practices that I espoused as an artist/educator/researcher, I created provocations for them. On one winter afternoon, an inviting lump of natural clay sat on the chalkboard table that I had refinished. They sat and played while I observed and recorded in my usual manner through digital photography. I attempted to more equitably share the power balance in the space with them but found it difficult when they began to push back in various ways: pushing objects not intended to get wet into the clay, pushing the clay into their skin and hair, pushing one another off of the chairs and onto the floor. *Trying to retain my composure and to remember to use my positive parenting strategies was a challenge: I modeled taking deep breaths and setting appropriate boundaries.* I could not let them push one another in Hop Studio. I validated how easy it was to become frustrated when making art but that the solution was not to push a sibling off the chair. The baby was an especially easy target for my older children. At one point, my oldest declared, 'I HATE art!' as his little brother toppled to the ground. I spent late evenings vacuuming dried clay bits out of the floor and scraping acrylic paint from the counters. At times, I struggled to merely tolerate what I envisioned fully embracing. Five minutes that felt like a lifetime later, I might feel the kind of out-of-body experience of overflowing joy that I might have previously considered hyperbole.

My strong aesthetic sense of what was a desirable engagement for my children in art-making bled into how I presented our work together in Hop Studio. I would recoil when I saw myself, exhausted and unkempt, in the video pieces that the children made, seemingly unaware of my presence. I edited myself totally out of our shared record even though I was almost always in the camera's view and of course my children's view of me each day. Like the mothers who were saving 'face' in DeGroot & Vik's study *Fake Smile: Everything is under control*, I was initially focused on what my imagined and highly critical 'global audience', or inner shadow thought of me rather than on what my interpersonal partners (my children) thought about me (p. 46).

Yet, over the first year of our residency and now into its waning last month, Hop Studio has become decidedly abject. My provocations are totally absent: neglected around the fourth week of our residency. Much of the time I sit just outside Hop Studio where I have made a makeshift home office with a chair as my laptop desk. Still teaching my university courses from home for most of the residency, I worked on my own work and sometimes intervened as their shouting reached crescendo. If something is too high to be reached, they climb before asking for assistance. There is no longer a door because my one-year-old purposefully pushes his fingers in the jamb. A 'stink bug' who has moved in and perished under a piece of wooden train track now has his own tiny hobbit home and has remained remarkably free of decomposition. The brown marmorated stink bug was accidentally introduced to the Pennsylvania landscape where it

Figure 8.4 Stella's altered dolls in Hopscotch Studio.

has thrived, noted for the odour that it produces when threatened. This is why it cannot be moved.

One morning, I notice the tables and chairs have been thrown about. No one will tell me what happened. There is fresh red oil pastel ground on the carpeted floor. A decapitated, Sharpie-bloodied hand-me-down Barbie head drowns face-down in her dream pool which was earlier used to give the family dog a bath (Figure 8.4). I am too tired to clean it up. As I do most mornings, I sit down to write in the early morning hours and plan to get back to it at some other time. I can't quite remember the last time that I showed publicly anything made in Hop Studio, which has a shared partial relationship to the sheer busyness of my days and my children's growing awareness of online consent. Yet Hop Studio overflows living with half-authored expressions and playscapes in punctuated motion.

One still morning before the children arose, I decided to photograph Hop Studio rather than make my usual note to clean it up. To observe this space and many of its interactions in which my children have spent nearly a year making art daily. To unhide me by deprioritizing myself while simultaneously embedding myself within the intricacies of this space, and embracing what unfolds.

As I scan the photographs, I see: a dragon robe and a home-sewn dinosaur tail neatly hung on hooks. A hook that once held a Darth Vader mask now holds a cat photo frame with its cat face painted over carefully with muddied metallic acrylic paint. The tables and chairs have been drawn on with permanent marker; the chair seats are dirty with wet footprints from the dog's bath. The sticky machine lays abandoned on the floor with its plastic top akimbo. The sink is full of potion-making gear: plastic cookie cutters, a measuring cup, a plastic pitcher I last used for mixing grout for the bathroom tile floor, empty ice cube trays once used for homemade baby food and puppy shampoo. On the counter is collaborative unicorn drawing, the outline made by my partner who is also an artist and whose presence permeates Hop Studio just slightly less than mine. Stella has filled in the outline with a jagged rainbow. The open sketchbook sits adjacent to half a metal easter egg, a Paw Patrol Marshall figure that we need to return to our neighbour, half of a wooden zucchini from the kitchen playset, a barely-filled capless squeeze bottle of acrylic paint, a ripped box of crayons and a strip of floor tile painted and coloured with paint and markers. There are actually several of these floor tile strips and they interest me so I note to ask about it later when the older children return home from preschool. A fold-out Disney Frozen colouring sheet from the inside of a disposable pull-up box fills almost all the floor space and as I scan around, I find my one-year-old in his bib and footed pyjamas. I'm not sure how he is already conditioned to smile for a camera, beaming at me with a wide strawberry applesauce grin. I set my phone aside to write this paragraph while he opens the camera and creates a series of selfies (Figure 8.5). His accidental documentation comprises much of the year's material record of Hop Studio. My presence is not centrally visible but like Jennifer's hands, I am everywhere. The materials that I carefully curated and presented – those that most align with my face of good mothering and good researching – have been absorbed by the entropy of the space. A genuine fossil found many years past and retrieved from my hope chest on an equal plane with a borrowed and a partially eaten board book (Figure 8.6).

In my work to become mutated, I acknowledge that these images, especially the latter with the chewed book, challenge my face as a mother and researcher. What kind of mother allows her children to roam so unsupervised that they eat books? What kind of educator would allow a book to be treated in such a way? What kind of mother/educator would not even know it had occurred until she happened upon it like a crime scene investigator? What could all of this mean for my purpose to now think differently as an artist/educator/researcher with young children?

Hidden Mothering 153

Figure 8.5 One of Luca's selfies in Hopscotch Studio.

Osgood's proposition of embracing the partial in doing research with young children provided me with the confidence that I needed to embrace my slow mutation. As she asks, how might I 'pull at strings that offer a speculative account of *what else* is going on when we allow ourselves to ask *what if* and so work beyond the limits of recognition and representation (p. 120, original emphasis)'.

Throughout this chapter, I draw attention to my own centring of myself and my aesthetic preferences, my dreams of motherhood and my attachment to young children's art-making by asking *what else* my discomfort with the disorder of Hop Studio offers. To de-centre and to deprioritize myself to open space for my children and other, non-human actors in the space, I sit with this discomfort in my writing and in my observations as I let go of hidden mothering to become mutated. What else I found was the immense pressure that I feel as a mother and as an educator to produce a particular view of childhood even within my professed ambition to do precisely the opposite. *What if* we accept that childhood

Figure 8.6 Hopscotch Studio at present.

art-making is unknowable, familiar and mutated at the same time? How might this acceptance allow us 'to recognize and take account of our entangled place in the world' (Osgood 2020, p. 114), to unhide ourselves as we engage in amore ethical practice in our endeavours to regenerate more equitable worlds?

Engaging in the work of becoming mutated in observations with young children has the potential to undo hidden mothering. It revels in the possibilities of slippages and tangles of knowing and becoming that emerge and move between adults, children, environments and materials endlessly. It valorizes hidden and shadow selves and labours of care as it directly challenges masculine modesty and objectivity. It opens and holds space for unexpected, unanticipated and situated experiences of knowledge and demands accountability towards all of the human and non-human actors in our shared work.

References

Clayton, L. (2012). Artist residence in motherhood manifesto. ARIM. https://static1.squarespace.com/static/56e03c0b044262cdb87af698/t/57200f699f7266fe4512c551/1461718908827/arim_manifesto.pdf

DeGroot, J., & Vik, T. (2021). 'Fake smile. Everything is under control': The flawless performance of motherhood. *Western Journal of Communication, 85*(1), 42–60. https://doi.org/10.1080/10570314.2019.1678763

Osgood, J. (2020). Becoming a 'mutated modest witness' in early childhood research. In C. Schulte (Ed.), *Ethics and research with young children: New perspectives* (pp. 113–128). Bloomsbury Academic.

Sakr, M. (2021, November 3). *Light play: Reconceptualizing shadow work through observations of childhood art* [Video]. Center for the Study of Childhood Art. https://www.centerforthestudyofchildhoodart.com/childhood-art-speaker-series

9

Posthuman Babies

Reconceptualizing a Baby's First Year

Sara Sintonen and Alexandra Nordström
Faculty of Educational Sciences, University of Helsinki

Introduction

In this chapter we ask how to engage critically with adults' conceptions and observations of babies and the first months or years of growth, and how to open new ways of thinking about childhood and babies' first year in general. As Murris (2016, p. 46) argues, children need to be considered as citizens, not citizens-to-be, expressing a postdevelopmental view of childhood. This is important, so the idea of the posthuman child mobilizes an openness and critical alertness to the diverse ways in which our categorizations and own childhood experiences shape educational theories and practices (Murris, 2016, p. 60).

We will focus on posthuman children and especially posthuman babies through our considerations of constructions and reconceptualizations of a baby's first year. Following Murris (2016) and her discussion of constructions of the child and childhood, the posthuman child is an entanglement, composed of social, political, biological and cultural concepts and material forces without clear boundaries. Paramount for the posthumanist orientation is that it works against binaries such as object/subject or nature/culture. The posthuman child is 'rich in potential in the now/present, engaged in lived experimental encounters and relations with human and nonhumans' (Kuby et al., 2018, p. 9). Some posthuman theorists have argued that children could be approached as the missing peoples of posthumanism (i.e. Murris, 2020a), as dominant figurations of the child position children as epistemically and ontologically inferior and 'becoming' human, instead of being human (Lee, 2001). We would like to expand this argument and claim that very young children (i.e. babies) have been missing from these discussions to an even larger extent, which is why we brought out and used the concept of *posthuman babies*.

We will bring our notion of postdevelopmental approaches to childhood observation by focusing on reconsidering the idea and meanings of the concepts of posthuman babies and child figurations. We attempt to explore the phenomenon through a posthumanist lens and are using journaling a baby's first year (baby journals and memory books) as a sample case. Considering how popular baby journals and memory books are among young parents, and how the market offers a wide variety of them, baby journals and memory books are an understudied phenomenon. Baby journals and books often cover a baby's first twelve months of life or a child's first few years of growth. The idea is that parents fill in blank pages with various topics and milestones to create lifelong memories by observing and documenting. Many parents use baby journals or memory books to document and track their baby's development and moments of joy and growth. In this chapter, we use four different Finnish baby books as tools to think-with and reflect upon the phenomenon of baby journaling.

Baby journals and memory books are a cultural and textual sample of the way we think about and conduct childhood observations and they are deeply connected with dominant developmental paradigms in early childhood observations. We believe that most baby journals and memory books represent the developmental discourse that has dominated the thinking of childhood and early childhood education and care during the greater part of the twentieth century. This still dominates all over the world. We think baby journals and memory books guide and teach parents and other adults to observe a child in a certain way. One could say that baby journals and memory books support parents' thinking of the adults' role to observe, and often also compare, a child's biological process of development towards adult maturity. Is there a need to change this culture?

Theoretical Starting Point

We have based our writing on the idea of thinking with theory (Jackson & Mazzei, 2012) allowing us to rethink the phenomenon of baby observations. This way our process has been more of a shared, reflective, philosophic inquiry than other qualitative approaches or analyses. Thinking with theory (Jackson & Mazzei, 2012, pp. 118–136) as a part of our exploration of the phenomenon entailed a means of experiencing aspects of observation through thinking and feeling within the possibilities of the phenomenon (see also Leander & Boldt, 2013). This approach thus entails resisting the separation of theory and method in a reflexive move to think-with theory (Gunnarsson & Bodén, 2021; Jackson & Mazzei, 2012).

The developmental discourse that has dominated the thinking of childhood is also relevant to rethinking early childhood education and practices. Barad (2007, 2015) emphasized mutual relationality: things are because they are in relation to and influence each other. As we consider baby journals and memory books as cultural and textual artefacts with the potential of guiding and teaching, it is also important to reconsider the educational meaning of the phenomenon. As Lee (2001) argues, in educational practices, children are often understood in the terms of lack, incompleteness and dependence on other humans. This has its roots in early childhood, as we tend to concentrate on a child's development and achievements compared to other babies and children rather than appreciate the here and now, and the child and childhood as precious and complete in itself.

A prevailing view of children and childhood has been that children are incomplete individuals who are in the midst of their development towards the ultimate goal, which is adulthood. Adults, on the other hand, have been seen as complete and fully developed individuals. The terms 'human beings', for adults, and 'human becomings', for children, have been used to signify these contrasting figurations (Lee, 2001). The difference between children and adults in this view is that human beings are considered stable, mature and unchanging while human becomings are considered to be unstable, immature and in a constant state of change. Children are mainly seen as future adults. Lee (2001) also points out that social changes, such as industrialization, have had an impact on these figurations, and that adults are now considered to be in the middle of their own development, and thus still incomplete (Lee, 2001).

In our thinking, posthuman lenses help us to refocus our gaze. According to Snaza et al. (2014), posthumanism transforms educational thought, practice and research in three related ways. First, it forces us to reckon with how resolutely humanist almost all educational philosophy and research is. Second, it allows us to reframe education to focus on how we are always already related to animals, machines and things within life in schools at the K–12 and university levels. Third, building on and incorporating these first two insights, it enables us to begin to explore new, posthumanist directions in research, curriculum design and pedagogical practice (Snaza et al., 2014). However, as Taylor (2016) writes, the challenge of doing posthumanist research is evident, because 'posthumanism proposes different starting points for educational research and new ways of grasping educational experience than those afforded by humanism' (p. 5). Posthuman knowledge moves towards material ways of thinking and being, and posthuman research is as much about what knowledge is as it is how knowledge comes to be (Ulmer, 2017).

Our posthumanist lenses also guide us in thinking about what and who counts as (fully) human or a human being and not as a becoming (Lee, 2001; Murris, 2016; Osgood and Robinson, 2019). At the same time, we can zoom out to take the more-than-human into consideration and zoom in on the child and childhood. According to Braidotti (2018), the missing people of humanism are 'real-life subjects whose knowledge never made it into any of the official cartographies' (Braidotti, 2018, p. 21). The knowledge and understanding of missing people, like babies, are marginalized and thus often subsumed. Further, Murris (2020a) argues that children could be considered to be missing peoples of posthumanism as well, as when referring to humans, they are commonly assumed to be adults of a specific age and their forms of knowledge.

We develop thinking around postdevelopmental approaches to childhood observation by reconceptualizing adult-child-observation as adult-child-connection. Replacing the idea of observation with the idea connection has led us to think of Barad's term 'intra-action', which is ontologically different from 'interaction' (see e.g. Murris 2018, pp. 40–1). Barad (2003) reworked the traditional notion of causality and explained how intra-action enacts an agential cut, a local resolution within the phenomena. Observation can be seen as a form of interaction. This 'knowing in being' can be transformative with regard to how a person interacts with and lives in the world (Garber, 2019). The concept of intra-action is also interesting from the materialist point of view, as it reframes materiality from design affordance to a cycling interplay produced by the physicality, fluidity and messiness of entangled bodies, things and places (Wohlwend et al., 2017, p. 447). 'Matter is promiscuous and inventive in its agential wanderings: one might even dare say, imaginative', as Barad (2015) writes (p. 287).

According to Murris (2018, pp. 40–1) Barad's 'intra-action is different from "interaction" in that "nature" and "culture" are never "pure", are never unaffected by each other, but are always in relation – a sympoietic system, Haraway (2016, p. 58) would say ("entanglement" for Barad)'. Murris continues by noticing that we can't reach a child in reality as it is not present, it can only be re-presented. This leads to a state of past, present, and future (e.g. the milestones) being always intra-actively threaded through one another (Barad, 2007). How does intra-action influence baby observation?

Sympoiesis is similarly situated and dynamic, responsive and intra-active (Haraway, 2016, p. 58). According to Haraway (2016, p. 58), this simple word means 'making-with', which according to our understanding differs radically from 'preparing-with' (growing a child towards adulthood). In sympoiesis the requirements in the connection of chronological time are put aside. Sympoiesis is making-with through experiences, always in the process of becoming (Murris & Haynes, 2020, p. 24). From the observer's point of view, sympoiesis is challenging the whole concept of observation as 'sympoietic systems are unbounded "complex amorphous entities", have "distributed control" with an "evolution within systems", and are "unpredictable"' (Murris & Haynes, 2020, p. 28).

Posthumanism attempts to decentre the human and seeks common good for all life systems. This helps us to see life as a dynamic force unfolding vital flows of connections and becomings, and an ethics of joy 'taps into that flow' (see Braidotti, 2018). For Barad (2007) agency emerges when things and bodies come together: humans and non-human entities become agents only by way of each other. As Oulanne (2018) explained, 'There is no bicycle rider without a bicycle and a ground on which it can be ridden; these are features we add, in our interpretive imagination, to even fictional evocations of the event of bicycling. Equally, there is no reader without the nonhuman agencies of the text and the book, other environmental contributors of the event of reading, or the influence of its cultural and linguistic context' (p. 25). This means a pragmatic engagement with the present with the potential to construct and produce collectively conditions for social horizons of joy (Braidotti, 2018). The life force of a newborn baby, often referred to as a 'bundle of joy', could be also considered as a boost of action and agency; how can we support parents as observers and emphasize the child-adult connection instead?

How Current Baby Books Guide Us to Observe

In this chapter, we consider four Finnish popular baby memory books, especially focusing on their depiction of (post)human babies. We have chosen a selection of baby books that are popular and/or traditional and/or recently published. All four selected memory books are printed books and are currently and readily available in several books stores and online.

A) Book 1. *Kulta-aika lapsuuden* [The golden age of childhood] is one of the most traditional baby memory books in Finland. The first edition was published in 1949. (Wsoy, Arvo Lehtovaara and Maija Karma https://www.wsoy.fi/kirja/maija-karma/kulta-aika-lapsuuden/9789510081020)

B) Book 2. *Vauvakirja – Muistoja vauvavuosista koulun aloitukseen* [Baby book – Memories from the baby years to the start of school]. The first edition was published in 2008. (Otava, Mauri Kunnas https://otava.fi/kirjat/vauvakirja/)

C) Book 3. *Pienen oma kirja – Muistoja ensi vuosistani* [A small one's own book – memories from my first years]. in the first edition was published in 2018. (Kirjapaja, Outi Virtanen https://lkkp.kauppakv.fi/sivu/tuote/?id=2277537)

D) Book 4. *Alku – Vauvakirja* [Beginning – Baby book]. The first edition was published in 2019. (Kosmos, Jussi Pekka and Kiira Keski-Hakuni https://www.kosmoskirjat.fi/kirjat/alku-vauvakirja-kovakantinen-kirja/)

The overall goal is to describe the characteristics of a phenomenon. Our aim is not to compare the four memory books, but to seek a better understanding of the issues concerning posthuman babies by engaging with each of these books. Each book was first reviewed for the overall image by cover and illustration, and the content. Next, the pages with the idea of 'the firsts' (achievements) were examined, and finally, we looked across the entire text for points of interest in relation to the idea of postdevelopmental figurations of the child.

The visual content in the most traditional baby book (A) shows the handprint of the illustrations recognizable from children's books and materials, as the illustrator of the work, Maija Karma, is familiar to many Finns from her numerous children's book illustrations. Karma illustrated her main work in the 1950s and 1960s, so the popularity of the work may be based in part on a sense of familiarity and nostalgia.

The rich illustrations resemble drawings and there are many pictures of nature, flowers, animals and the forest. The illustrations also show child characters, as well as toys and games. Further, the illustrations support the textual content in the evocation of a religious tone (e.g. christening bowl, candles, angels). Throughout the illustrations, the work exudes a normative tone, and the illustration reflects the Finnish culture of the 1940s and 1950s. The child characters depicted seem smiling, content and kind. Overall, the book illustrations point towards a deeply traditional ideal of childhood and family life in mainstream Finnish culture.

Mauri Kunnas is also a well-known Finnish children's author and his works have been translated into numerous languages around the world. Our second sample baby book (B) has a characteristic, recognizable illustration style for

Kunnas, and many of the characters are familiar from his children's books. The images with a lot of details serve mainly as illustrations, and the colour scheme of the work is fresh and earthy. The characters convey different emotions and, to some extent, vivid and radical actions. Compared to the previous one, this book represents much modern interpretation of a child, childhood and play as it is more playful and nonnormative.

Our third example (C) represents a more neutral tone (it is mainly black and white with some pastel highlight colours) and a 'cute' bunny character plays a key role in the illustration. The illustration is organic throughout and utilizes many natural elements (e.g. leaves, trees, waves), partly in an abstract and ornamental style. In addition to the softness of the colouring, the drawing of the illustration is also softly round. The illustration conveys a gentle caring for others as well as small everyday joys. In some of the openings in the work, the illustration and colours refer to a dreamlike world and in turn, a romanticized construction of childhood as a dreamlike time.

The fourth baby book (D) is remarkably minimalist compared to the previous three. It has no illustrations at all, just pastel colour empty pages with a title and some text. The cover is bare and has an area bounded by a black line, like a photo frame. The design gives the impression of a technical, well-organized notebook, and it looks like an interior design element of a well-organized, minimalistic home. Of the four, this one emphasizes the technical dimension of recording the first year.

It is interesting to notice that each book represents its own era if we look at the visual elements, colours and illustrations. Although these four baby journals represent a cultural change in this sense, the content has remained remarkably similar. In each book, adult observers are encouraged to record similar details concerning a baby's first months and growth. These are hand and footprints as well as pieces of hair and tooth growth as related to the baby's age. Also, each book encourages adults to record many 'firsts' and achievements: the first smile, teeth, words, steps, songs, visits, trips and so on.

It appears that the cultural idea of observing babies (and writing a baby journal) is still based on an entrenched view of childhood and is still deeply connected with dominant developmental paradigms where what matters most is when things happen and in what order. The content has remained the same even though the representations seem to have adapted to wider cultural and aesthetic change. At closer inspection, the baby journals guide parents to produce figurations of the child following a chronological model of childhood. The chronological model often entails, in detail, how the linear development of the child 'should' progress, with a strong focus on 'firsts'. This model suggests and indicates heavily that all children develop in the same way and at the same pace. This entails that baby journals guide parents to observe their child with a chronological mindset. Many journals represent a newborn child and the beginning of life as chronologically determined, and it is this notion we aim to challenge and rethink in the following theoretical considerations.

Notions and Thoughts of Current Baby Journaling Tradition

We argue that cultural and societal norms of the child and conceptions of childhood are narrow and reductive. For example, cultural expectations and norms suggest that a newborn baby brings a lot of joy to the family and babies are often referred to as a 'bundle of joy'. Of course, this is a simplified, generalizing and prescriptive view of families and babies, which does not take into consideration the diversity of families, parents, and babies (e.g. Segers & Cavaliere, 2021). We do recognize that not every family experiences joy in welcoming a newborn, but in this case we recognize the cultural association between joy and babies, that is, the tension between societal norms and lived experience.

What produces and generates joy, and how is it observed? In the context of the four baby journals we have looked at, joy is connected to an understanding of child development and chronological growth, and these daily, weekly and/or monthly *achievements* (e.g. skill-based development) of the child. The pre-written prompts and thought-starters guide parents to observe certain topics and happenings, milestones and achievements. In our thinking, this indicates the educational nature of journals as they 'guide and teach' parents to observe their babies in a certain way. Parents (and other adults) learn to tick off the developmental milestones that have been achieved. As a result, baby journals and memory books have the potential to seriously influence an adult's perceptions and views of childhood, children and the beginning of life in general.

Baby journals and memory books can be regarded as cultural images intimately tied to social relations. Besides the texts, illustrations, colours and layouts, they represent their own 'rhetorical voice' with the potential of modelling and guiding observation. Baby books can be regarded as multimodal ensembles of the baby's first twelve months and/or first few years. Parents can collect memories in the form of writing, photos, first tufts of hair and paint prints of tiny hands and feet. Many parents also want to keep maternity ward bracelets and other first documents as a memory. With the investment of the parent/carer, baby books emerge as treasured multimodal collages of joyful memories.

It is important to consider how baby journals and memory books guide parents, through the process of the multimodal collage, to produce figurations of the child which reinforce the conceptualization of child-as-chronology. Baby journals and memory books are artefacts that guide and teach parents to know what is meaningful, true and worthwhile, and they are focused on adults' viewpoint failing to consider babies as such.

In one sense, baby journals and memory books represent a 'do not miss anything culture' as they are also marketed with the idea of 'remembering all the firsts'. As a result, 'do not miss anything' becomes a mantra, a psychological certainty, guiding the parent's observation of the child. For example, in one sample book (C), the memory book asks parents to fill the whole page listed with various 'firsts': the baby's first smile, bath, wave, going out, laugh, first words, first moment of crawling, sitting, taking the first steps and many other firsts. Nothing should pass the observers' attention. This directs observers to focus on all the first times and wait for them to happen.

The Pressure to Observe

New parents know how the first year forms the basis of the child's development and most of them consider the first year as significant in a child's growth and development. This might also cause parental stress, and according to research, being a parent, especially during the child's first year, can be experienced as overwhelming (e.g. Lee et al., 2014; Nyström & Öhrling, 2004). New parents, especially mothers, might also experience social exclusion as their babies are solely dependent on them. It is also known from earlier research that being a parent for the first time is hard work, despite the support received from a wide range of sources (Leahy-Warren et al., 2012).

Especially in Western societies, motherhood is mythically considered to be a universally fulfilling experience, but many new mothers (and fathers) have intensely ambivalent feelings (e.g. Leahy-Warren et al., 2012; Kruger, 2003). In this complex experience, a rollercoaster of mixed feelings and new responsibilities (e.g. Lee et al., 2014), parents cannot be required to be critical about various sources of information and models of baby observation. In parents' minds, baby journaling and keeping baby memory books might be even connected to 'good parenting' and some parents might be motivated by baby memory books as they can share the achievements through observation and documentation to other adults (see also Kumar & Schoenebeck, 2015). This phenomenon can also be recognized in digital culture as many new parents share photos and other documents online. According to one piece of research, many mothers share baby photos online, as sharing helps them enact and receive validation of 'good mothering' (Kumar & Schoenebeck, 2015). However, little is yet known about what kinds of baby photos new parents share and what motivates them most.

As baby journals and memory books support parents' conceptions of adults' role as observers, and often prompt the comparison of a child's biological process of development towards adult maturity, the situation might cause extra stress to the parents. What if my baby does not grow up according to the guidebooks and measurement timetables? What if I miss all the important milestones and first moments? Whose achievement is a child's own growth?

It is also interesting to note how some baby journals and memory books are advertised as physical, material things – as beautiful objects that suit your style and interior: 'If your baby memory book is going to live on a shelf on your dresser, by your bedside table or in baby's nursery, you want it to fit in, right? Look for one that suits your personal style and the decor of your home.'[1] This only highlights the external purposes and motives of purchasing baby journals and memory books and overrides the original purpose. From the market's point of view, the family acts as a key organizing force that shapes our behaviours and experiences in the marketplace, and the market follows and affects parents' choices which thus represent cultural ideals and normative beliefs about parenthood. As Epp (2018, p. 66–7) points out, the market interacts with families across all life stages and the market often facilitates intimate family relations, and it can be a site of both destructive and productive relationships with family. She continues that these tensions emerge from the basic understanding that family exists in the intimate sphere, governed by logic of intimacy, love and self-sacrifice, whereas the market exists in the economic sphere, governed by a logic of monetary exchange, profit motives, and competition (Epp, 2018, p. 67). Epp (2018, p. 66) also mentions competitive parenting as one aspect of this phenomenon.

Parental stress is also connected to the need to control, which might cause extra pressure to observe. As mentioned earlier, baby journals and memory books represent the 'do not miss anything culture' as they are marketed with the idea of 'remembering all the firsts'. This also resonates with the need to control and keep things in order, which Somerville and Powell (2019) recognize in early childhood learning centres. They suggest that we need to become immersed in the emergent worlds and play of young children and pursue understanding of the ways in which seemingly fixed spaces and territories of learning are constantly being territorialized and de-territorialized by emergent play. If parents only concentrate on noticing and remembering all the firsts and they are keen on observing babies in the sense of 'not missing anything', they might be narrow-eyed and too concentrated only on certain things. These distinctions might lead to maintaining stereotypes and hierarchies. Instead of causing parental stress, observation of babies' first months could emphasize sensing vital flows of connection, recognizing and being part and welcoming various becomings.

Re-constructions of Childhood and Posthuman Babies

The Western idea and model of childhood is narrow and contains many assumptions and knowledge on behalf of babies and children. As mentioned earlier, and as Bohlman and Hickey-Moody (2018, p. 1) have noted, Western thought about childhood is dominated by a view of the child as developmentally deficit in comparison to adults; it is based on a binary logic positioning children in contrast to adults. Bohlman and Hickey-Moody continue by describing childhood as 'undergoing a stage-delineated process of maturation that prepares them for being the adult they are supposed to become' (p. 1). This sets a developmental framework, which in turn resonates through mainstream practices of baby journaling and keeping a memory book.

General ideas, notions and representations about childhood and adulthood change radically in time and place and are thus connected to our cultural understanding of the child, childhood and growth. Rethinking the journaling of a baby's first year requires the re-constructions of childhood and new thinking about/with posthuman babies. As Annalisa Caputo (2020, p. 107) remarks 'childhood *in itself* does not exist'. She continues, how it is inevitably '*related to us*', and points out that 'also an adult-being *in itself* does not exist, except in relation – among other things – to childhood'. From this point of view, baby observation as an adult-led activity is not a solid base for intra-action especially if we follow posthuman thinking of childhood in relation.

Posthumanist thinking breaks dichotomies and calls us to join, to world-with, to be in company (Haraway, 2016). Barad's intra-action enacts an agential cut, a local resolution within the phenomenon which challenges observers to appraise lived experimental encounters and relations. Murris' (2016) definition of the posthuman child offers a starting point for the definition of posthuman babies. She sees the child as having the potential to be engaged in lived experimental encounters and relations. Although babies and children are flesh and blood, childhood is not a biological process but a conceptual one. Entering this process demands that the rational models of developmental appreciation and measurement be put aside. As Murris (2016, p. 128) remarks, the posthuman child is 'bodymindmatter and *at the same time* linguistic, social, political, natural, material and cultural'. The posthuman child is 'in a process of becoming with/in others and with/in the world', says Murris (2020b, p. 173). She emphasizes how a posthuman child emerges through material and discursive intra-actions. According to her, understanding child-adult as an entanglement helps us to decentre the child as a being (Murris, 2020b). The posthuman figuration of child challenges our normative and stereotypical child-to-be-adult orientation. It is much more mobile, dynamic and living in the moment – leaving much more space for seeing the child as a rich potential engaged in lived experimental encounters and relations.

What is worth noting is that sympoiesis reconfigures learning as a relational material-discursive worlding process in between human and non-human bodies. It is important to bring babies' embodied thoughts closer to our perceptions (which is important considering especially non-talking babies), forcing us to pay attention to baby's body movements, gaze, sounds, body temperature and other wordless acts, not only as signs of deviation but also as efforts to intra-action. Babies are interestingly unpredictable companions if we are willing, open and prepared to receive the unpredictable. Sympoiesis forces us to focus and be in the moment without any expectations, comparisons or appraisings. Adult–child connection is living, dynamic and amenable, and in that intra-action also the baby is sympoietical.

Implications

Emphasizing adult–child connection (instead of an adult–child observation) and the process of becoming (recognizing the relevant at the moment) can act as the basis for child observation, but only if we are prepared to see beyond the dominant figurations of the child position placing children as epistemologically and ontologically inferior rather than as full human beings.

It is important to critically consider the ways and means in which parents, societies and the market make meanings and inform actions through all forms of texts, materials and experience. This has also a foundational educational implication. We need a deeper educational appreciation of a baby and a child including nonrepresentational and joyful understandings of the processes of becoming through connection with others and in observing and documenting these.

We need to consider parents' and other adults' observations as constantly forming in unforeseen ways (e.g. Coole & Frost, 2010) leaving space for dynamic, not pre-directed, notions. Instead of thinking of childhood observation as a relation between a subject and an object, our aim is to shift the focus to their entanglement. As Barad (2007) said, things are because they are influencing each other. For example, thinking of baby journaling and baby books only as resources or affordances does not offer enough multidimensional focus to understand the state of constant intra-action of parent–child connections.

It is also worth recognizing that rich material resources can inspire imagination (Alesina & Lupton, 2010). Ready-made baby journals and memory books are popular cultural artefacts intimately tied to social relations and figurations of the child. They respond to and construct popular conceptualizations of the child, childhood and childhood observation. On the other hand, baby journals and memory books are educational tools as they guide parents and other adults to pay attention and observe certain topics, milestones and achievements.

Many people think of a baby as an infant, the beginning of a human, without the capacity to share anything. Etymologically infant refers to 'unable to speak' which reveals the role of language in child figurations. A posthuman perspective offers an opening for culture in which making sense of other beings and being in relation to them is not a linguistic matter. Understanding posthuman babies is also therefore about respecting a wide range of beings (see Weston, 2004) and non-verbal sensing and sense-making. Respecting babies' multimodal communication and interaction enables new opportunities for connection to emerge.

If we shift our minds towards connection in baby observations, babies are also much more capable of learning themselves. As Berger and Argent (2020, p. 200) suggest in the Ingoldian way, there is no idea to observe irrelevant moments not connected to the living lines of a world. They continue with the quotation from Tim Ingold saying that they enact the mode of observation in which 'to observe is to bring our lifeline into closer correspondence with those of lines of materials' (p. 201). According to Berger and Argent (2020, p. 201) witnessing a special encounter is 'joining with the processes of their ongoing formation'.

For example, in one book (sample book C) parents are inspired to write down 'some thoughts about me [their baby]'. In the same memory book, there is an open page for remembering 'joint family moments'. These two samples hint at the beginnings of what a posthuman practice of baby journaling might look like, where parents record their own feelings, thoughts and memorable moments. But there is no place for parents' own milestones and growth, and there is not even one question concerning what a baby means in parents' minds or how the relationship with a baby has changed them, or how they describe their joining with (sympoiesis) and becoming with.

Conclusion

In our reconceptualization of posthuman babies and a baby's first year, we have been trying to ask how to engage critically with adults' conceptions and observations of babies and the first months or years of growth, and how to open new ways of thinking about childhood and babies' first year in particular. It is obvious that parents' thinking is shaped by their beliefs, feelings and thoughts (e.g. Gottman et al., 1996) which also has cultural meanings. The first year of a child's life is significant for development and growth. But it should be significant also per se, without any expectations.

Childhood cultures, with observation as a dominant mode of enquiry, guide and educate parents as observers. The posthuman child mobilizes an openness and critical alertness to the conceptualizations and categories that shape how we go about observation as part of our everyday life. By thinking with the posthuman child, we can challenge the dominance of developmental and chronological paradigms and we can move towards postdevelopmental approaches of childhood observation.

Through the recognition of how we formulate childhood observations, we need to start rethinking the approaches through which we are connected to childhood in general and ask what it would be to grow and be educated without normative expectations. This also concerns early childhood education practitioners and institutions. Approaching observations in new, experimental and innovative ways can enable us to expand the emergent field of postdevelopmental theorizations and modes of inquiry in early childhood education. There is a need to develop a new culture of postdevelopmental observation with the focus on staying with moments in action, joining the connection of the living lines of a world and life itself. Researchers and educators need to search for alternative modes for deeper appreciation of connections and joining withs. Joining with the processes of their ongoing formations is not easy, as it requires openness for the unpredictable. But it will teach us to listen to alternative narratives and to better illuminate the everyday experiences of parents, children and families.

From a parent's point of view, joining with also means parents' becoming, a vital flow of mutual connections.

It is also worth considering how parenting should not be dependent on competition and comparison, documented milestones and skill-based achievements by a baby. As caretakers and a baby's companion, posthuman parents are not thinking of the ideal child, but focusing on and experiencing entanglements and wordlings together. Sympoiesis needs to be respected with an understanding that adult–child connection exists in the intimate sphere, filled with mutual intimacy, love and self-sacrifice.

Note

1 https://www.whattoexpect.com/baby-products/best-baby-memory-books/

References

Alesina, I., & Lupton, E. (2010). *Exploring materials: Creative design for everyday objects*. Princeton Architectural Press.

Barad, K. (2003). Posthumanist performativity: Toward an understanding of how matter comes to matter. *Signs, 40*(1), 801–831.

Barad, K. (2007). *Meeting the universe halfway: Quantum physics and the entanglement of matter and meaning*. Duke University Press.

Barad, K. (2015). Transmaterialities: Trans*/matter/realities and queer political imaginings. *GLC: Journal of Lesbian and Gay Studies, 21*(2–3), 387–422.

Berger, I., & Argent, A. (2020). Life as a pedagogical concept. In W. O. Kohan & B. Weber (Eds.), *Thinking, childhood, and time: Contemporary perspectives on the politics of education* (pp. 195–207, Vol. 195). Rowman & Littlefield.

Braidotti, R. (2018). Joy, ethics of. In R. Braidotti & M. Hlavajova (Eds.), *Posthuman glossary* (pp. 221–224). Bloomsbury Academic.

Bohlmann, B., & Hickey-Moody, A. (Eds.). (2018). *Deleuze and children*. Edinburgh University Press.

Caputo, A. (2020). Philosophia ludens for children: A proposal to play and to think. In W. O. Kohan & B. Weber (Eds.), *Thinking, childhood, and time: Contemporary perspectives on the politics of education* (pp. 105–116). Lexington Books.

Coole, D., & Frost, S. (2010). Introducing the new materialisms. In D. Coole & S. Frost (Eds.), *New materialisms: Ontology, agency, and politics* (pp. 1–43). Duke University Press.

Epp, A. E. (2018). Family and collective identity. In E. J. Arnoud & C. J. Thompson (Eds.), *Consumer culture theory* (pp. 65–89). Sage.

Garber, E. (2019). Objects and new materialisms: A journey across making and living with objects. *Studies in Art Education, 60*(1), 7–21. https://doi.org/10.1080/00393541.2018.1557454

Gunnarsson, K., & Bodén, L. (2021). *Introduktion till postkvalitativ metodologi.* Stockholm University Press.

Gottman, J. M., Katz, L. F., & Hooven, C. (1996). Parental meta-emotion philosophy and the emotional life of families: Theoretical models and preliminary data. *Journal of Family Psychology, 10,* 243–268. https://doi.org/10.1037/0893-3200.10.3.243

Haraway, D. (2016). *Staying with the trouble: Making Kin in the Chthulucene.* Duke University Press.

Jackson, A. Y., & Mazzei, L. (2012). *Thinking with theory in qualitative research: Viewing data across multiple perspectives.* Routledge.

Kruger, L.-M. (2003). Narrating motherhood: The transformative potential of individual stories. *South African Journal of Psychology, 33,* 198–204.

Kuby, C. R., Spector, K., & Thiel, J. J. (Eds.). (2018). *Posthumanism and literacy education: Knowing/becoming/doing literacies.* Routledge.

Kumar, P. & Schoenebeck, S. (2015). The modern day baby book: Enacting good mothering and stewarding privacy on Facebook. In *Proceedings of the 18th ACM conference on computer supported cooperative work & social computing (CSCW '15)* (pp. 1302–1312). Association for Computing Machinery. https://doi.org/10.1145/2675133.2675149

Leahy-Warren, P., McCarthy, G., & Corcoran, P. (2012). First-time mothers: Social support, maternal parental self-efficacy and postnatal depression. *Journal of Clinical Nursing, 21*(3–4), 388–397.

Leander, K., & Boldt, G. (2013). Rereading "a pedagogy of multiliteracies" bodies, texts, and emergence. *Journal of Literacy Research, 45*(1), 22–46.

Lee, N. (2001). *Childhood and society: Growing up in an age of uncertainty.* Open University Press.

Lee, E., Bristow, J., Faircloth, C., & Macvarish, J. (2014). *Parenting culture studies.* Springer.

Murris, K. (2016). *The posthuman child: Educational transformation through philosophy with picturebooks.* Routledge.

Murris, K. (2018). Posthuman child and the diffractive teacher: Decolonizing the nature/culture binary. In A. Cutter-Mackenzie-Knowles et al. (Eds.), *Research handbook on childhoodnature: Assemblages of childhood and nature research* (pp. 1–25). Springer.

Murris, K. (2020a). The 'missing peoples' of critical posthumanism and new materialism. In K. Murris (Ed.), *Navigating the postqualitative, new materialist and critical posthumanist terrain across disciplines* (pp. 62–84). Routledge.

Murris, K. (2020b). Posthuman child: De(con)structing western notions of child agency. In W. O. Kohan & B. Weber (Eds.), *Thinking, childhood, and time: Contemporary perspectives on the politics of education* (pp. 161–178). Lexington Books.

Murris, K., & Haynes, J. (2020). Troubling authority and material bodies: Creating *sympoietic* pedagogies for working with children and practitioners. *Global Education Review*, 7(2), 24–42.

Nyström, K., & Öhrling, K. (2004). Parenthood experiences during the child's first year: Literature review. *Journal of Advanced Nursing*, 46(3), 319–330.

Osgood, J., & Robinson, K. H. (Eds.). (2019). *Feminists researching gendered childhoods: Generative entanglements*. Bloomsbury.

Oulanne, L. (2018). *Lived things: Materialities of agency, affect and meaning in the short fiction of Djuna Barnes and Jean Rhys* (Academic dissertation). University of Helsinki, Faculty of Arts. https://helda.helsinki.fi/bitstream/handle/10138/234783/LivedThi.pdf?sequence=1&isAllowed=y

Segers, S., & Cavaliere, G. (2021). Parenthood: Norms and experiences. *Digest - Journal of Diversity and Gender Studies*, 7(2), 2–5.

Snaza, N., Appelbaum, P., Bayne, S., Carlson, D., Morris, M., Rotas, N., Sandlin, J., Wallin, J. & Weaver, J. A. (2014). Toward a posthuman education. *Journal of Curriculum Theorizing*, 30(2), 39.

Somerville, M., & Powell, S. J. (2019). Thinking posthuman with mud: And children of the anthropocene. *Educational Philosophy and Theory*, 51(8), 829–840.

Taylor, C. A. (2016). Edu-crafting a cacophonous ecology: Posthumanist research practices for education. In C. A. Taylor & C. Hughes (Eds.), *Posthuman research practices in education* (pp. 5–24). Palgrave MacMillan.

Ulmer, J. B. (2017). Posthumanism as research methodology: Inquiry in the anthropocene. *International Journal of Qualitative Studies in Education*, 30(9), 832–848. https://doi.org/10.1080/09518398.2017.1336806

Weston, A. (2004). Multicentrism: A manifesto. *Environmental Ethics*, 26, 25–40.

Wohlwend, K. E., Peppler, K. A., Keune, A., & Thompson, N. (2017). Making sense and nonsense: Comparing mediated discourse and agential realist approaches to materiality in a preschool makerspace. *Journal of Early Childhood Literacy*, 17(3), 444–462. https://doi.org/10.1177/1468798417712066

10

Experimental Analysis of Photography and Video in Postdevelopmental Observations of Early Childhood Art in the Family Home

Thinking with Barthes' *Camera Lucida*

Mona Sakr
Middlesex University

Introduction

This chapter explores how to approach analysis of photography and video as part of postdevelopmental childhood observations. I argue that experimenting with the way that we analyse photographs and videos as part of childhood observation can be a generative approach to disrupting the dominant developmentalist logic surrounding childhood observation. When we play with how we analyse photographs and videos that are part of childhood observation, we are opening up, questioning and deconstructing a much deeper set of assumptions about children and childhood. Theory can support us in this experimentation and in this chapter, I explore the invitations to think differently about photographs offered by Barthes in his work *Camera Lucida*. Taking Barthes' reconceptualizations of photography as a starting point, I experiment with analysis of a four-second video fragment of my nephew E engaged in art-making in the family home. I show how, when thinking with Barthes, my focus re-orientates to new details in the action and interaction which in turn opens up new lines of questioning. Rather than putting the child in the evaluative gaze of the adult, these new lines of questioning create a foundation for authentic curiosity and co-presence – two potential pillars of a postdevelopmental approach.

The chapter begins with a brief overview of how I understand a postdevelopmental approach to childhood art and how thinking about and doing photography and video differently may be a way to cultivate a postdevelopmental practice of childhood observation. I then introduce some of the main ideas put forward by Barthes in *Camera Lucida* before outlining the particular childhood art context towards which I am gearing my experimental analysis. I then take a series of invitations put forward by Barthes in *Camera Lucida* for thinking about photography and use these as the basis for experimenting with the analysis of a four-second video fragment that I made as part of an observation of childhood art in the family home. I suggest, on the basis of this experimental analysis, a series of work-in-progress principles that can be applied to postdevelopmental childhood observations, particularly when they involve photography and video.

Postdevelopmental Pedagogies of Childhood Art

When we look at childhood art through the lens of postdevelopmentalism, we are committing to moving beyond our fascination with developmental milestones in children's experiences and behaviours. We are instead endeavouring to engage with the messy richness of children's actions, experiences, meaning-making, play and learning as it unfolds in the 'here and now' of art-making (Osgood & Sakr, 2019). I understand postdevelopmentalism as an umbrella term referring to theoretical orientations that challenge the dominance of developmental psychology as a means through which to make sense of children and childhood. We need to challenge developmental psychology as *the* paradigm through which to view children and childhood for two reasons.

First, the paradigm of developmentalism is built around normative trajectories on which children are expected to neatly fit. When children do not develop according to these trajectories, they are perceived and treated as problematic cases that need to be 'fixed'. The children most likely to endure this 'fixing' are those who are already encountering systematic inequalities and experiencing disadvantages (Burman, 2016). Thus, a fixation on development exacerbates, rather than ameliorates, their marginalization. Rejecting and challenging developmentalism is therefore a social justice issue, where we seek to validate the experiences of all children and not just those who look and behave in a way deemed appropriate for their age.

Second, developmentalism turns childhood into a project of 'becoming-adult' and in doing so, misses much of what is happening in childhood experiences. Childhood art is a rich site of being that involves thinking, feeling and moving (Wright, 2001; Schulte & Park, 2021). It is a place in which children can construct and express their identity, collaborate with others and learn about their own and others' cultures (Sakr et al., 2018). When we look exclusively for what children can and cannot do and position ourselves in the role of helping them to do what they cannot yet do, we miss so much of what is actually happening. Schulte (this volume) celebrates the potential of asking the question 'What's happening here?' as a way to engage with the multitude of possibilities and meanings in childhood art. Postdevelopmental pedagogies position authentic curiosity – a faith in the richness of what children do and experience – at the heart of childhood observation.

In mainstream formal education, observations are often used as a way to 'pin down' what a child can and cannot do and record this as part of a linear 'learning journey' (Kind, 2013). In postdevelopmental pedagogies, observation is a non-linear process of 'knot-knowing' (Osgood, 2019), where we accept that the reality of childhood experience (indeed, reality in all aspects) is beyond representation and capture; it is not something that can ever be truly disentangled. Observation as 'knot-knowing' is an exploration of what is happening without a desire to reach a particular endpoint. When Osgood uses the term 'knot-knowing', borrowing the concept of the 'knot' from Donna Haraway, she highlights the potential of sitting with an authentic curiosity in which we accept that we will never truly disentangle the reality that is in front of us. It will remain messy and tangled despite our observation work. Postdevelopmental pedagogical observations do not seek to neaten the edges of childhood experience but instead act as a means through which to immerse ourselves in childhood experience and to bring us closer and deeper into the messiness of what unfolds there.

Photography and video play a key role in the use of mainstream childhood observation as a means to 'pin down' children's development. Sylvia Kind (2013) discusses the way in which cameras are not neutral instruments of representation but have a deep and unsettling history of being used in exploitation and to evaluate others' worth in relation to oneself. Colonialists used cameras as a means to 'capture' Otherness and display it to the world, without consent, for their own exploitative purposes. Thus, when we are working with the camera from a postcolonial, postmodernist perspective, we are aware of this troubled history and we aim to disrupt it and challenge it by using the camera in new ways. For Kind, this involves drawing children into the taking of photographs and the analysis of photographs – so that rather than looking at a child's photograph in order to assess, as an adult, what it shows to us, we can engage with children in looking at and responding to photographs. Kind found that when she invited children's responses to the photography of other children, the nature of the image changed – children responded in bodily ways to the feelings evoked by images rather than obsessing over the content of the representation.

Similarly, when we think about postdevelopmental observations, we can play with the norms and tendencies that we associate with photography and video in traditional sites of developmentalist logic, such as the classroom. For example, I have suggested in previous work the importance of playing with the frame of the camera in time and space and being prepared to see the ways in which the observation extends beyond what we think is the spatial and temporal frame (Sakr, 2021). A willingness to experiment with photography and video indicates a willingness to experiment with our perceptions of the observation and to use it as a means of opening up questions rather than capturing a representation desired or needed by an adult. When we think in this way about camera work in pedagogical observations, a fruitful line of inquiry and thinking is to consider how others have thought about photography and to use this as a jumping-off point from which to enrich and extend the analysis. To experiment with new ways of doing observation through new ways of being with the camera as part of the observation, I consider the invitations offered by Barthes in his work *Camera Lucida*.

Barthes' *Camera Lucida*

Barthes wrote and published *Camera Lucida* in 1980. It is an investigation into the *noeme* (or special nature) of Photography[1] He explores the *noeme* of Photography through his own reaction to photographs, both those created by artists and those that are of a more personal nature. Barthes develops an understanding of why some photographs seem to prompt such a strong affective response and why others do not, organizing this potential into two central concepts: the *studium* (the subject matter and its interest) and the *punctum* (the details in the image that evoke a strong response and further questions). Although Barthes is not writing about photographs that are used for research or pedagogical purposes, it can be helpful to think about his work on Photography as a means to unsettle what we think we know about using photographs in observation. By considering Barthes' ideas on Photography and putting these into dialogue with photography and video in pedagogical observation, there is the opportunity to find new ways of doing things and of practising photography and video, which in turn introduces new possibilities for observation. It is with this intention that I introduce the work of Barthes here – as a means for unsettling what we think we know about pedagogical observations and doing this in a way that invites practical change and experimentation. The remainder of the chapter looks at the invitations that are alive in Barthes' writing and uses these as a basis for the experimental analysis of pedagogical observation of one instance of early childhood art in the family home. More detail about this particular context is offered as follows.

Context: Childhood Art in the Family Home

To explore the potential of thinking with Barthes' *Camera Lucida* in the context of pedagogical observations, I want to explore a particular observation of childhood art in the environment of my family home. The observation involved five children – three of my own (L aged five, I aged four and R aged eighteen months) and two of my sister's children (E aged four and S aged eight). I was also present in the observation, as was my sister. The observation took place one Sunday afternoon at the end of summer of 2021. It is not unusual for this group of individuals to gather together in this way for an art-making activity and so the environment and set-up were familiar to everyone involved.

I have written previously about involving my own children and my sister's children in observations of childhood art (Sakr, 2021). My recent research has tended to focus on the informal educational environment of the family home and reconceptualizing childhood art in this space as an entanglement. This means that rather than positioning the dynamics of the family home, including my own close relationship to those I am observing, as 'noise' to be filtered out, it often becomes a focus in the research and exploration. For example, my previous work has looked at emphasizing rather than downplaying the 'ethics of care' that surrounds childhood art in the family home, so that we are seeing the ways in which physical and emotional labour intra-act with art-making (Sakr, 2021).

In this particular observation, I focused on a session of free-flow art-making with a selection of materials including acrylic paint, strips of white cloth, some large sponges, a roll of brown paper, a palette knife and some paint brushes. The materials were laid out on the kitchen table on top of a table cloth used regularly for art-making. To record the observation, I positioned one static camera on a tripod on a separate surface. I also used my cameraphone to take photographs (eight in total) and a series of brief videos, each no longer than twenty seconds (four in total). In the following analysis, I work with the photographs and videos that I took using my cameraphone. The reason for this is theoretical since

Barthes' *Camera Lucida* focuses so particularly on the *noeme* of Photography and its distinction from cinema. Barthes suggests that Photography is special because of the time we have to reflect on the image in front of us, while with cinema, the image continues to move and change without the same potential for reflection. Bearing this in mind, I decided to work with the photographs and video fragments on my phone rather than trying to unpick the continuous film captured through the static videocamera, which lasted for longer than an hour.

The experimental analysis that follows is a dialogue between my reading of Barthes' *Camera Lucida* and the four short videos and eight photographs taken through my cameraphone. What follows is an account of this dialogue, moving back and forth between Barthes' conceptualizations of Photography and the 'data' that emerged from this particular observation of childhood art in the family home.

Affective Response

In *Camera Lucida*, Barthes is clear that he is not attempting to explain or outline a technical language of Photography. For him, the key to Photography lies in the affective response that a particular photograph will evoke. Looking through photographs, both those in the public eye and those that are more personal to him, he finds that some photographs seem to reach out: they prompt 'an internal agitation, an excitement, a certain labor too, the pressure of the unspeakable which wants to be spoken' (p. 23). To describe this response, Barthes uses two terms. First he talks about 'animation', in that some photographs have an animating effect – 'it animates me, and I animate it . . . ' (p. 24). Second, animation leads to 'adventure', in which the photograph prompts seeing, feeling, noticing, observing and thinking (p. 26). What Barthes expresses is that we can go on a journey with a photograph, but only if it reaches something deep within us. When photographs hold us, it is not just the photograph at play but our own subjectivity – some photographs provoke a response because of 'an erotic or lacerating value buried in myself' (p. 20). Barthes' discussion of the affective response to photographs reminds me of Maggie MacLure's writing on 'glow' as part of post-qualitative approaches to analysis. MacLure (2013) describes how, when working with 'data', we can use our affective response as a means of analysis. Rather than writing our responses out of the equation, those parts of what we have found that seem to 'glow' can be those which we stay with and investigate further. This places an emphasis on intensity and saturation as opposed to a more numerical understanding of validity, where a 'theme' matters more if it is spoken of more frequently. Barthes reminds us then, in the context of research and pedagogical observation, that an affective response is an excellent starting point for both selecting which photographs/moving images to explore further, and also paying attention to this affective response to see whether we can learn anything from it.

Thinking about this as I look at the photographs and video fragments on my phone, showing the children as they engage in the art-making activity at home, I am aware that some of the images prompt a more powerful response than others. This is not something that I am immediately able to understand. Images that seem to be similar in terms of what they show can prompt a contrasting reaction because of small details that lead to an affective response, whether this is a facial expression or a figure in the background or a detail in the movement of the hands. In the 'data' on my phone, I find myself drawn particularly to a four-second video fragment showing my nephew E rubbing frantically at his left hand using his right hand. There are two discarded wipes on the table, as well as the sponge that he has been covering in strips of white cloth and acrylic paint. He picks up, with his right hand, one of the used wipes and rubs it vigorously across the left hand. While Barthes writes powerfully about the potential of Photography (when compared with Cinema) to enable spaces for reflection and responsiveness, I find that this four-second video fragment creates a similar reflective space for me. This effect is strengthened through the way in which the video displayed on my phone plays itself over and over on a continuous loop. This offers the video fragment a characteristic more similar to Barthes' description of Photography, not just in the ability to stop and ponder what is happening, but also in the powerful feeling of co-presence, which Barthes describes when looking at photographs. With the invitation of prioritizing affect in my response to the photographic and video observation, I choose to focus on this four-second clip for the further layers of experimental analysis.

Staying With

Do I add to the images in movies? I don't think so; I don't have time: in front of the screen, I am not free to shut my eyes; otherwise, opening them again, I would not discover the same image; I am constrained to a continuous voracity; a host of other qualities, but not pensiveness; whence the interest, for me, of the photogram.

(Barthes, 1980 [2020], p. 67)

Barthes was particularly enamoured with Photography because of the potential it offers to stay with an image of something that has existed in the world. As a result of its stillness, Photography enables 'pensiveness' so that the viewer can stop and think-with the image in front of them. This is why Barthes explained that Photography and Cinema, while they may use some of the same technological frameworks, are so different in terms of culture and individual affect.

I wonder what Barthes would make of the four-second video fragment, taken using my cameraphone, that I have chosen to focus my analysis on. At the time he was writing, there was little in between Photography and Cinema. Now, with the advent of digital recording, and particularly the ease of making both photographs and videos on a smartphone, there is a whole range of experiences and representations that sit in between traditional photography and traditional cinema. The four-second fragment, which plays on a continuous loop when it is open on my phone (much like a Tik Tok video would), is one of those 'in the middle' kinds of representation and experience. Of course, in addition to the four-second video fragment not fitting into either of the categories understood and presented by Barthes, there is the additional complexity of the ease with which we can bring more pause into moving image footage that exists on our phones or computers. We can pause the film as it plays, but we can also easily use freely available apps to take stills from the video, to slow it down or speed it up. These tools are all potential aides in pensiveness, though only if they are used with that approach in mind.

In the four-second fragment, even watching it on a continuous loop, it is amazing how quickly the action actually unfolds. As you watch the video replay itself, the following actions seem to rush past: E's action of picking up the wipe and rubbing his hand, as well as the way in which his whole body and particularly his head moves, alongside the changes in facial expression. To support pensiveness, and to again borrow from Maggie MacLure's (2013) emphasis on luxuriating in 'data' I used software on my laptop to both slow down the video and also create a series of stills (shown in Figure 10.1) that helped me to identify what actually happens in the four-second fragment and in what order. This is not for the purpose of a multimodal analysis, where I am unpicking bodily details and the sequence in which they unfold and understanding communication and interaction as this unfolding, but rather using this manipulation and understanding as a way to 'pensiveness' – a starting point for understanding what is important here to me, and what I would like to further investigate. One of the main details that emerged for me in this process was the stillness of E's left hand as he waits to pick up the wipe with his right hand. The left hand is held aloft as a contaminated

Early Childhood Art in the Family Home   183

Figure 10.1 Series of stills showing E's action.

object would be; it looks mechanical, artificial and no longer a part of the body's flow of movement. Through playing with the fragment, in a way that was not available to Barthes or his contemporaries, I find the details that captivate but are not necessarily immediately visible or discernible.

Punctum

In explaining why some photographs have a more powerful effect on us than others, Barthes builds the idea of two types of work carried out by each photograph: the *studium* and the *punctum*. The *studium* relates to the subject matter shown in the photograph and the way in which this does or does not correspond to our own interests. If I am interested in fashion for example, I am much more likely to respond to fashion photography as the *studium* is aligned. However, Barthes is clear that *studium* is not nearly enough for Photography to prompt its full affective response and it also cannot explain why some photographs, superficially unaligned with our interests, still lead to a strong affective impulse. He puts this down to the *punctum*. These are the accidental details that exist in a photograph that provoke a reaction. He uses the Latin *punctum* because it conjures the image of multiple points across the image, which are also pricks or cuts in the viewer's psyche. That is, they prompt an affective response because they relate to wounds or sensitive points in our deepest selves:

> 'for punctum is also: sting, speck, cut, little hole – and also a cast of the dice. A photograph's punctum is that accident which pricks me (but also bruises me, is poignant to me).' (p. 33)

Barthes' description of the *punctum* suggests feelings of discomfort and disruption rather than parts of an image that we feel particularly warm to. In the four-second fragment of E rubbing his hands, it is the immobility of the left hand that seems to pierce its way out of the video and affect me deeply. The limp way that he holds his hand, as though it is something separate from his body and lifeless, waiting to be cleansed, has a startling effect on me. The more I watch the video, the more this detail seems to take over the whole of the video. Barthes talks about this as the metonymic effect of the *punctum*, where a detail appears to consume the whole image to the point where, for the viewer, it is 'the thing'. The immobile left hand becomes 'the thing' I see and it leaves me asking many questions about both the hand and its place in art-making (in this case the left-out, contaminated, sedated left hand) but also about why this particular detail has the power over me that it does. To use Barthes' terms, what are the wounds and marks in myself to which this 'sting/speck/cut/little hole' relates?

Going Beyond

While the *punctum* is a detail, it has the potential to expand the viewer's experience of a photograph. Barthes explains that the *punctum* 'takes the spectator outside its frame, and it is there that I animate this photograph and that it animates me. The *punctum*, then, is a kind of subtle beyond – as if the image launched desire beyond what it permits us to see' (p. 71). These details point towards something that exists well beyond the spatial and temporal frame of the image. They challenge us to ask questions about what is really happening both in the image and in ourselves as a spectator. This resonates with the introduction to postdevelopmentalism that I offered earlier in the chapter, where I suggested that engaging with childhood experience as an entanglement provokes us to see well beyond the traditional spatial and temporal frame of that experience. We might go into an observation with a clear idea in our mind of what the 'centre' is but in the process of 'knot-knowing' we seek a de-centring experience where new centres and alternative frames come to light. This is what the *punctum* also seems to offer – a chance to re-orientate and see new possibilities, to continue to open up the viewpoint on childhood experience and in this case, childhood art.

If we take the detail of E's immobile left hand, we can ask what new lines of questioning and exploration emerge when we engage with this point in the observation. In Barthes' 'moving beyond', these ideas and feelings tumble through our minds and bodies. I find it useful to engage in a stream of consciousness writing as a way to follow some of these lines of questioning to see where they will lead. Here is an excerpt from my stream of consciousness writing as I repeatedly watch the detail as it plays in the video fragment:

> *Mess, contamination, discomfort with the body as it engages in art-making and different sensory experiences – what are the messages about mess surrounding E – where do these ideas about mess come from, do they belong to him or do they belong to us – who is squeamish, us or him, or both – is he protecting us (the adults) by wiping away the mess or is he protecting himself and we have brought the mess? Both ways. We have brought the mess and we have brought the message that the mess is intolerable, with the wipes there, constantly there waiting to clear up – just as we, the caretakers, wait in the wings ready to clear up and clean up the mess. Who is passive here? What is passive? The left hand held aloft, regal but immobile, pandered to by the right hand, the furious right hand which scrubs away the acrylic paint – futile. The right hand worries at the left hand, rubbing it raw. What has the left hand done? What mess has the left hand created that the right hand must clear up?*

Further questions emerge about the dualities that reveal themselves through this stream of consciousness: mess/cleanliness, activity/passivity and mobility/immobility. How do such dualities feed into our practices, our pedagogies, our ways of being with children and our commitment to the postdevelopmental project? Moving beyond, from the starting place of the *punctum*, is therefore also a way to move beyond the dominant developmentalist desire to impose order and assume a position of greater knowledge and understanding in relation to the child. In this analysis, it is *my/adult* knowledge which is under question and the dualities that structure *my/adult* perceptions, rather than the child's actions.

Co-Presence

For Barthes, the *noeme* of Photography is its capacity to enable us to exist simultaneously with a record of what has been. This is so powerful that it arrests ours senses and our thoughts: 'time is engorged . . . a strange stasis, the stasis of an arrest' (p. 110). A photograph turns off, temporarily at least, our capacity to interpret or analyse because the experience of co-presence is more consuming. Barthes describes how with old family photographs, particularly those of his mother, he tries repeatedly to enter into the photograph, to uncover its secrets, to find a way through its mystery (or the mystery of the figure it shows), but the reiteration of the realization that this is impossible. The photograph both allows us to be with the subject and holds us away from the subject, violently:

> The Photograph is violent: not because it shows violent things, but because on each occasion it fills the sight by force, and because in it nothing can be refused or transformed. (p. 111)
>
> it is precisely in this arrest of interpretation that the Photograph's certainty resides. (p. 130)

This echoes my feelings as I watch and re-watch the video fragment of E as he wipes furiously at his left hand. I am with E, co-present with him, but unable to penetrate the moving image to understand what is *really* going on. I can dance around the reality, as I did in the previous section, thinking about the new lines of questioning that open up as a result of focusing on the *punctum*, but I am ultimately held at bay. Rather than positioning this as frustrating (though it may be), this may be an aspect to celebrate as part of a postdevelopmental approach to childhood observation. Recognizing that we cannot know the child, that we cannot define them, categorize them, decide where they can and cannot fit, is a stepping stone to a new way of being with children in the moment. Co-presence is therefore about a deep and authentic curiosity, that bubbles up from an affective response to what we see in front of us, while at the same time holding us away from our desire to colonize children through developmental charts and ticklists. Through this lens, photography and video can become something vastly different from what they are currently – the handmaidens in the representation of development – and instead become a 'no trespass' sign to the adult, holding the adult at bay from the desire to colonize the child's experience of the world.

Pedagogical Observation Inspired by Barthes' *Camera Lucida*

Earlier in the chapter, I proposed postdevelopmentalism as an umbrella term used to refer to a diverse range of theoretical orientations all of which have in common the wish to disrupt and challenge the dominance of developmentalism as a lens through which to see the child and childhood. Because postdevelopmentalism is an umbrella term, there is still a need to develop concrete ways of applying postdevelopmentalism in pedagogy and practice. One of the main ways that we can seek to do this is by developing a method and/or approach for pedagogical observation that invites the richness of childhood experience and refrains from attempting to classify or assess children. The analytical experiments earlier, thinking with Barthes, as I engage with a video fragment from an observation of childhood art in the family home, act as a starting point for developing a process for postdevelopmental video and/or photographic observation that can be used by others in different situations. The key tenets of this process can be summarized as follows:

- **Affective Response.** The process highlights the potential of working with photographs or video fragments that you, the individual observer, find particularly captivating. Our affective response is not a rational response and it does not need to be justified – as with MacLure (2013), Barthes gives permission to pay attention to the affective response that we have. We seek to notice it and respond to it practically (e.g. by selecting the photographs and/or video fragments that prompt the most powerful response, selecting these for further analysis), as well as taking it as an entrance into 'knot-knowing'.
- **Staying With.** Barthes' fascination with Photography, as compared with Cinema, was due to what he saw as the power of photography to induce pensiveness in the viewer. This is important for the postdevelopmental approach, where we wish to practice being more in the moment with children. It suggests that we need to cultivate this pensiveness and that one of the practical ways to do this is to use photographic and video methods that emphasize stillness and space for reflection. This means emphasizing selectivity both at the point of taking photographs/videos and at the point of

deciding which to keep and think about further. A few photographs and/or very brief video fragments can support us to stay with the moment, and to stay with the child in the moment.

- **Punctum and Moving Beyond.** *Punctum* are the details in a photograph that seems to 'prick' the viewer with their intensity and can come to dominate the entirety of the perception of the image. This is subjective, but it is also generative. By staying with the *punctum* and allowing our attention to focus in on these details, we can expand our understanding and lines of inquiry around childhood experience. *Punctum* are *punctum* because of their potential to open up questions, associations and even wounds that we are carrying. In turn, these are vital elements of our wider pedagogical approach. *Punctum* are therefore a way to move beyond what is just happening in the image to ask deeper questions about the pedagogical context, most importantly taking time to reflect on our constrained ways of seeing and living with children.
- **Co-Presence.** The most important lesson from Barthes it seems, for a postdevelopmentalist pedagogue, would be that we can stay with our record of the child and we can learn from it deeply, but that we must repeatedly acknowledge to ourselves that we cannot know the child. We cannot enter into the photograph or video, however many times we look at it, or however many different ways we manipulate it. This teaches us co-presence, which becomes a fundamental facet of a postdevelopmental approach to being with children. Our explorations of childhood are rich and meaningful, but there will always remain a distance between ourselves and the child. Rather than being frustrating or something that needs to be overcome, the distance is the only way for the child to enhance their voice, participation and citizenship – to resist the colonizing attempts of the adult.

The earlier points are not a set process to be followed without question and experimentation. I offer the list as some ideas that may be helpful to others as they attempt postdevelopmental pedagogical or research childhood observations. It is a work in progress that can be adapted and developed through engagement with various theorists and – of course – how it fares in the world.

Conclusion

In this chapter, I have suggested that moving forward with postdevelopmental childhood observations depends on working with theory on experimental practices of observation and analysis of observation. I have taken inspiration from Barthes' *Camera Lucida*, which highlights the power of Photography and offers an emergent framework for engaging with it as a medium on an affective and subjective level. Looking at an observation of childhood art in the family home, with particular focus on a four-second video fragment of my nephew E as he wipes his left hand with his right hand, I have tried to use Barthes' ideas of staying with, *punctum*, moving beyond and co-presence as a way to engage, analyse and interpret in a way that stays true to the postdevelopmental commitment to being with the child in the moment. These experiments have reminded me of the power of unsettling our practical ways of doing things as a way to more deeply unsettle our approach to childhood art (and childhood pedagogies more generally) which may otherwise go unquestioned. Rather than dissecting the child through the observation, this approach encourages us to deconstruct our own perceptions and ways of thinking which define and limit what we can see through the observation. Most importantly, working with Barthes has suggested the possibility that childhood observations may be an intentional act of co-presence, where we seek to be with the child without defining them.

Note

1 As Barthes capitalizes Photography, when I am discussing his ideas, I also capitalize the word. At other points in the chapter, when I am discussing my own ideas and perspective, I do not capitalize the word.

References

Barthes, R. (2020 [1980]). *Camera Lucida* (trans. R. Howard). Penguin Random House.
Burman, E. (2016). *Deconstructing developmental psychology*. Routledge.
Kind, S. (2013). Lively entanglements: The doings, movements and enactments of photography. *Global Studies of Childhood*, 3(4), 427–441.
MacLure, M. (2013). The wonder of data. *Cultural Studies? Critical Methodologies*, 13(4), 228–232.
Osgood, J. (2019). You can't separate it from anything!: Glitter's doings as materialised figurations of childhood (and) art. In M. Sakr & J. Osgood (Eds.), *Postdevelopmental approaches to childhood art* (pp. 111–136). Bloomsbury.

Osgood, J., & Sakr, M. (2019). Introduction. In M. Sakr & J. Osgood (Eds.), *Postdevelopmental approaches to childhood art*. Bloomsbury.

Sakr, M. (2021). Reconceptualizing early childhood art as entanglement: Playing with chalk in the home. In C. Schulte & H. Park (Eds.), *Visual arts with young children* (pp. 11–23). Routledge.

Sakr, M., Federici, R., Hall, N., Trivedy, B., & O'Brien, L. (2018). *Creativity and making in early childhood: Challenging practitioner perspectives*. Bloomsbury.

Schulte, C., & Park, H. (2021). Introduction. In C. Schulte & H. Park (Eds.), *Visual arts with young children*. Routledge.

Wright, S. (2001). Guiding learning processes in the integration of the arts. *Contemporary Issues in Early Childhood, 2*(2), 225–238.

Index

Aboriginal knowledges 59, 65, 72–3, 75
adult-child connection 160, 168
affect 9, 18, 22
agency 64, 76
agentive objects 120–2
art-making 27, 106, 141, 147, 150, 176, 184
assemblage 15, 19, 21, 87
attachments 99, 100, 110
attention 93
attunement 16, 38

baby journaling 158, 164–5
becoming 9, 14, 18, 21–2, 54, 135, 154, 159–61, 167–71

cameraphone 179–80, 182
childhood geographies 90–3
choreographies 40, 52
co-presence 186, 188
curiosity 41, 129, 177, 186

derive 130
desire 99, 103–5, 113, 114
documentation 28–9, 31–3, 37, 43
drawing 38–9

ecological sense-making 81, 94
emergent curriculum 34
encounters 11, 14, 148
entanglements 12, 17, 22
ethics 13, 17, 22
ethnography 13

fluxus artists 123
forceful seeing 107, 109

hacking 60, 66–7, 69, 71–2, 74–5

inequity 11
intra-action 14, 19, 21, 88–9, 160

'knot-knowing' 187

learning stories 81–2, 84–6

literacy workshop 11, 13

mapping 123–6
mothering 143
mutated modest witness 142, 149, 152

objects of childhood 104–5
objects of desire 99, 104, 113

permeable curriculum 13
photography 186–7
place literacies 60, 67, 72–5
place-making 66, 76
posthuman 86–8
posthuman babies 157–8, 167–8
posthumanism 159, 161
posthumanist 9, 13, 17, 20, 92, 94
posthuman pedagogies 87
power 29, 31–2
provocations 27, 32
punctum 183, 188

relational complexity 87
relations 48, 57, 59, 60, 64–7, 69, 73–6
relationships 30–1
research creation 122

speculate 15, 21
speculative 100, 110, 114
speculative act 100, 112, 114
speculative gestures 99, 114
studium 178, 183
sympoiesis 161, 168
synaesthesia 133

Te Whāriki 82–4, 86–7, 92
thing power 18–20
thinking with theory 158–9
threshold 32–4
video 147, 175–6, 178
virtual 18
vitality 9, 22
voluntary art-making 27, 32

www.ingramcontent.com/pod-product-compliance
Lightning Source LLC
Chambersburg PA
CBHW052119300426
44116CB00010B/1713